Biological Aspects of Mental Disorder

Biological Aspects of Mental Disorder

SOLOMON H. SNYDER, M.D.
Distinguished Service Professor of Psychiatry and Pharmacology
The Johns Hopkins University School of Medicine

New York / Oxford
OXFORD UNIVERSITY PRESS
1980

Library of Congress Cataloging in Publication Data

Snyder, Solomon H   1938–
  Biological aspects of mental disorder.

  Bibliography: p.
  Includes index.
  1. Psychology, Pathological—Physiological aspects.
2. Drug abuse—Physiological aspects.   3. Brain—
Diseases.   4. Medicine, Psychosomatic.   5. Sexual
disorders.   I. Title.   [DNLM: 1. Mental disorders.
2. Biology.   WM100 S765b]
RC455.4.B5S6   616.8'5   80-11981
ISBN 0-19-502715-9

Printed in the United States of America

To Elaine,
whose loving support
has made feasible this book
as well as everything else

Preface

I was one of those medical students who never wanted to be a real "doctor," viewing medical school simply as an obstacle which must be surmounted on the road to my true profession, that of the psychiatrist. Any involvement in basic biomedical research was an accident. A guitar pupil of mine who happened to be doing biochemical research at the NIH needed a technician for the summer, which happened to be the summer before I began medical school. It seemed convenient to work during electives and summer periods at the NIH, so I continued doing this throughout medical school. I became a research associate for a period of two years in the laboratory of Dr. Julius Axelrod in the National Institute of Mental Health largely in an effort to avoid the doctor draft. However, working in the stimulating environment of this Nobel laureate's laboratory addicted me to the basic research enterprise. Research in a laboratory at the forefront was vastly different from the boring science of classes and textbooks.

Despite its great attractions, my NIH research experience still did not deter me from the long held goal of becoming a clinical psychiatrist with a special interest in psychotherapy. At the time I began my residency at Johns Hopkins in 1965 I viewed basic research in psychopharmacology as quite distant from the clinical practice of psychiatry. There was little that biological studies of brain function could contribute to practical problems in the clinical treatment of patients. Indeed, basic research didn't even appear to offer much in the way of enhancing our understanding of how the brain mediated normal and abnormal emotional behavior. I viewed myself as a practitioner of two separate and quite distinct vocations, science and psychiatry, with the two having very little in common.

The past fifteen years have been gratifying ones. My two vocations more and more seem to fuse. I am constantly amazed at how basic research on neuro-transmitters and drug interactions can bear directly on theoretical and practical aspects of everyday psychiatric practice. True, we don't yet know the locus of the specific lesion that explains the genetic vulnerability for at least some forms of schizophrenia and affective disorder. Nonetheless, the mental health profes-sions can be proud that mechanisms of action of psychotropic drugs are proba-bly at least as well worked out as the mechanisms for many of the principal drugs in general medicine. Identifying specific sites of actions of drugs at molecularly defined receptors has permitted the tailoring of drugs with greater therapeutic potency and fewer side effects. Clarification of neurotransmitter synthesis, release, and inactivation has considerably enhanced our understand-ing of how the brain processes emotional behavior. Genetic studies have in-creased our appreciation of what determines vulnerability to various forms of major mental illness. In a word, the biological and psychological aspects of mental disorders have drawn closer and closer.

Traditionally, there have been controversies between those espousing "biological" and those favoring "psychological" views of mental illness. In my perception, increased scientific understanding in both areas demonstrates convincingly that most of these disputes are built on mutual ignorance and misunderstanding. Today a far more integrated view of normal and abnormal mental functioning is possible. In reading numerous texts of abnormal psychol-ogy I became concerned that this integrated view has not yet reached many volumes written for undergraduates, graduate students, or professionals. In an attempt to provide this view of the "new biology of behavior," I have written the present book.

I owe a special debt to Jeffrey House, my editor through three books, who has provided kind, courageous, and incisive advice over the past ten years. Sections on sexual behavior benefited greatly from the advice of John Money, while Paul McHugh provided valuable suggestions relating to organic brain disorder.

Baltimore   S.H.S.
February 1980

Contents

Biological Aspects of Mental Disorder

1. Affective disorders: Phenomenology

The term *affect* refers to feeling state. Every person suffering from emotional distress experiences some sort of affective disturbance. Varying degrees of depression are ubiquitous in all societies of the world. Chronic anxiety almost invariably merges into a state of depression as the sufferer becomes demoralized from his or her failure to attain relief. When schizophrenics confront the gravity of their disturbance, they often experience severe depression. Many people, however, suffer from emotional disturbances in which the primary abnormality involves their affective state. There may exist several distinct types of such primary affective disorders, some with and others without a genetic basis.

Though any number of affective disorders may exist, there appear to be only two major abnormal affective conditions, mania and depression. *Mania* signifies an elated feeling state, while *depression* refers to severe dejection.

Josh Logan

Feeling states are not readily conveyed by formal lists of symptoms. Their essential features may be better understood by descriptions of individual patients. The eminent stage director Joshua Logan has suffered from both mania and depression. To diminish the public stigma associated with mental illness, he has talked about his emotional disorders before professional and lay audiences and has written about them openly in his biography, *Josh*. Mr. Logan's first manic attack began at the time of a major professional success, his direction of the Broadway production of *Charlie's Aunt*. The overexcitement which accompanies a Broadway smash success seems to have played, to some degree, a precipitating role in his breakdown (Logan, 1976).

Charlie's Aunt continued to be my entree everywhere. My checks were accepted easily. I handed tickets out like handbills—to a shoe salesman, a stenographer . . . I sent flowers by the carloads and I began investing in plays, which merely increased the script load and seekers of advice. I had a self assurance that was incredible even to me, and I seemed able to convince anybody of anything. It was as though I was speaking someone else's lines. I'd say to a girl in a store, "You're coming to bed with me tonight at 8:00—here's my card." And she came. My wishes were granted almost too easily. Life was a fantasy of utter freedom.

One of the most difficult aspects for a family member, friend, or mental health professional attempting to deal with a manic person is that, as in Mr. Logan's case, there is usually some apparent justification for the elation. As he or she gradually progresses to severe mania, the victim is, for a good while, witty and bubbling over with new ideas, some of which seem reasonable. Friends and relatives may even conclude that the patient is the talented and clever one and that they, the onlookers, are just kill-joys. Manic individuals may "feel so good" that it is difficult to convince them that something is seriously wrong and that they require medical treatment. When told by a psychiatrist that he was sick and required hospitalization, Mr. Logan was puzzled:

There was no way I could make him understand that this high whizzing feeling I had now delighted me. It was true that when people crossed me I turned nasty, but as long as I got my way I considered myself the nicest guy in the world. I was full of extra warmth for taxi drivers, waitresses, clerks, anyone who was helpful—and I kept talking nice, no matter how nervous my behavior made them. I was forever offering everyone free dinners or seats to *Charlie's Aunt*. If this sense of freedom and expansiveness was manic, then manic was what I'd been hoping for all my life.

Logan finally acknowledged that something was wrong enough for him to requires hospitalization. But still he did not feel "sick," as he had earlier during a depressive episode: "Now for the first time I really believed I might be mentally disturbed, though I certainly felt fine. I remembered how dark blue I had been during the rehearsals of *Higher and Higher*. At that time I was in a different frame of mind. I knew I was in trouble. But why now when I felt so soaringly happy?"

During manic attacks, individuals can often do a lot of productive work in a remarkably short period, provided they are experiencing only a mild episode. In rehearsing for a play thirteen years after his first manic breakdown, Logan suffered another manic episode. In its initial phases, he continued to be professionally effective:

Still, I found I had extraordinary energy. Although I wasn't aware of it, I exhausted everyone who tried to keep up with me. Again I was directing—as I had directed *Charlie's*

Aunt—quickly, efficiently and with seemingly effective ideas. The whole cast took on my excitement and if they suspected I was in a strange state, they never showed it to me.

It was an exhilarating time for me. I was extremely productive, perhaps overly so, but it was the best thing I think I've ever done in my life. I doubt if I've ever had the freedom of thought and unfettered ideas which really connect with an audience than I had during that time.

As mania develops, the patient's judgment deteriorates gradually or rapidly. When Logan's second manic illness was beginning, James Mitchener approached him at a restaurant and proposed a musical show based on nis new novel, *Sayonara*. Though he knew nothing about the book, Logan responded instantly: "I almost leaped at it. . . . All I wanted to know from Jim was what I had to pay to secure the rights (which was $250,000). I said, ignoring Nedda's worried look, 'I accept! I'll write you a check right now!' "

As often happens in effective illnesses, Logan's depressive episodes developed insidiously. This pattern may delay proper treatment since patients assume that their bad feelings stem solely from external circumstances. Logan describes it in this way: "My first impression was that something had sneaked up on me. I had no idea I was depressed, that is mentally. I knew I felt bad, I knew I felt low. I knew I had no faith in the work I was doing or the people I was working with, but I didn't imagine I was sick. It was a great burden to get up in the morning and I couldn't wait to go to bed at night even though I started not sleeping well."

Logan's first depression occurred while he was directing a Broadway play. He could take no joy in the production and concluded wrongly that he felt unhappy only because the play was so terrible: "I can remember that I sat in some sort of aggravated agony as it [the play] was read aloud the first time by the cast. It sounded so awful I didn't want to direct it. I didn't even want to see it. I remember feeling so depressed that I wished that I were dead without having to go through the shame and defeat of suicide. I couldn't sleep well at all and sleep meant, for me, oblivion, and that's what I longed for and couldn't get."

Because patients themselves misperceive the nature of the depression, their friends and family may also fail to respond appropriately. The most common, and least helpful, action taken is to admonish the patient that things aren't really so bad and he or she accordingly ought to "perk up." In the case of Mr. Logan:

I didn't know what to do and I felt very lost. I remember asking a friend of mine who was the company manager to walk around the block with me during lunch, because I didn't want to have to converse with the cast lest they sense my feelings. I told my friend that the play was awful. He said, "No, no it's not so bad. I don't know what's the matter with you, you're looking at things wrong. Come on now, just buck up." It seemed to me that all friends of the average human being in depression only knew one cure—and that was a slap on the back. "Buck up." It's just about the most futile thing that could happen to you when you are depressed. My friends never even hinted to me that I was really ill.

Joshua Logan is representative of the many patients with manic-depressive illness in whom the continuous, prophylactic administration of the metal ion lithium has prevented the recurrence of both manic and depressive episodes: "I have now been taking lithium carbonate for four and a half or five years, and I've not been conscious of the slightest highs or lows out of what would be considered a normal proportion. And yet, I seem to be as productive as I've ever been. I've collaborated this past year on two different musical comedies, and I'm writing my own autobiography" (Logan, 1973).

John Custance

Most people feel "depressed" at one time or another. But the intensity of dejection experienced by an individual with clinically severe depression is different. Again, a firsthand description is illuminating. The English writer John Custance suffered from manic-depressive illness and vividly reported his experience of severe depression. "I was utterly miserable and wanted to die, but my fears, troubles and words were of normal human mischances which might happen to anybody. I feared poverty, failure in life, inability to educate my children, making my wife miserable, losing her, ending up in the gutter as the most revolting type of beggar and so on. My fears had in fact become so overpowering as to appear to me like certainties, but they were only earthly human fears" (Custance, 1951). While some depressions are precipitated by definite environmental setbacks, more often patients, much like Mr. Custance, become depressed and worry endlessly over things which under normal circumstances would be no cause for concern.

In their extreme form, depressive thoughts can be so unrealistic that they constitute delusions. At such times the depression is considered to be psychotic. In the case of Mr. Custance:

I had now become quite convinced that I was finished for good and all. There was no possible chance of my coming out of the hospital alive. In fact, though not actually dead, I was as good as dead. For some inscrutable reason, perhaps because I had committed the "unforgivable sin" or just because I was such an appalling sinner, the worst man who had ever existed, I had been chosen to go alive through the portals of Hell in an ordinary English lunatic asylum. . . . I was a sort of opposite of Jesus Christ. Satan's job had been to catch a man, get him to sell his soul to him completely and utterly like Faust, and then take him down alive into the pit. That was a sort of necessary counterway to the resurrection of Jesus and the elect. I was the man.

The delusions of a depressed patient differ from those of a schizophrenic in that the former focuses his or her delusional thoughts upon depressive themes. Distinguishing depression from schizophrenia can sometimes be difficult, especially in the occasional depressed patients who develop hallucinations. Mr. Custance's apparent hallucinations seemed to emerge out of the same depressive thoughts:

A crumpled pillow is quite an ordinary everyday object, is it not? One looks at it and thinks no more about it. So is a washing rag, or a towel tumbled on the floor, or the creases on the side of the bed. Yet they can suggest shapes of the utmost horror to the mind possessed by fear. Gradually my eyes began to distinguish such shapes, until eventually, which ever way I turned, I could see nothing but devils waiting to torment me, devils which seemed infinitely more real than the material objects in which I saw them.

Symptoms

Depression

Accounts of the symptoms of depression have been remarkably constant over the centuries. About 200 A.D. Plutarch pictured the typically melancholic individual as follows: "Leave me, says the wretched man, me the impious, the accursed, hated of the Gods, to suffer my punishment. He sits out of doors, wrapped in sack cloth or in filthy rags. Ever and anon he rolls himself, naked, in the dirt confessing about this and that sin. He has eaten or drunk something wrong. He has gone some way or other which the divine being did not approve of" (Plutarch, 1941).

Beck (1976) has classified the symptoms of depression as emotional manifestations, cognitive manifestations, and vegetative or physical manifestations.

The presenting complaint of most depressed patients relates to feelings of hopelessness, desperation, and general misery. In one study, about 53 percent of moderately depressed patients complained first of such feelings to the physician (Beck, 1967). The fact that only about half of patients complain primarily of depressive symptoms highlights the impression of clinicians that many depressed patients do not recognize that they are suffering from depression. Many center their complaints instead on physical symptoms—usually those one would expect to derive from a depressed mood. For instance, some patients complain of diminished appetite, loss of sexual desire, and general fatigue. Others report symptoms that seem to be associated with physical disease: localized pain, apparently severe digestive disturbances, and difficulty in breathing. Careful physical examination ordinarily reveals no physical abnormality.

Upon probing, an interviewer can usually detect a genuine dejection of mood. Patients typically also have a negative self-image, describing themselves

as worthless, no good, wicked, deserving to die. At the same time, they derive
no pleasure from activities which formally brought enjoyment. Eating, sex,
work, and recreational activities are now devoid of gratification. Not surprisingly, depressed individuals lose their sense of humor; nothing seems funny or
even mildly amusing any longer. Not only activities but also other people bring
no satisfaction so that depressed persons no longer care about others. Often
they will separate from their spouse, sensing a loss of love without realizing
that they are depressed.

Most symptoms of depression increase in severity as patients vary from mild
or *neurotic* to severe or *psychotic* depression. One symptom that seems to
diminish as depression becomes more severe is crying. Frequent crying spells
are characteristic of women with mild and moderate depression. Some even say
that they can't understand why they are crying; they don't feel terribly depressed but simply have an urge to cry. Severely depressed patients tend not to
weep. Their capacity for overt emotional expression seems "washed out."
Some weep but without tears.

Cognitive manifestations
Though depression is usually regarded as a disorder of mood in contrast to
schizophrenia, a disorder of thought, there are cognitive disturbances in depression. Self-devaluation is a *sine qua non* of depression. Patients tabulate their
past and present wrongdoings or inadequacies and consistently judge themselves deficient. Religious patients chronicle their sins. As bad as the present is
for a depressed individual, the future seems even bleaker. The failure to perceive any likelihood of future improvement, a complete loss of hope, lies at the
root of the impulse to commit suicide. An important element in the psychotherapy of depression is to emphasize again and again, "While I know you feel
awful now, remember one thing—depression is always temporary and will
surely get better with time."

Along with their low self-esteem, patients often develop a distorted body
image. Women, for example, become preoccupied with their ugliness.

Depressed individuals are notoriously indecisive. Though some of them have
a premorbid obsessive personality, the difficulty depressives have in making
decisions appears somewhat different from the experience of an obsessional
neurotic in going over and over the same ground. Because they expect to make
the wrong decision, depressed persons weigh various alternatives, each of
which seems to presage a bad outcome. In addition, because they have a deficit
of emotional energy, depressed persons do not feel motivated strongly enough
to think through a decision-making process.

Motivational manifestations

Depressives appear as devoid of motivation for pursuing any of life's activities as they are devoid of pleasure. They tend to be remarkably passive and dependent. They are often described as having a "paralyzed will" and in severe cases even have difficulty rousing themselves to eat or use the toilet. It is sometimes necessary to feed, wash, and dress depressed patients much as one would handle an infant.

Depressives frequently recount that they have lost the desire to go on living, but in line with their general passivity and dependence, most are not actively suicidal. They may "wish" they were dead, but usually they do not take action. Or they may say that they don't care whether they live or die, or even beg the physician to kill them. The most severely depressed individuals have the least interest in going on living, but paradoxically they may also be lower suicidal risks. Suicides are most often reported as patients gradually emerge from depression and then muster up the energy required to carry out an effective suicidal act.

Physical manifestations

Almost all severely depressed patients lose appetite. A diminished interest in eating and loss of weight is often the first sign of an oncoming depression. Some severely depressed patients would starve to death if they were not fed by tube in the hospital. At the same time, bowel movements slow so that patients are constipated. This can become part of a delusional system in which patients envision that "my entire insides are blocked up with a stone."

Difficulty in sleeping is also a hallmark of depression. Though there may be numerous patterns of depressive insomnia, the most typical involves early morning awakening.

Psychomotor retardation gives most depressed persons a sort of inertia. Thinking and movements are greatly slowed. On the other hand, some depressives are agitated. They frequently pace the floor, wringing their hands, crying, and imploring everyone they meet to help them.

Most depressed persons lose interest in sex. Many enter sex therapy clinics with a chief complaint of impotence. Only upon careful interviewing are moderately severe depressive symptoms elicited.

Physical symptoms usually improve after treatment with antidepressant drugs before the depression lifts. This well-established clinical feature suggests that the physical aspects of depression may reflect abnormalities in centers of the brain which regulate internal organs of the body and secondarily elicit the psychological symptoms rather than vice versa.

In summary, depression invades many spheres of mental, emotional, and physical activity. No one knows which disturbance is primary. Perhaps the situation varies in different patients. For instance, one might speculate that vegetative disorders are preeminent in patients with a strong genetic component. Cognitive features could play an initiating role in patients whose condition has some characteristics of schizophrenia. In others who have suffered disappointments in life, dejected mood might be primary.

Mania

In many ways the symptoms of mania are exact opposites of those of depression, except that both manic and depressive patients have difficulty sleeping.

One can group these symptoms in the same categories applied to depression. The chief emotional symptom of mania is elation. Manics gain gratification from a wide variety of experiences and are so intensely "up" that minor hindrances to their frantic activities sometimes provoke irritable outbursts which can border on paranoia. In contrast to the self-depreciation of depressives, manics feel themselves to be wonderful and most important individuals. Whereas depressives have lost contact with others, manics regard everyone they meet as their special friend. While depressives tend to be deathly serious, manics are full of fun, telling jokes and making rhymes.

In the cognitive sphere, manics think positively about themselves and the future. They never blame themselves for anything and deny personal weaknesses. Far from having a paralyzed will, manic individuals make frequent impulsive decisions of a grandiose sort, extravagant spending sprees being common. In striking contrast to the nihilism of depressives, manics feel on top of the world and may think they can do anything within human reach.

Manics tend to talk almost incessantly, running things together end-on-end in a characteristic "flight of ideas." Though the associations may be tangential, they do make sense, in contrast to the bizarrely disordered thinking of schizophrenics.

Manics seem to display a super-excess of motivation. They are constantly embarking on new activities, seemingly free of self-doubt or any wavering of will. Physically, they have boundless energy. Many patients have worked at an incredibly fast pace for weeks on end with hardly any sleep. Manics seem to have an increased sex drive and are often flagrantly promiscuous. While manics sleep very little, they do not complain of insomnia. They will wake up after three or four hours of sleep full of energy and new projects so that they have no desire to stay in bed.

Classification

Being depressed is an experience that a large proportion of the population undergoes in some form. Many people are chronically depressed to a mild or moderate degree all their lives. Others appear quite normal for most of their childhood and adult lives but then develop extremely severe depressive episodes that can be classified as psychotic. Some people are depressed on many occasions, while others have only one depressive episode. Some patients are only depressed, while others alternate between mania and depression. Patients with other psychiatric or medical problems frequently become depressed. Up to 50 percent of alcoholics may suffer a depression as severe as individuals with pure depression (Cadoret and Winokur, 1972; Kielholz, 1969). Upon emerging from an acute psychotic episode, schizophrenics often develop a severe *post-psychotic* depression (Bowers and Astrachan, 1967; McGlashan and Carpenter, 1976; Stern et al., 1968). Depression is also common among opiate addicts (Weissman et al., 1976). Some depressed states begin soon after and apparently as a result of some life event, an environmental precipitating factor, while others seem to arise on their own, independent of the person's situation in life. Certain depressives have a clear loss of contact with reality and are presumably psychotic, but most only distort without breaking away from reality.

Because of these varied patterns, most clinicians assume that the affective disorders are not a single clinical entity. In many conditions, such as alcoholism, another disorder seems to dominate the individual's life and to provide a "good reason" to be depressed. Of course, one could also argue that the heavy drinking follows from depressive tendencies. At the other end of the spectrum, there is strong evidence of a major genetic component in some depressives whose families have a high incidence of affective disorder.

Primary and secondary affective disorders

Investigators have proposed a variety of classification systems in an effort to identify clusters of patients who suffer from specific, unitary affective disorders. To separate individuals in whom depression is secondary to other problems, such as schizophrenia, alcoholism, and drug addiction, some investigators have made two groupings: *primary affective disorder* and *secondary affective disorder* (Feighner et al., 1972; Guze et al., 1971; Robins and Guze, 1972). A primary affective disorder is one that occurs in a patient in whom no other psychiatric illness preceded the affective illness. Any depression that occurs in the course of a severe medical illness or episode of drug abuse would be classified as a secondary affective disorder. Thus, the distinction between "primary" and "secondary" does not depend on the patient's affective symptoms so much as on the presence of other abnormalities. In general, the symptoms of primary and secondary depression do not differ markedly (Weissman et al., 1977). However, there is a somewhat higher incidence of successful suicide attempts in patients with primary affective disorder.

Because several different kinds of affective disorders probably exist, investigators have attempted to distinguish various subtypes. Feighner et al., (1971) recommend specific criteria that restrict the diagnosis of depression to those individuals whose symptoms suggest the presence of a distinct psychopathologic entity. These include a depressive mood for at least two to four weeks and a minimum of four of the following associated symptoms: anorexia or weight loss, loss of energy, agitation or psychomotor retardation, sleep difficulty, self-reproach or guilt, loss of interest in usual activities, diminished ability to think or concentrate, and recurrent thoughts of death or suicide.

Unipolar and bipolar affective disorders

A straightforward classification which has proved useful in biological studies, and gained validity from them, divides patients into *unipolar* and *bipolar* affective disorders. Leonhardt et al. (1963) labeled as "bipolar" those patients who experience both mania and depression, calling those who suffer only depression "unipolar." This classification was initially proposed on the basis of family history. Bipolar illness is much more frequent in relatives of bipolar patients than it is in relatives of unipolar patients. Psychosis and suicide are also more prevalent in the families of individuals with bipolar illness. In one study, 11 percent of first-degree relatives of bipolar patients had bipolar illness and only 0.5 percent had unipolar illness, while 7 percent of the first-degree relatives of unipolar patients suffered unipolar illness and only 0.4 percent had bipolar illness (Perris, 1968; Winokur et al., 1969); Winokur et al. interviewed all available first-degree relatives of sixty-one patients who had been diagnosed as having mania and thus were bipolar. The risk of having primary affective disorders was 56 percent in the mothers of these patients and 13 percent in the fathers, and other relatives also had a high incidence of bipolar and unipolar illness. By contrast, relatives of unipolar patients had a much lower frequency of affective disturbance. These studies suggest that bipolar illness is more likely to have a genetic component than unipolar illness.

Clinical symptoms during the depressive phase also differentiate bipolar from unipolar patients. Bipolar individuals tend to become ill at an earlier age than unipolar patients. Their first episode occurs at an average age of twenty-eight years, compared to thirty-six years for unipolar patients. In general, the depressive periods of bipolar patients tend to be "retarded," while agitation and anxiety are more common in unipolar patients.

Psychotic and neurotic affective disorders

Another classification system distinguishes between *psychotic* and *neurotic* depressions. Neurotic depressions develop in response to external stresses and so are "reactive" or "exogenous," while psychotic depressions stem from some innate constitutional factor and so are "endogenous." Thus, the neurotic-psychotic and reactive-endogenous dichotomies usually distinguish between the same two groups of patients. In one sense, the distinction is based on severity of the symptoms, psychotic patients simply being sicker than neurotic ones. Some investigators have questioned whether such a distinction has any more validity than separating strep throat into two diagnostic categories of mild and severe. Kraepelin, who first defined manic-depressive illness as a single entity, felt that psychotic and neurotic depressions were differences of degree rather than of kind: "We include in the manic-depressive group certain slight and sightest colorings of mood, some of them periodic, some of them continuously morbid, which are to be regarded as the rudiments of more severe disorders" (Kraepelin, 1913).

Nevertheless, several clinical and experimental observations suggest that separate disorders of neurotic and psychotic depression may exist. When psychological rating scales are administered to a large number of depressed patients, there is a bimodal distribution of scores apparently reflecting neurotic and psychotic differences (Carney et al., 1965; Kiloh and Garside, 1963; Sandifer et al., 1966). There is evidence that electroconvulsive shock and antidepressant drug treatment are more effective in psychotic than neurotic depressions (Hordern, 1965; Mendels, 1965), although some clinicians feel that the drugs are just as useful in both (Klerman and Cole, 1965; Kline, 1965).

Other workers feel that there is no inherent difference in the symptom patterns of psychotic and neurotic depressions. In one classic study, Aubrey Lewis (1934) found that neurotic symptoms occur just as frequently in psychotic as in neurotic depressives. Many years later, careful analysis of specific symptoms in 253 patients provided a possible explanation for the psychotic-neurotic dichotomy (Guze et al., 1977). Among patients with unipolar depression no demographic, family history, or parental home variables distinguished between those with or without psychotic symptoms. Since bipolar patients can be differentiated by genetic and personality variables from other patients with affective disorder, the inclusion of unipolar individuals might explain the apparent difference between psychotic and neurotic groups.

Depression occurring about the time of menopause in women has been referred to as *involutional psychotic reaction*. It is thought that this may represent a distinct entity in which the depression is triggered by hormonal changes or by the various interpersonal losses which often occur at this time of life. Clinicians have often emphasized that involutional depressives tend to be agitated rather than retarded. Before their depression develops, these patients display personality traits such as meticulousness, stubbornness, and overconscientiousness more often than other types of depressives. Several investigators question whether involutional melancholia represents a distinct disorder. Estrogenic replacement therapy does not alleviate the patients' symptoms. Moreover, symptom analyses suggest that agitation is no more common in involutional melancholia than in other types of depression (Beck, 1967; Cassidy et al., 1957; Hopkinson, 1964).

Many patients seem to have features of both schizophrenia and depression. This has led to the diagnosis of *schizo-affective psychosis*.

Such patients usually have a more acute onset of psychotic symptoms, better premorbid adjustment, and a better prognosis than most schizophrenics. Whether these individuals suffer primarily from schizophrenia or affective disorder or whether they in fact possess both illnesses is unclear. When schizo-affective illness recurs after a remission, symptoms are often typical of depression or mania (Clayton et al., 1968). Family history studies disclose an increased prevalence of affective disorder but not of schizophrenia among relatives of these patients (Clayton et al., 1968; Cohen et al., 1972). Thus, it seems that the fundamental disturbance in most schizo-affective patients is affective disorder rather than schizophrenia.

The DSM-III classification

The DSM-III does not deal with the dichotomies of primary-secondary, neurotic-psychotic, endogenous-reactive, or agitated-retarded depressions. Instead, *episodic affective disorders* in which patients suffer a defined episode of severe illness are distinguished from *intermittent affective disorders* in individuals with a lifelong history of a depressive or hypomanic personality. A category of intermittent bipolar disorder refers to individuals with *cyclothymic* personalities whose "up" and "down" fluctuations are more marked than those of the general population. Among the episodic affective disorders, mania, depression, and bipolar illness are listed separately. By restricting its classifications to purely descriptive features, the DSM-III attempts to diminish the role of subjective judgments and theoretical considerations in making diagnoses.

The criteria for a diagnosis of depression in the DSM-3 are similar to those for primary affective disorder described above. First, individuals should have suffered a depressed mood for at least one week not in response to simple bereavement. Symptoms suggesting schizophrenic or organic mental disorder should be absent. In addition, at least four other symptoms must be present from the following group:

1. Poor appetite or weight loss or increased appetite or weight gain (change of one pound a week or ten pounds a year when not dieting).
2. Sleep difficulty or excessive sleeping.
3. Loss of energy, fatigue, or tiredness.
4. Psychomotor agitation or retardation.
5. Loss of interest or pleasure in usual activities or decrease in sexual drive.
6. Feelings of self-reproach or excessive or inappropriate guilt.
7. Complaints or evidence of diminished ability to think or concentrate, such as slow thinking or indecisiveness.
8. Recurrent thoughts of death or suicide or any suicidal behavior, including thoughts of wishing to be dead.

For a diagnosis of mania, patients should have displayed a predominantly elevated, expansive, or irritable mood for at least a week. There should be no evidence of schizophrenia or organic mental disorder. In addition, at least three of the following symptoms must be present:

1. More active than usual—socially, at work, sexually, or physically restless.
2. More talkative than usual or feeling a pressure to keep talking.
3. Flight of ideas or subjective experience that thoughts are racing.
4. Inflated self-esteem (grandiosity, which may be delusional).
5. Decreased need for sleep.
6. Distractability—i.e., attention too easily drawn to unimportant or irrelevant external stimuli.
7. Excessive involvement in activities without recognizing the high potential for painful consequences (e.g., buying sprees, sexual indiscretions, foolish business investments, and reckless driving).

References

Beck, A. T. *Depression, cause and treatment.* University of Pennsylvania Press, Philadelphia, 1967, p. 12.
Bowers, M. B., and Astrachan, B. M. Depression in acute schizophrenic psychoses. *Am. J. Psychiat., 123:*976–979, 1967.
Cadoret, R. and Winokur, G. Depression in alcoholism. *Ann. N.Y. Acad. Sci., 233:*34–39, 1972.
Carney, M. W. P., Roth, M., and Garside, R. F. The diagnosis of depressive syndromes and the prediction of ECT response. *Br. J. Psychiat., 3:*654–674, 1965.
Cassidy, W. L., Flanagan, N. B., and Spellman, M. Clinical observations in manic-depressive disease: A quantitative study of 100 manic-depressive patients and 50 medically sick controls. *J. Am. Med. Assoc., 1644:*1535–1546, 1957.
Clayton, P. J., Rodin, L., and Winokur, G. Family history studies; III. Schizo-affective

disorder: Clinical and genetic factors including a one to two year follow up. *Comp. Psychiat., 9:*31–49, 1968.

Cohen, S. M., Allen, M. G., Pollin, W., and Hrubeck, Z. Relationship of schizo-affective psychosis to manic depressive psychosis and schizophrenia. *Arch. Gen. Psychiat., 26:*539–546, 1972.

Custance, J. *Wisdom, madness, and folly.* Farrar, Straus and Cudahy, 1952. Reprinted in *The inner world of mental illness,* ed. B. Kaplan. Harper & Row, New York, 1964, p. 56.

Feighner, J., Robins, E., Guze, S. B., Woodruff, R. A., Winokur, G., and Munoz, R. Diagnostic criteria for use in psychiatric research. *Arch. Gen. Psychiat., 26:*57–63, 1972.

Gibson, J. K., Ebert, M. H., and Bunney, W. E., Jr. Mental effects of reserpine in man: A review. In *Psychiatric Complications of Medical Drugs,* ed. R. Shader. Raven Press, New York, 1972, pp. 73–101.

Guze, S. B., Woodruff, R. A., and Clayton, P. J. Secondary affective disorder: A study of 95 cases. *Psychol. Med., 1:*428–436, 1971.

Guze, S. B., Woodruff, R. A., and Clayton, P. J. The significance of psychotic affective disorders. *Arch. Gen. Psychiat., 32:*1147–1150, 1977.

Hopkinson, G. A genetic study of affective illness in patients over 50. *Br. J. Psychiat., 110:*244–254, 1964.

Hordern, A. The antidepressant drugs. *N. Eng. J. Med., 272:*1159–1169, 1965.

Kielholz, P. Alcohol and depression. *Br. J. Addict., 565:*187–193, 1969.

Kiloh, L. G., and Garside, R. F. The independence of neurotic depression and endogenous depression. *Br. J. Psychiat., 109:*451–463, 1963.

Klerman, G. L., and Cole, J. O. Clinical pharmacology of imipramine and related antidepressant compounds. *Pharmacol. Rev., 17:*101–104, 1965.

Kline, N. Practical management of depression. *J. Am. Med. Assoc., 190:*732–740, 1965.

Kraepelin, E. *Textbook of psychiatry.* Trans. by R. M. Barclay, Livingston, Edinborough, 1913.

Leonhardt, K., Karff, I., and Shulz, H. Temperament in den famillien der monopolaren und bipolaren, phasischen, psychosin. *J. Psychiat. Neurol., 143:*416–434, 1963.

Lewis, A. Melancholia: A clinical survey of depressive states. *J. Ment. Sci., 80:*277–278, 1934.

Logan, J. Address to the American Medical Association, 1973. In *Mood Swing* by R. R. Fieve. Bantam Books, New York, 1976, pp. 30, 34.

Logan, J. *Josh.* Delacorte Press, New York, 1976, pp. 154, 159, 161, 363, and 365.

McGlashan, T. H., and Carpenter, W. T. Post-psychotic depression in schizophrenia. *Arch. Gen. Psychiat., 33:*231–239, 1976.

Mendels, J. Electroconvulsive therapy and depression. *Br. J. Psychiat., 3:*675–681, 1965.

Perris, C. Genetic transmission of depressive psychosis. *Acta Psychiat. Scand.* suppl. *203:*45–52, 1968.

Plutarch, quoted in Zilboorg, G. *A history of medical psychology.* Norton, New York, 1941.

Robins, E., and Guze, S. B. Classification of affective disorders: The primary-secondary, the endogenous-reactive and the neurotic psychotic concepts. In *Recent advances in psychobiology of the depressive illnesses: Proceedings of a work-shop sponsored by the NIMH,* eds. Williams, T. A., Katz, M. M., and Shield, J. A. U.S. Government Printing Office, Washington, D.C., 1972.

Sandifer, M. G., Jr., Wilson, I. C., and Green, L. The two-type thesis of depressive disorders. *Am. J. Psychiat., 123:*93–97, 1966.

Stern, J. J., Brunschwig, L., Duffy, J. P., Agle, D. P., Rosenbaum, A. L., and bidder, T. G. Comparison of therapeutic effects and memory changes with bilateral and unilateral ECT. *Am. J. Psychiat., 125:*294–304, 1968.

Weissman, M. M., Plobetz, F., and Prusoff, B. A. Clinical depression among narcotic addicts maintained on methadone in the community. *Am. J. Psychiat., 133:*1434–1438, 1976.

Weissman, M. M., Pottenger, M., Kleber, H., Ruben, H. L., Williams, D., and Thompson, W. D. Symptom patterns in primary and secondary depression. *Arch. Gen. Psychiat., 34:*854–862, 1977.

Winokur, G., Clayton, P., and Reich, T. *Manic depressive illness.* C. V. Mosby Co., St. Louis, 1969.

2. Affective disorders: etiology and treatment

Affective disorders are so varied in their manifestations that they probably represent a collection of diverse entities. This tentative conclusion fits with evidence that a wide range of genetic, biochemical, and psychological mechanisms are implicated in these conditions.

Genetic factors

The most impressive evidence for genetic determination of a vulnerability to affective disorders has been obtained for bipolar illness. Twin studies show a higher concordance for all types of affective disorders in monozygotic (identical) as opposed to dizygotic (fraternal) twins. Most strikingly, there is also a high correlation between the type of affective disturbance in monozygotic twins. If one twin is manic-depressive and the other develops affective disorder, it will almost invariably be manic-depressive (Cadoret and Winokur, 1975; Price, 1968; Slater and Cowie, 1971; Zerbin-Rudin, 1968). This is particularly striking when one considers that bipolar affective disturbance is much less common than unipolar illness.

In a summary of twin studies of affective illness, Allen (1976) noted that the overall concordance rate for bipolar illness in monozygotic twins was 72 percent while the corresponding figure for dizygotic twins was only 14 percent. In unipolar affective disorder the concordance rate for monozygotic twins (40 percent) also exceeded that for dizygotic twins (11 percent). However the magnitude of the difference between monozygotic and dizygotic twins was greater for bipolar than unipolar affective illness. This observation is consistent with the assumption that bipolar and unipolar disorders represent distinct entities and that the genetic loading is greater for bipolar illness.

In several large-scale studies, the incidence of bipolar illness has been much higher among the relatives of bipolar patients than among the relatives of unipolar patients (Angst and Perris, 1972). Bipolar patients also have family members with a high frequency of hypomanic personality traits, an elated state less pronounced than mania, even in the absence of clear affective disorder. In unipolar families, on the other hand, depressive personality traits are more common (Cadoret, 1972; Cadoret et al., 1970).

Studies of genetic linkage have shed light on the mode of inheritance of affective disorders. In these investigations, known genetic markers are utilized to delineate other genetically more questionable traits. If the trait in question is located on the same chromosome close to the marker gene, then one may be able to follow through several generations correlations between the trait being studied and the marker gene. X-chromosome traits such as particular antigens and red-green color blindness are distributed through several generations of certain families together with a diathesis, or vulnerability, for developing bipolar illness (Cadoret and Winokur, 1975; Rich and Winokur, 1969). These findings suggest that at least in some manic-depressive families the vulnerability to fall ill is transmitted on the X-chromosome as a dominant gene. In other family studies, X-linked transmission could not be demonstrated (Perris, 1968).

Genetic studies of unipolar affective disturbance are less extensive. In one study of 100 families, patients with an earlier onset of depression had a larger number of first-degree relatives with affective illness than did those with a later onset (Winokur et al., 1971).

Evidence that unipolar affective disorder may represent more than one disease entity derives from findings of a much higher frequency of alcoholism and sociopathy among the relatives of patients whose depression has an early onset than among the general population.

Common illnesses with genetic components such as diabetes are usually determined by several different genetic factors. Results of the various genetic studies suggest such a pattern for affective disorder, which afflicts 5 to 8 percent of all people some time in their lives.

These genetic studies establish that some people have a specific vulnerability to affective disorder, which is most striking in the case of bipolar patients. However, this vulnerability is only a disposition toward illness. Clearly environmental factors must also play a role. Since only about half the identical twins of patients with severe depression develop the same disorder, abnormal genes alone are insufficient to cause the disease.

Many clinicians feel that depression is precipitated by certain life events, especially personal losses. Several studies have compared the frequency of life events out of the normal range in depressed patients, normal controls, and other psychiatric patients or hospitalized medical patients. Depressed patients report two to three times as many disruptive life events as normal controls or other psychiatric patients (Levi et al., 1966; Paykel et al., 1969). Schizophrenics report far fewer precipitating stresses in the six months before hospitalization than do depressives (Beck and Worthen, 1972; Jacobs et al., 1974). The stresses that typically occur before the onset of a depressive episode appear to be events that pose threats. These threats most often involve separation, as with middle-aged women who see their children growing up and leaving home (Brown et al., 1973; Deykin et al., 1966).

Though stressful life events, especially separations, occur more often among depressed patients than among others, one cannot invariably link the occurrence of depression to a precipitating environmental factor. In one study, separations increased the probability of depression by five to six times, but even so, less than 10 percent of people experiencing wrenching separations became depressed (Brown et al., 1973). Individual personality type also increases vulnerability. Obsessional people tolerate change poorly. Dependent personalities are particularly threatened by increased responsibility. Adults who experienced a parental loss during childhood may be especially sensitive to losses. This latter relationship was demonstrated elegantly in a study that revealed a combination of early childhood and recent adult separations in a large number of suicidal patients (Levi et al., 1966).

Psychological theories

Psychoanalytic theories of depression seem to be predicated on a few specific clinical observations. First of all, Freud emphasized the resemblance between depression and mourning. He compared the sequence of psychological events during bereavement to what might be going on in the mind of a depressed person. Second, clinicians have consistently noted how much depressed patients, especially retarded depressives, behave like helpless infants. They may refuse to take care of themselves and can be extremely dependent. Though they berate themselves for being ineffective and helpless, they are in effect powerful manipulators of their family, friends, and physicians.

In focusing on the idea of loss in depression as in mourning, Freud had to deal with the fact that most depressives do not suffer concrete losses; so he concluded that depression might follow "the loss of some abstraction which has taken the place of one [real object] such as one's country, liberty, an ideal and so on.'' To explain why patients indulge in so much self-reproach, often appearing to be angry with themselves, Freud noted that ''if one listens patiently to a melancholic's various self-accusations, one cannot in the end avoid the impression that often the most violent of them are hardly applicable to the patient himself, but that with insignificant modification they do fit someone else, someone whom the patient loves or has loved or should love.'' Thus, Freud concluded that the self-reproaches were not directed at the patient but at the introjected image of the lost love object. In other words, like a small child, the depressed patient is enraged at his beloved for leaving him (Freud, 1957).

Other psychoanalysts, especially Karl Abraham, felt that the *recalcitrant obstinacy* of the depressed individual reflects a fixation at the anal stage. The traditional psychoanalytic view, on the other hand, is that the helpless, dependent behavior, the begging to be cared for by others, resembles the oral stage of psychosexual development. Most psychoanalytic formulations of depression involve various combinations of these themes. The oral components of depression have been broadened by recent analysts to include a wide variety of psychological needs related to self-esteem. Analysts such as Rado and Bibring have suggested that depressives differ from other people in deriving more of their self-esteem from external sources—the approval, affection, appreciation, and love of others—instead of from their own inner strength (Bibring, 1953; Rado, 1928).

One detailed psychoanalytic study supports the notion that individuals with bipolar illness require for their self-esteem substantial approval from their parents, friends, and professional associates. Cohen et al. (1954) intensively investigated the personality characteristics and family interactions of twelve of their bipolar patients and found a typical family background. As children, the patients were used by their parents as a means of gaining social acceptability. The children were expected to be better behaved than others in the neighborhood, and they complied. In adult life before the onset of mania or depressive episodes, these patients appeared to be extremely dependent individuals who managed to maintain emotional equilibrium by working hard to gain acceptance from others. They apparently felt a need to meet extremely high standards in order to merit love and so felt chronically inferior. They were ''conventionally well behaved and frequently successful'' and were typically hard working and conscientious; indeed, at times this overconscientiousness and scrupulousness led to their being called ''obsessional.'' They were ''typically involved in one or more relations of extreme dependence.''

Cohen et al. (1954) felt that manic-depressive episodes were triggered in such persons by real or imagined losses because their ''principal source of anxiety is the fear of abandonment.'' These psychiatrists disagreed with Freud and

Abraham in contending that rage and hostility were not major ingredients. They felt that hostility, whether directed outward or inward, was only a secondary reaction which arose when needs to achieve acceptance and love were frustrated.

Based on detailed clinical evaluations including rating scales, Beck (1967) suggested that cognitive rather than affective factors may be important in depression. He demonstrated that depressed patients think illogically in evaluating their self-worth, resulting in low self-esteem and depressive affect. The logical errors he found included overgeneralizing, magnifying, and minimizing events, as well as basing conclusions on highly selective components of available data. Whether these cognitive aberrations give rise to depressive feelings rather than the reverse is a chicken-egg dilemma which is not readily resolved.

Biochemical theories

The existence of genetic elements in at least some cases of affective disorder implies an associated biochemical abnormality. No such change has ever been conclusively identified in the brains or body fluids of any patients. The evidence that permits one to formulate biochemical theories derives largely from the influence of drugs on depressive symptoms and on neurotransmitters—chemicals that transmit nerve impulses from cell to cell—in the brain (Maas, 1975; Schildkraut and Kety, 1967).

Drugs that can cause symptoms closely resembling those of severe depression produce effects upon brain neurotransmitters that are virtually the opposite of the changes elicited by antidepressant drugs. The neurotransmitters which have been implicated are serotonin (5-hydroxytryptamine) and norepinephrine (see Figure 6.2). Both of these neurotransmitters are localized in parts of the brain known to be involved in the regulation of emotional behavior, specifically the limbic system and hypothalamus. These transmitters are contained within specific neurons and are highly concentrated in vesicles within nerve terminals (see Figure 6.1). Reserpine, a widely used antihypertensive drug, weakens the binding sites for serotonin and norepinephrine within the vesicles so that the transmitters gradually leak out into the synapse—the gap between nerve cells—and are destroyed by enzymes. After a period of a day or so, the brain may be completely depleted of its serotonin and norepinephrine content. Strikingly, a large number of hypertensive patients treated with reserpine develop depressive symptoms. In about 15 percent of cases, these symptoms are sufficiently severe that they can be clinically indistinguishable from psychotic depression. Thus, a depletion of serotonin and norepinephrine may be associated with depressive symptoms.

Two major classes of drugs are used in the treatment of depression. The monoamine oxidase (MAO) inhibitors block the activity of the enzyme mono-amine oxidase, which can destroy both norepinephrine and serotonin (see Figure 6.6, 6.7). Administration of these drugs results in a buildup of serotonin and norepinephrine concentrations. Some of the accumulated transmitter molecules spill out into the synaptic cleft to act on receptor sites (see Figure 6.1). While reserpine results in a deficiency of these transmitters, monoamine oxidase inhibitors produce an excess.

Tricyclic antidepressants are the most widely used antidepressant drugs. They exert their effects by preventing the inactivation of serotonin and norepinephrine molecules which have been released into the synapse through normal nerve impulse flow. Though monoamine oxidase and other enzymes can degrade serotonin and norepinephrine, these transmitters are inactivated after synaptic release primarily by a pumplike mechanism that takes them back into the nerve ending from which they had been released (see Figure 6.1). The tricyclic antidepressants block this reuptake mechanism, potentiating the actions of released transmitters. Thus, like the monoamine oxidase inhibitors, these drugs produce an excess of synaptically active serotonin and norepinephrine.

Electroconvulsive shock therapy, which is highly effective in relieving depression, causes neurons all over the brain to fire. One can readily envision how increased firing of serotonin and norepinephrine neurons following such treatment might relieve depression, which fits well with neurotransmitter hypotheses of depression.

Since reserpine, monoamine oxidase inhibitors, and tricyclic antidepressants affect both serotonin and norepinephrine, it is difficult to distinguish between the roles of these two transmitters in depressive disorders. Administration of tryptophan, the amino acid precursor of serotonin (see Figure 6.7), can increase the formation of serotonin without increasing norepinephrine. Trials of tryptophan in depressed patients have indicated a therapeutic effect, though there is a certain amount of controversy about the efficacy of this agent (Carroll, 1971; Coppen et al., 1972; Goodwin et al., 1972). While the therapeutic effects of tryptophan in depression suggest a unique role for serotonin, the effects of another agent indicate that norepinephrine also mediates the symptoms of depression. The drug α-methyl-dopa (Aldomet) is used to treat high blood pressure. It interferes with the formation and release of norepinephrine but not of serotonin. As with reserpine, a substantial number of patients treated with α-methyl-dopa develop depression.

Some studies have provided direct evidence of a serotonin abnormality in certain depressed patients. Spinal fluid levels of 5-hydroxyindoleacetic acid, a breakdown product of serotonin (see Figure 6.1), are an indirect reflection on the amount of serotonin released in the brain. Spinal fluid analyses in depressed patients reveal a biphasic distribution (Asberg et al., 1976). Some possess normal levels of this compound, while others display extremely low levels. Clinically, the patients with low levels of 5-hydroxyindoleacetic acid appear to be retarded depressives. In one study that provided more direct evidence for neurotransmitter hypotheses, levels of serotonin were reported to be low in the brains of patients who had committed suicide, compared with the brains of individuals dying of other causes (Bourne et al., 1968).

Most theoretical formulations of affective disorder based on studies of neurotransmitters assume that a deficit of norepinephrine and serotonin in depressed states is complemented by an excess during mania. The fact that antidepressents sometimes cause the symptoms of bipolar depressed patients to switch abruptly to mania is consistent with this notion. However, the remarkable effects of lithium ions are difficult to explain. Administered acutely, lithium relieves the symptoms of mania. Administered chronically, it prevents the recurrence of depressive episodes. In a sense lithium "normalizes" patients, which does not fit simply with the above theories.

In summary, one can alter the symptoms of affective disorder by manipulating levels of neurotransmitters. This by no means proves that abnormalities in these transmitter systems are primarily responsible for the symptoms of the disease. However, research stimulated by an interest in the actions of antidepressant drugs has contributed greatly to the increased understanding of the neurotransmitter systems that regulate emotional behavior. Moreover, an understanding of the mechanisms of action of antidepressants has made possible a scientific biochemical approach to the development of more effective agents.

Treatment

One fact about affective disorders is crucial for therapy, even with extremely sick patients: These disorders are *episodic*. Before the advent of modern treatment techniques, manic and depressive conditions gradually improved, though recovery might require a year or more. In those days treatment was largely supportive. With severely depressed patients, heroic efforts such as tube feedings were often made to keep the patients from starving to death. Physical restraints and heavy sedation prevented excessively manic patients from killing themselves through overactivity. Extreme precautions were necessary to prevent suicide attempts. Much more effective methods of treatment are available now.

Electroconvulsive therapy

To the general public, "hooking a person's brain to the house current" may seem like a barbaric form of treatment. One wonders how physicians would have come to use such methods. Actually, they have a long history. Inducing convulsions to treat mental illness was initiated in 1785 by Oliver, who employed camphor as a convulsant drug. In the 1920s Von Meduna reported success in treating schizophrenic patients with camphor-induced convulsions. Camphor was unreliable, however, as it produced overly severe seizures in some patients and no convulsions in others. Convulsive therapy came into wide use only after Cerletti introduced electroconvulsive treatment (ECT) (Cerletti and Bini, 1938). Throughout the 1940s ECT was applied frequently in the treatment of schizophrenia, and psychiatrists experimented with its use in many other conditions. Gradually, it became apparent that ECT offered no selective therapeutic benefit in schizophrenia, but it did relieve depression. Subsequent controlled studies have validated these claims.

ECT is now generally recognized as the most effective treatment of depression. In well-controlled studies comparing ECT with tricyclic antidepressants and monoamine oxidase inhibitors as well as placebos, ECT is consistently more effective (Greenblatt et al., 1964; McDonald et al., 1966; Shepherd, 1965; Wittenborn et al., 1962). Psychotic depression seems to respond best to ECT. Even when patients with various kinds of depression are evaluated, however, ECT is effective in 75 to 90 percent of cases (Ilaria and Prange, 1975). In addition, the therapeutic effects of ECT occur more rapidly than those of antidepressant drugs. For this reason, ECT may be the treatment of choice for severely depressed, suicidal patients or for patients in danger of extreme malnutrition or death because they do not eat. Treatment with ECT is usually combined with prolonged administration of antidepressant drugs for up to a year after completion of the course of ECT. This regimen has been shown to prevent relapses of depression (Kay et al., 1970; Seager and Bird, 1962).

The popular conception of ECT involves patients responding to the electric current with gross convulsions, complete with flailing limbs. In fact, ECT is conventionally utilized in conjunction with the muscle relaxant succinycholine. Though convulsive electrical activity occurs within the brain, the limbs do not move at all. When ECT was first introduced, appropriate muscle relaxants were not available so that some patients suffered fractures of the vertebrae, a side effect which no longer occurs. Presently ECT treatments are usually administered every two or three days for a total of about six treatments. After the seizure ends, the patient is alert in about ten minutes. Before the electric current is applied, patients are put to sleep with an intravenous barbiturate.

The dangers of ECT are relatively small. The likelihood of death is no greater than with general anesthesia—about one in 3,000 cases. The major side effect of ECT is its effect on memory. For a few days after treatment, patients are somewhat confused. Abnormalities in memory functioning persist for about a month. These involve both retrograde and anterograde amnesia for events before and after the ECT. Short-term memory appears normal, but if the interval between exposure to an item and attempts at its recall is increased, the amnesia is evident (Cronholm, 1969; Dornbush et al., 1971; Ottoson, 1960). There have been anecdotal accounts of patients with some irreversible memory loss, but these have not been apparent in well-controlled clinical studies.

Recently unilateral ECT has been applied as a means of reducing memory deficit. If ECT is used only on the nondominant hemisphere, there is much less amnesia (Inglis, 1969; Lancaster et al., 1958; Strain et al., 1968; Zomora and Kaelbling, 1965). Several studies indicate that the therapeutic effect of unilateral ECT is equivalent to that of bilateral ECT (Bidder et al., 1970; Fleminger et al., 1970). Thus, unilateral ECT appears to be the treatment procedure of choice when electroconvulsive therapy is indicated for the patient.

Antidepressant drugs
Though ECT is more effective than antidepressant drugs, the greater ease of using drugs and the general social revulsion against "shock" therapy have restricted its application. Thus, antidepressant drugs have become the primary mode of treatment for patients with severe or moderate depression. With mild depression, some physicians prefer to rely exclusively upon psychotherapy.

The first monoamine oxidase inhibitor, iproniazid, was synthesized as an analogue of the valuable antituberculosis drug isoniazid. When iproniazid was administered to tuberculosis patients, astute physicians noticed that some patients seemed happier than could be accounted for simply by the relief of tubercular symptoms. Only later was the drug shown to be an inhibitor of monoamine oxidase. Thereupon, pharmaceutical companies synthesized many potent inhibitors of monoamine oxidase, all of which were found to be effective antidepressants.

Certain side effects of the monoamine oxidase inhibitors have restricted their use so much that they are rarely employed today in the United States. These drugs inhibit the ability of the enzyme monoamine oxidase to destroy amine compounds such as serotonin and norepinephrine. However, naturally occurring amines are present in the diet. One of them is tyramine, which is contained in many foods such as certain wines, cheeses, and bananas. Tyramine is potent in raising blood pressure. Most dietary tyramine is rapidly destroyed by monoamine oxidase in the intestine and liver. In patients treated with monoamine oxidase inhibitors, however, dietary tyramine remains intact and can produce hypertension, on rare occasions severely enough to result in sudden death (Blackwell et al., 1967). Accordingly, the extensive dietary restrictions needed to prevent the ingestion of tyramine make the monoamine oxidase inhibitors impractical drugs.

The tricyclic antidepressants are the major drugs now in clinical use. Somewhat paradoxically, their acute effects include sedation. Clinicians take advantage of the sedative actions by administering the major portion of the daily dose at bedtime, which helps relieve insomnia, a frequent problem for depressed patients. For reasons which are as yet unclear, one to three weeks usually elapse before the full antidepressant effects of tricyclic drugs, as well as monoamine oxidase inhibitors, are evident. This lag phase may preclude the use of these agents in highly suicidal patients, for whom ECT may be preferable.

The major side effects of tricyclic agents involve actions resembling those of the anticholinergic drug atropine. These include a dry mouth, blurry vision, and difficulty in urinating.

A substantial number of patients undergo relapse. Controlled studies demonstrate that continued treatment with tricyclic drugs tends to prevent such relapses (Klein and Davis, 1969).

Lithium

This simple metal ion is one of the most remarkable drugs in psychiatry. Its effects in manic-depressive patients are astonishing. Lithium was discovered as a treatment for mania serendipitously by an Australian physician, John Cade, in 1949 (Cade, 1949). At the time, lithium was utilized in the treatment of cardiac patients as a means of reducing their sodium retention. With very high doses of lithium—no one knowing then what the normal range should be—the total sodium balance of the body was disrupted and several fatalities ensued.

American physicians were reluctant to test such a risky drug. A Danish investigator, Mogens Schou, followed up on Cade's findings in extensive clinical studies which confirmed that lithium was indeed effective in treating mania. At that time, the only way to cope with the disruptive behavior of manics was by massive sedation. In contrast, lithium did not cause any alteration in the patients' level of consciousness. Instead, it seemed to normalize them (Schou et al., 1954). In the late 1960's lithium was introduced into the United States, and its dramatic efficacy in the treatment of mania was again demonstrated (Bunney et al., 1968; Fieve et al., 1968).

Equally remarkable was the discovery of Schou and his associates that prophylactic administration of lithium prevented the recurrence of depression both in manic-depressive patients and in unipolar patients with recurrent depression (Braastrup and Schou, 1967). These findings were confirmed by numerous groups (Coppen et al., 1971; Prien et al., 1973).

Besides its practical therapeutic benefits, lithium may advance our understanding of fundamental abnormalities in affective disorders. It is easy to imagine how a "stimulating" drug might relieve depression even if it did not act at the specific site of abnormality in the brains of depressed patients. Similarly, one can see how a "quieting" drug might ease the symptoms of mania. A drug that normalizes patients, preventing both manic and depressive episodes, would seem to be acting at some site closely linked to the fundamental abnormality of the manic-depressive disorder.

Psychotherapy

During an active manic phase or in the throes of severe depression, patients with affective disorder are not accessible to insight-oriented psychotherapy. The manic individual simply doesn't "stay put" mentally long enough to communicate in a psychotherapeutic relationship. Depressed patients are often unable to focus emotional energy upon the work of psychotherapy. Any apparent insights tend to make them feel more guilty (Cohen, 1975; Freyhan, 1960).

Though there is no evidence from controlled studies that psychotherapy alone can accelerate the recovery from a severe depressive episode (West, 1975), supportive elements of psychotherapy in conjunction with physical therapy can be important in facilitating recovery. One of the most difficult problems in conducting psychotherapy with depressed patients is to develop appropriate rapport. Though depressed patients become very dependent on their therapists, they tend not to feel emotionally close. The detached "blank wall" approach of psychoanalytically oriented therapists may be useful in dealing with some neurotics, but it is often counterproductive with depressed patients. If the therapist does nothing, the patient will also say nothing and may spend the therapeutic hour privately ruminating about his or her guilt and misery. With depressed patients, the therapist often must do much of the talking. Reassurance is an important element of treatment. Patients should be informed clearly that theirs is a self-limited disorder because most depressed individuals are convinced that they will never get better. Following recovery, many patients have told their therapist that reassurance of eventual recovery made their existence much more tolerable and kept them from committing suicide (Ayd, 1961; Beck, 1967).

Left to their own devices, severely depressed patients, especially retarded ones, may do nothing but sit and bemoan their fate. Agitated patients will pace and cry a lot. It is best that the therapist structure the patient's time with various activities, provided that these are not unduly demanding. Even though they may take no pleasure in a hobby or physical exercise, the ability to be active at all provides reassurance that some day they will again indulge in these activities spontaneously.

A crucial task in dealing with a depressed patient is to recognize and cope with the suicidal risk (Castelnuovo-Tedesco, 1967; Friedman, 1962). Some therapists may not want to mention suicide for fear of giving patients the idea of killing themselves, but this merely increases the emotional distance between patient and therapist since the patient realizes that the therapist is not attentive to his or her most serious feelings.

When patients crystallize a firm intention to kill themselves, they often hide it from their friends and therapist and may even put on a cheerful facade. The suicidal risk actually may increase as a person emerges from depression and galvanizes adequate emotional strength to carry out the act. Accordingly, therapists must be attuned to subtle hints of farewell messages. They should also recognize the increased danger of suicide attempts at times of separation, such as the therapist's vacation.

In summary, though organic treatments such as lithium, antidepressant drugs, and ECT are the most effective method of treatment for severe mania or depression, supportive psychotherapy should always be incorporated into the treatment program. In relatively mild cases of depression, psychotherapy alone may be adequate.

References

Allen, M. G. Twin studies of affective illness. *Arch. Gen. Psychiat., 33:*1476–1478, 1976.

Angst, J. and Perris, C. The nosology of endogenous depression—Comparison of the results of two studies. *Int. J. Ment. Health, 1:*145–158, 1972.

Asberg, M., Thorén, P., Träskman, L., Bertilsson, L., and Ringberger, V. Serotonin depression—a biochemical subgroup within the affective disorders? *Science, 191:*478–480, 1976.

Ayd, F. J., Jr. *Recognizing the depressed patient.* Grune and Stratton, New York, 1961.

Beck, A. T. *Depression, cause and treatment.* University of Pennsylvania Press, Philadelphia, 1967, p. 12.

Beck, J. C., and Worthen, J. C. Precipitating stress, crisis theory and hospitalization in schizophrenia and depression. *Arch. Gen. Psychiat., 26:*123–129, 1972.

Bibring, E. The mechanism of depression. In *Affective disorders,* ed. P Greenacre. International University Press, New York, 1953.

Bidder, T. G., Strain, J. J., and Brunschwig, L. Bilateral and unilateral ECT: Follow-up study and critique *Am. J. Psychiat., 127:*373–745, 1970.

Blackwell, B., Barley, E., Price, J., and Taylor, D. Hypertensive interactions between monoamine oxidase inhibitors and food stuffs. *Br. J. Psychiat., 113:*349–365, 1967.

Bourne, H. R., Bunney, W. E., Jr., Colburn, R. W., Davis, J. M., Shaw, D. M., and Coppen, A. J. Noradrenaline, 5-hydroxytryptamine and 5-hydroxyindoleacetic acid in hindbrains of suicidal patients. Lancet, Oct. 12, 1968, pp. 805–808.

Braastrup, P. C., and Schou, M. Lithium as a prophylactic agent: Its effect against recurrent depressions and manic-depressive psychosis. *Arch. Gen. Psychiat., 16:*162, 1967.

Brown, G. W., Sklair, F., Harris, T. O., and Birley, J. L. T. Life events and psychiatric disorders. Part I: Some methodological issues. *Psychol. Med., 3:*74–87, 1973.

Bunney, W. E., Goodwin, F. K., Davis, J. M., and Fawcett, J. A. A behavioral study of lithium treatment. *Am. J. Psychiat., 125:*499, 1968.

Cade, J. F. J. Lithium salt in the treatment of psychotic excitement. *Med. J. Australia, 1:*195, 1949.

Cadoret, R. J. Family differences in illness and personality in affective disorder. In *Life history research in psychopathology,* eds. M. Roff, L. Robins and M. Pollack. University of Minnesota Press, Minneapolis, 1972.

Cadoret, R., and Winokur, G. Genetic Studies of affective disorders. In *The nature and treatment of depression,* eds. F. F. Flach and S. C. Draghi. Wiley and Sons, New York, 1975, pp. 335–346.

Cadoret, R. J., Winokur, G., and Clayton, P. Family history studies VII. Manic-depressive disease vs. depressive disease. *Br. J. Psychiat., 116:*625–635, 1970.

Carroll, B. J. Monoamine precursors in the treatment of depression. *Clin. Pharm. and Thera., 12:*743–761, 1971.

Castelnuovo-Tedesco, P. Brief psychotherapeutic treatment of the depressive reactions. *Int. Psychiat. Clin., 3:*197–210, 1967.

Cerletti, V., and Bini, L. L'Elettroshock. *Arch. Gen. Neurol., Psichiat, Psicoanal, 19:*266–268, 1938.

Cohen, M. B., Baker, G., Cohen, R. A., Weigert, E. V., and Fromm-Reichmann, F. An intensive study of 12 cases of manic-depressive psychosis. *Psychiatry,* 17:103–137, 1954.

Cohen, R. A. Manic depressive illness. In *Comprehensive textbook of psychiatry II,* eds. A. M. Freedman, H. I. Kaplan, and B. J. Sadock. Williams and Wilkins, Baltimore, 1975, pp. 1012–1024.

Coppen, A., Noguera, R., Bailey, J. Burns, B. H., Sivani, J. S., Hare, E. H., Gardner, R., and Maggs, R. Prophylactic lithium in affective disorders. *Lancet, 2:*275, 1971.

Coppen, A. Whybrow, P. C., Noguera, R., et al. The comparative antidepressant value of L-tryptophan and imipramine with and without attempted potentiation by liothyronine. *Arch. Gen. Psychiat., 26:*234–241, 1972.

Cronholm, B. Post-ECT amnesia. In *The pathology of memory,* Academic Press, New York, 1969.

Deykin, E. S., Jacobson, S., Klerman, G. L., and Solomon, M. The empty nest: Psychosocial aspects of conflict between depressed women and their grown children. *Am. J. Psychiat., 122:*1422–1426, 1966.

Dornbush, R., Abrams, R., and Fink, M. Memory changes after unilateral and bilateral convulsive therapy. *Br. J. Psychiat., 119:*75–78, 1971.

Fieve, R. R., Platman, S. R., and Plutchik, R. R. The use of lithium in affective disorders I. Acute endogenous depression. *Am. J. Psychiat., 125:*487, 1968.

Fleminger, J. J., Horne, D. J., Nair, N. P. V., and Nott, P. N. Differential effect of unilateral and bilateral ECT. *Am. J. Psychiat., 127:*4, 1970.

Freud, S. *Mourning and melancholia,* standard ed. London, Hogarth Press, *14:*237–260, 1957.

Freyhan, F. A. The modern treatment of depressive disorder. *Am. J. Psychiat., 116:*1057, 1960.

Friedman, P. Some considerations on the treatment of suicidal depressive patients. *Am. J. Psychiat., 16:*379–386, 1962.

Goodwin, J. K., Ebert, M. H., and Bunney, W. E., Jr. Mental effects of reserpine in man: A review. In *Psychiatric complications of medical drugs,* ed. R. Shader. Raven Press, New York, 1972, pp. 73–101.

Greenblatt, M., Grosser, G. H., and Wechsler, H. Differential response of hospitalized depressed patients to somatic therapy. *Am. J. Psychiat., 120:*935–943, 1964.

Ilaria, R., and Prange, A. J. Convulsive therapy and other biological treatments. In *The Nature and Treatment of depression,* eds. F. F. Flach and S. C. Draghi. Wiley and Sons, New York, 1975, pp. 271–308.

Inglis, J. Electrode placement and the effect of ECT on mood and memory in depression. *Canad. Psych. Assoc. J., 14:* 1969.

Jacobs, S. C., Prusoff, B. A., and Paykeles, E. S. Recent life events in schizophrenia and depression. *Psychol. Med., 4:*444–453, 1974.

Kay, D. W., Fahy, T., and Garside, R. F. A seven month double blind trial of amitriptyline and diazepam in ECT treated depressed patients. *Br. J. Psychiat., 117:*667–671, 1970.

Klein, D. F., and Davis, J. M. *Diagnosis and drug treatment of psychiatric disorders.* Williams and Wilkins, Baltimore, 1969.

Kline, N. Practical management of depression. *J. Am. Med. Assoc., 190:*732–740, 1964.

Lancaster, N., Steinert, R., and Frost, I. Unilateral electroconvulsive therapy. *J. Ment. Sci., 104:*221–227, 1958.

Levi, L. D., Fales, C. H., Stein, M. and Sharp, V. H. Separation and attempted suicide. *Arch. Gen. Psychiat., 15:*158–165, 1966.

Maas, J. W. Biogenic amines and depression. *Arch. Gen. Psychiat., 32:*1357–1361, 1975.

McDonald, I. M., Perkins, M., Merjerrison, G., and Podilsky, M. A controlled comparison of amitriptyline and electroconvulsive therapy in the treatment of depression. *Am. J. Psychiat., 122:*1427–1431, 1966.

Meduna, L. J., Von, and Friedman, E. The convulsive, irritative therapy of the psychosis. *J. Am. Med. Assoc., 112:*6, 1939.

Ottoson, J. Experimental studies of memory impairment after electroconvulsive therapy. *Acta Psychiat. Neurol. Scand., 145:*103–127, 1960.

Paykel, E. S., Myers, J. K., Dienelt, M. N., Klerman, G. L., Lindenthal, J. J., and Pepper, M. P. Life events and depression: A controlled study. *Arch. Gen. Psychiat., 21:*753–760, 1969.

Perris, C. Genetic transmission of depressive psychosis. *Acta Psychiat. Neurol. Scand.,* suppl. *203:*45–52, 1968.

Price, J. The genetics of depressive behavior. In *Recent developments in affective disorders,* eds. A. Coppen and A. Walk. *Br. J. Psychiat.,* Special Publication No. 2, 1968.

Prien, R. F., Caffey, E. M., and Klett, C. J. Prophylactic efficacy of lithium carbonate in manic-depressive illness. *Arch. Gen. Psychiat., 28:*337, 1973.

Rado, S. The problem of melancholia. *Int. J. Psychoanal., 9:*42–438, 1928.

Rich, T., and Winokur, G. Family history studies V: The genetics of mania. *Am. J. Psychiat., 125:*1358–1369, 1969.

Schildkraut, J. J., and Kety, S. S. Biogenic amines and emotion. *Science, 156:*21–30, 1967.

Schou, M., Juel-Nielsen, N., Stromgren, E., and Voldby, H. The treatment of manic psychosis by the administration of lithium salts. *J. Neurol. Neurosurg. and Psychiat., 17:*250, 1954.

Seager, C. P., and Bird, R. L. Imipramine with electrical treatment in depression: Controlled trial. *Br. J. Psychiat., 108:*704–707, 1962.

Shepherd, M. Clinical trial of the treatment of depressive illness. *Br. Med. J., 1:*881, 1965.

Slater, E., and Cowie, V. *The genetics of affective disorders.* Oxford University Press, London, 1971.

Strain, J. J., Brunschwig, L., Duffy, J. P., Agle, D. P., Rosenbaum, A. L. and Bidder, T. G. Comparison of therapeutic effects and memory changes with bilateral and unilateral ECT. *Am. J. Psychiat., 125:*294–304, 1968.

West, L. J. Integrative psychotherapy of depressive illness. In *The nature and treatment of depression,* eds. F. F. Flach and S. C. Draghi. Wiley and Sons, New York, 1975, pp. 161–181.

Winokur, G., Cadoret, R. J., and Dorzob, J. Depressive disease: A genetic study. *Arch. Gen. Psychiat., 24:*135–144, 1971.

Wittenborn, J. P., Plante, M., Burgess, F. and Maurer, H. A comparison of imipramine, electroconvulsive therapy and placebo in the treatment of depressions. *J. Nerv. and Ment. Diseases, 135:*131–137, 1962.

Zerbin-Rudin, E. Zur. Genetik der depresiven Enkrankungen. In *Das depressive Syndrome,* eds. H. Hippius and H. Sellbach. International Symposium, Berlin, 1968.

Zomora, E. N., and Kaelbling, R. Memory and electroconvulsive therapy. *Am. J. Psychiat., 112:*545–554, 1965.

3. Suicide

Suicide is usually defined as the conscious, intentional taking of one's own life. It implies a powerful urge to terminate living, and to commit suicide there must, of course, be an act, the ultimate one in a person's life. One would think that only intolerable anguish would provide sufficient reason for committing suicide. Yet, in analyzing the rationale underlying many cases of suicide, investigators often find that the victim's problems were far from insoluble, that many people confront similar dilemmas with optimism. So why do suicide victims kill themselves? For many cases of suicide, one can reasonably argue, "They must have been crazy to kill themselves!" And yet psychiatric analysis of suicide cases shows only a limited incidence of severe mental illness. Many do not warrant any conventional psychiatric diagnosis.

Confronted with the contradiction between the seemingly irrational, pathological act of suicide and the inability to assign a psychiatric label to most victims, some researchers suggest that the repeated, irresistible impulse to end one's life constitutes a specific emotional disorder in its own right, a new disease. To the extent that many suicide victims suffer from endogenous depression of the sort which is thought to have genetic, hence biological, antecedents (see Chapter 2), suicide is related to a mental illness with biological concomitants. Morever, even among severe depressives, hormonal secretion patterns differ in those who are most suicidal. Urinary excretion of adrenal steroid hormones in depressives who subsequently commit suicide is so markedly elevated that it is virtually a marker of suicidal potential (Bunney and Fawcett, 1968). In these studies of adrenal steroid excretion, one patient was given a weekend pass because her depression had begun to lift. When extraordinarily high urinary adrenal steroid levels were detected the day after she left the hospital, the physicians hurriedly contacted her home only to learn that she had just killed herself. This hypersecretion of adrenal steroids indicates that the suicidal state is one of extraordinary emotional stress. Conceivably it is an abnormality in the biological stress response that brings some individuals to the point of suicide even though their apparent psychiatric illness is substantially less severe than that of others who never attempt suicide.

Determining the extent to which suicidal individuals represent a homogenous or heterogeneous population and searching for underlying causes has considerable importance for psychopathology and public health. Vital statistics indicate that suicide is one of the five leading causes of death in the United States. Moreover, these data probably underestimate the true incidence. Many whose reckless driving results in their death may well have been suicidal. Since social stigma attends suicide, coroners often avoid using the term when the circumstances leave any room for doubt as to the cause of death. With this consideration in mind, one can be sure that suicide is a major determinant of motality in our country.

Fallacies

Perhaps because suicide is so hard to accept for family and friends, so emotionally disruptive, a good deal of conventional wisdom has grown up to ease their burden. Or perhaps this mythology of suicide has developed because as Camus said, it is "the only serious philosophical problem."

According to one familiar aphorism, "people who talk about it never commit suicide." Obviously this idea could comfort those close to someone who seems to harbor a suicidal intent. And, of course, there is a grain of truth in it. Only a small minority of those who contemplate and talk of suicide ever go through with the final act. But it is equally true that those who do commit suicide have talked about it, usually many times before ending their lives. Stengel (1964) estimated that about 75 percent of people who ultimately kill themselves give definite warnings of their suicidal intentions at one time or another. The simple deduction from this is that one should take suicide threats seriously.

Another common notion is that when a person improves after a suicidal crisis, he has been "shocked" out of the attitude that ending his life is the only solution to his problems and he will now deal with them in more constructive ways. Although recovery from a suicidal crisis does indeed provoke a reorientation toward life for many people, this is a misconception. Once a person has attempted suicide, he or she is at least three times more likely to try again than someone who has not (Stengel, 1964).

Because suicide is such a decisive, final action, many people assume that victims possess an unshakable will to die, so that they are not likely to be dissuaded. A possible corollary to this view is that victims have made a well-informed decision about their own lives and one has no right to interfere. Again, there is a grain of truth in this. Some severely depressed individuals have an overwhelming urge to end their lives and, if thwarted, will try again and again. Yet even those individuals who seem so sure of their suicidal intent while they are deeply depressed may view life much differently after drug and psychological therapy has relieved their depression. Moreover, for the great majority of suicides, motivation is not unequivocal. Victims are extremely ambivalent. Shneidman (1973) has remarked, "It is possible—indeed prototypical—for a suicidal individual to cut his throat and to cry for help at the same time." According to a related myth, once a person is suicidal, he or she will always be suicidal. The great ambivalence of most people who try to kill themselves belies this idea. Moreover, there are countless reports of individuals who recovered from a serious suicide attempt and gone on to lead long and productive lives. The literary critic A. Alvarez survived an almost lethal ingestion of forty-five sleeping pills and went on to recognize that his life situation had changed for the better, that his outlook had matured:

The truth is, in some way I died. The overintensity, the tiresome excess of sensitivity and self-consciousness, of arrogance and idealism, which came in adolescence and stayed on and on beyond their due time, like some visiting bore, had not survived the coma. It was as though I had finally, and sadly late in the day, lost my innocence. . . . Then, as the months passed I began gradually to stir into another style of life, less theoretical, less optimistic, less vulnerable. I was ready for an insentient middle age (Alvarez, 1972).

Who commits suicide?

At one time or another, about 2 to 5 percent of the population attempts suicide. This exceeds the incidence of schizophrenia and severe depression. Only about one out of eight suicide attempts, however, results in death. In general, attempts at suicide reflect different motivations than successful suicides. Attempts are usually meant to attract the attention of others to the individual's plight. Usually, those who make such attempts don't really want to die, though this may be the inadvertent result.

This distinction between suicide attempts and completions is reflected in demographic statistics. Among successful suicides, males predominant by a ratio of about 3 to 1. Among attemptors, the ratio is reversed, women predominating by a 3 to 1 ratio. Nevertheless, there has been a tendency for the gap between the sexes to close, perhaps reflecting the movement of women toward a social and professional status like that of men (Diggory, 1976).

Social factors are also apparent in the changing suicide rate among blacks. Traditionally, blacks have had rates only about one-third those of whites. Studies in which black and white survivors of suicide attempts were interviewed indicate that for whites, especially white males, suicide often follows a perceived failure to attain professional and/or social success. These factors are not evident in most black suicides, who tend to have lower aspirations than whites and whose commitment is more to simple survival than to any form of success. Since the late 1950s, however, suicide rates among blacks have risen markedly, especially among younger individuals (Grier and Cobbs, 1968; Hendin, 1969; Myrdal, 1944; Pederson et al., 1973; Swanson and Breed, 1976). Now, in the age group below forty years, suicide rates are about the same for blacks and whites. In older age groups, however, black rates are still substantially lower than white rates. It would seem that recent social changes have exposed young blacks to tensions or forces similar to those which lead to suicide in young whites.

Age is a major factor in suicide. Among white males, suicide rates increase about 600 percent between the ages of twenty and seventy. While the incidence of male suicide increases progressively into the seventies, rates for women stabilize at their highest point at about age fifty and then change little or even decline. For men, the erosion of feelings of self-worth is greatest in the years following retirement. Perhaps for women the early fifties, associated with menopause and the departure from home of grown children, are the peak period of self-devaluation. Close family ties do seem to protect against suicide, for married people with children have the lowest suicide rates. Among those who are unmarried, suicide is more frequent in divorced than in single individuals.

Though statistics on suicide provide strong hints as to underlying psychological and social factors, one must be cautious in drawing conclusions. For reasons mentioned above, suicide statistics are less reliable than most other demographic information.

The sociology of suicide

The striking differences in rates of suicide among various social groups indicate that social factors may be just as important as psychological stresses in determining the propensity of individuals to take their own lives. The father of the sociological approach to suicide was the French social philosopher Emile Durkheim. Durkheim was the first researcher to collect data systematically on suicide rates among different groups and then to attempt an explanation of the variations. Subsequent research has tended to confirm most of his findings. Among these were the following: that old people have a higher suicide rate than the young; that males commit suicide about three times more frequently than females; that Protestants have higher suicide rates than Catholics, while rates are still lower among Jews; and that rates are higher among the unmarried, especially the divorced, than among those with stable marriages (Durkheim, 1951).

Durkheim was impressed that traumatic life events, including alcoholism and insanity, had so little influence over rates of suicide: "Individual peculiarities could not explain the social suicide rate; for the latter varies in considerable proportions, whereas the different combinations of circumstances which constitute the immediate antecedents of individual cases of suicide retain approximately the same frequency. They are, therefore, not the determining causes of the act which they precede." In his subsequent search for social forces that shape suicidal tendencies, Durkheim came to the conclusion that there are two major determinants. One is a lack of meaningful social interaction, which he called *egoism*. The other arises when the social group itself fails to provide adequate social regulation. Durkheim referred to this lack of social constraint upon group members as *anomie*. Egoistic suicides would be those who, for one reason or another, lacked group ties, such as divorced or widowed individuals, expatriated or unemployed persons, or other isolated, lonely people. Suicides related to anomie would be apparent in times of social disintegration, such as the great depression in Germany following World War I.

A small group of suicides, in Durkheim's view, derive from motivations that seem the opposite of egoism and anomie. These cases, though less frequent, often have the most dramatic impact upon the social conscience of the rest of the community. One type is the *altruistic* suicide, which represents the antithesis of egoistic suicide. An altruistic suicide victim is perhaps too well integrated into the social group, a virtual martyr. The best examples of altruistic suicide are found in Japan, where cultural tradition seems to attach less stigma to self-destruction than Western cultures do. Hara-kiri and the Japanese kamikaze pilots of World War II are familiar instances. *Fatalistic* suicide may be viewed as the opposite of anomic suicide, a self-inflicted death in apparent conformity with excessive regulation by society. The suicide of blacks jailed by repressive Southern towns has been cited as an example of such motivation (Maris, 1976).

The importance of social integration in determining suicide rates is strikingly evident in a major study of suicide in different areas of London (Sainsbury,

1955). In a very poor but relatively close-knit working-class area of London, the suicide rate was markedly lower than in the wealthier Bloomsbury district. Bloomsbury was populated at the time partly by upper-class persons in financial difficulty, experiencing decline in economic status.

Researchers have placed much emphasis on the role of economic factors in suicide. Durkheim had seen so many cases of suicide among the wealthy that he felt that poverty almost protects against suicide. Subsequent research suggests that what matters most are rapid changes. The poor are unlikely to become suddenly much poorer or richer than they are, while the wealthy are at greater risk of economic reversal. Pierce (1967) found a close relationship between U.S. male suicide rates from 1919 to 1931 and fluctuations in stock prices on the New York Stock Exchange, whether they were increases or decreases. Several researchers have detected a relationship between suicide rates and downward social mobility (Breed, 1963). Others have been struck by the association of suicide with upward as well as downward mobility (Porterfield and Gibbs, 1960).

There are a couple of widespread myths about the sociological aspects of suicide. San Francisco is often cited as a city with an extraordinarily high suicide rate, presumably because of the "far out" life style of its residents, which is reflected in a high incidence of homosexuality and alcoholism. Recent studies suggest that suicide is not really more frequent in San Francisco than in other American cities. Instead, it appears that the coroner's office in San Francisco is simply more conscientious in registering suicide as a cause of death. Critics of socialism have pointed to high rates of suicide in Denmark and Sweden, claiming that life in a welfare state presents little challenge to people so that more often than elsewhere they lose initiative, become bored, and kill themselves. This overlooks the fact that suicide rates in Norway are only a third of those in Denmark and Sweden, although Norway is just as much a welfare state as they are. Moreover, when the welfare system was initiated in Denmark, suicide rates declined (Hendin, 1965).

Psychological features of suicide

Commiting suicide may seem the "craziest" thing a person could do, yet as we have seen, most suicides do not appear to derive from disturbances that would justify an unequivocal label of "mental illness." Extensive interviews with surviving relatives of suicide victims suggest that only about 5 to 20 percent of the victims would qualify for the diagnosis of psychosis or severe neurosis (Robins et al., 1959). Of course, the extreme anguish of a suicidal individual itself might warrant a psychiatric label, and perhaps for this reason some researchers have concluded that 90 percent of the suicides they were studying were psychiatrically ill at the time of the act (Dorpat and Riple, 1960). The one psychiatric category that is most consistently associated with suicide is depression. The suicide rate for seriously depressed individuals is six times higher than the rate for neurotics and three times that of schizophrenics. Among depressed patients the risk of suicide seems to be greatest as the patients begin to improve. Patients often commit suicide shortly after discharge from the psychiatric hospital. Psychiatrists theorize that in the deepest throes of depression, patients are too immobile to carry out a successful suicide. As they recover, they acquire the necessary drive. Indeed, a retrospective examination of depressives who commit suicide suggests that the final decision actually lifts their spirits, relieving somewhat the anxiety and dread experienced in ambivalent deliberation over the act.

The incidence of suicide among schizophrenics is surprisingly low, considering their extreme mental disturbance. The rate for schizophrenics is about 200 per 100,000, compared with 70 per 100,000 for elderly males in the general population (Tenouche et al., 1964).

Though suicidal individuals do not conform to conventional psychiatric diagnoses, they seem to have some characteristic psychological features. Thinking processes have been analyzed both by administering psychological tests to recovered attemptors and by studying the content of suicide notes. These studies indicate that victims tend to be rigid in their thinking and to perceive things in terms of highly polarized concepts. This rigidity in thinking is apparent in a large number of social attitudes and even in simple word association tests, in which suicidal individuals show less creativity and flexibility (Levenson and Neuringer, 1971). In another type of study, suicidal individuals were asked to rate various concepts on a seven-step scale from "very good" to "very bad," a technique known as *semantic differential*. Suicide attemptors tended to rate concepts in a more extreme fashion than did control subjects (Neuringer, 1967). Their attitudes were most polarized toward concepts related to the power of the environment in exerting influence over them. Forces about them were felt to be very powerful, and often malignant, or very weak. This all-or-none kind of thinking apparently does not merely reflect their mental state during the suicidal crisis, for when subjects were followed long after recovery from a suicide attempt, it did not change (Neuringer and Lettieri, 1971).

Suicide notes often reveal a peculiar illogic. Writers imply that they intend to gain attention by their act but seem to forget that they won't be around to enjoy it (Shneidman, 1967). One macabre aspect of suicide notes is their relative lack of emotion. The notes usually contain many neutral statements, especially instructions. One gets the impression that the writers have a sense of omnipotence, expecting readers to carry out all their orders, orders of a kind they would probably never give if they expected to remain alive. In this way, they hope to accomplish more dead than alive. An example of these tendencies is contained in the following note:

To Mary Jones: Please take care of my bills. Tell Tom I made enough money for him. He can take care of these small bills. Mary, I love Betty and I can't stand being without her. She's something I spoiled myself. Love, Bill. Mary, take this pen as Helen gave it to me when I went to the Army (Shneidman and Farberow, 1957).

Suicidal individuals seem to lack an ability to moderate their responses, to seek or find alternative ways of solving problems:

My darling, it's all my fault. I've thought this over a million times and this seems to be the only way I can settle all the trouble I have caused you and others. This is only a sample of how sorry I am (Shneidman and Farberow, 1957).

Psychologists have developed theories about the fundamental emotional mechanisms that determine suicidal behavior. Before discussing these theories, it is important to distinguish between different types of suicide. Though there is some overlap, individuals who commit suicide and those who make unsuccessful attempts have somewhat different personality characteristics. A distinction can also be drawn between those who make a suicidal "gesture," seeking attention without intending to die, and those who make more genuine suicide attempts. Even among those who sincerely want to kill themselves, there are several patterns. Some people have a long life expectancy but nonetheless wish to die. Others don't expect to live much longer, usually because of terminal illnesses. They simply initiate their impending death. Some individuals with mental illness don't really appreciate the fact that they are ending their existence. They ignore the reality of death, sometimes killing themselves in the belief that they will meet their dead spouses in heaven. Deaths that are not recorded as suicides but do involve suicidal motivation might be called "subintentioned" (Shneidman, 1967). These persons don't really want to live but are reluctant to kill themselves in a single, decisive act. As examples, one could cite severe alcoholics who have been warned that their lives are failing yet continue to drink a quart of whiskey a day, or diabetics who mismanage their diets or insulin regimen.

In a book called *Man Against Himself,* Karl Menninger (1938) developed a theory of suicide using some concepts of Freud, who did not write much about the subject himself. According to this theory, a person must have three distinct motivations in order to kill himself. First, he must wish to die. This is necessary but not sufficient, since many unhappy people may wish to die but do nothing about it. Second, he must have an urge to kill. Menninger argued that the act of suicide is indeed a genuine murder and cited the fact that until the nineteenth century in Europe the death sentence was often imposed as punishment for those who attempted suicide. Third, besides wanting to kill, the victim must desire to be killed. This often represents a desire to be punished for real or imagined wrongdoings.

No matter what the degree of intent, it is unlikely that any suicide victim is altogether of one mind about the deed. Even in the most serious suicide acts, ambivalence is a prominent feature.

Most people who commit suicidal acts do not either want to die or to live; they want to do both at the same time, usually the one more, or much more, than the other. It is quite unpsychological to expect people in states of stress, and especially vulnerable and emotionally unstable individuals who form the large majority of those prone to suicide, to live up to St. James' exhortation: 'Let your yea be yea and your nay, nay' (Stengel, 1964).

Intervention

Most people who commit suicide are not being treated by a mental health professional. Thus, preventing suicide cannot be regarded as the function of psychotherapists alone. Most suicide victims voice "cries for help." It is primarily the responsibility of friends and family to pay heed. In trying to determine the "lethality" of the situation, a number of risk factors should be borne in mind:

1. The danger is greater in men than women and in people older than age fifty.
2. Severely depressed individuals have the highest probability of committing suicide. Among those with a diagnosis of psychotic depression, the incidence of suicide is more than twenty-five times greater than that of the general population.
3. Serious sleep disturbance and alcoholism are also correlated with greater lethality.
4. A recent divorce, loss of a loved one, loss of a job, or serious illness all go along with serious suicidal potential.
5. Individuals without family or friends are in the most danger.
6. Finally, 10 percent of those who make unsuccessful attempts go on to kill themselves later.

The acute suicidal crisis, when the final decision is made and the act committed, is usually a period of only a few hours. News media reports of policemen and clergymen "talking" potential suicides away from the edge of a building or bridge underline the possibility of successful intervention.

The greatest success in dealing with suicides has been achieved by centers that primarily offer a sympathetic listener on call at a well-publicized telephone number twenty-four hours a day. In the United States about 200 suicide prevention centers have been established. The first was opened in Los Angeles in 1958 by Norman Farberow and Edwin Shneidman. Most of the work of these centers is conducted by volunteers who are supervised by mental health professionals and who can make referrals to professionals and institutions.

The few studies evaluating the impact of American suicide centers indicate that no major change in suicide rates has taken place as a result of their existence. However, this may be because there are relatively few centers and the public's awareness of them is limited. Follow-up studies of individuals suggest that suicide prevention centers have helped alleviate the problems of many callers, who have gone on to make good recoveries (Litman, 1970). The persons who are helped most by prevention centers are those with short-term problems. In a study comparing persons who contacted the Los Angeles Suicide Prevention Center and then went on to kill themselves with those who made recoveries, clear differences were apparent between the two groups. Those who subsequently killed themselves had more long-term, difficult problems, such as chronic alcoholism and severe depression (Litman et al., 1974).

To deal with high-risk, chronically suicidal individuals, the Los Angeles Suicide Prevention Center established a program in which steady contact was maintained with clients. At the minimum, they were telephoned at least once a week. Usually they were seen briefly but frequently, both at the center and at their own home, so that total contact averaged an hour each week. The contacts were not directed toward conventional psychotherapy. Instead, the center worker acted more as a friendly helper, assisting patients in rehabilitating themselves. A controlled study revealed that this type of program was more successful in terms of reduced loneliness, improved love relationships, and less depression than the standard, acute crisis assistance (Litman and Wold, 1976). Yet the continued contact did not actually change the frequency of suicidal thinking and suicide attempts.

Though the limited American experience has yet to provide firm evidence that intervention can change suicide rates, British efforts have succeeded in reducing the incidence of suicide. The Samaritan program of volunteers offering counseling to individuals in distress has had a major impact in Britain. This program was begun in 1953 by Chad Varah, then rector of St. Stephen's in London. Reverend Varah had established a small counseling service for individuals with sexual problems and had enlisted volunteers to make coffee for clients. After a while, he noticed that some of the clients appeared to get what they needed simply by talking to other clients or to the volunteers and would leave without seeing him at all. Accordingly, he developed a program in which volunteers befriend clients with any form of problem. The program has now spread throughout the British Isles and numbers about 200 Samaritan centers. It enjoys such wide public awareness that a 1975 survey found that 92 percent of adult British citizens were familiar with the program. In 1974 the Samaritans dealt with about one out of every 125 Britons so that about one family in 40 had contact with them. The Samaritans are available by phone, or clients may simply drop in for a visit.

The Samaritan movement has apparently influenced suicide rates more than any other factor in contemporary history. In the first six decades of the twentieth century, the suicide rate in Britain averaged about 10 to 12 per 100,000. There had been a peak of about 15 per 100,000 during the Great Depression and a low of about 9 per 100,000 during the early years of World War II. After the war, rates climbed back to their usual levels. Between 1963 and 1972, a period during which the Samaritan movement spread throughout the British Isles, there was a steady decline to a rate of 7.7 per 100,000. Researchers have ruled out many other factors as potential explanations for this decline. A systematic comparison of suicide rates in towns with or without Samaritan centers in the 1960s showed a decrease of about 6 percent in the Samaritan towns and a rise of about 20 percent in the control communities (Bagley, 1968, 1971; Fox, 1975; Sainsbury, 1973).

References

Alvarez, A. *The savage god.* Bantam Books, New York, 1973, pp. 268–269.

Bagley, C. The evaluation of a suicide prevention scheme by an ecological method. *Soc. Sci. Med., 2:*1–14, 1968.

Bagley, C. An evaluation of suicide prevention agencies. *Life Threatening Behavior, 1:*245–259, 1971.

Breed, W. Occupational mobility and suicide among white males. *Am. Soc. Rev., 28:*179–188, 1963.

Bunney, W. G., Jr., and Fawcett, J. A. Biochemical research in depression and suicide. In *Suicidal behaviors: Diagnosis and management,* ed. H. L. P Resnik. Little, Brown, Boston, 1968, pp. 144–159.

Diggor, J. D. United States suicide rates, 1933–1968: An analysis of some trends. In *Suicidology: Contemporary developments,* ed. E. S. Shneidman. Grune and Stratton, New York, 1976, pp. 25–70.

Dorpat, T. L., and Riple, H. S. Study of suicide in the Seattle area. *Comp. Psychiat., 1:*349–359, 1960.

Durkheim, E. *Suicide.* Trans. by J. A. Spaulding and G. Simpson. The Free Press, Glencoe, Ill., 1951, pp. 145–276.

Fox, R. The suicide drop—why? *Royal Society Health Journal 95:*9–13, 1975.

Grier, W., and Cobbs, P. *Black rage.* Basic Books, New York, 1968.

Hendin, H. *Suicide and Scandinavia.* Doubleday, New York, 1965.

Hendin, H. *Black suicide.* Basic Books, New York, 1969.

Levenson, M., and Neuringer, C. Problem-solving behavior in suicidal adolescents. *J. Consult. and Clin. Psychol., 37:*433–436, 1971.

Litman, R. Suicide prevention center patients: A follow-up study. *Bulletin of Suicidology, 6:*12–17, 1970.

Litman, R., Farberow, N. L., Wold, C., and Brown, T. Prediction models of suicidal behaviors. In *The prediction of suicide,* ed. A. Beck, H. Resnick, and D. Lettieri. Charles Press, Bowie, Md., 1974.

Litman, R. E., and Wold, C. I. Beyond crisis intervention. In *Suicidology: Contemporary developments,* ed. E. S. Shneidman. Grune and Stratton, New York, 1976, pp. 525–546.

Menninger, K. *Man against himself.* Harcourt Brace Jovanovich, New York, 1938.

Myrdal, G. *American dilemma.* Harper & Row, New York, 1944.

Neuringer, C. The cognitive organization of meaning in suicidal individuals. *J. Gen. Psychol., 76:*91–100, 1967.

Neuringer, C., and Lettieri, D. J. Cognitive attitude and affect in suicidal individuals. *Life Threatening Behavior, 1:*106–124, 1971.

Pederson, A., Awad, G., and Kindler, A. Epidemiological differences between white and nonwhite suicide attemptors. *Am. J. Psychiat., 130:*1971–1976, 1973.

Pierce, A. The economic cycle and the social suicide rate. *Am. Soc. Rev., 32:*457–462, 1967.

Porterfield, A. L., and Gibbs, J. Occupational prestige and social mobility in suicides in New Zealand. *Am. J. Soc., 66:*147–152, 1960.

Robins, E., Jassner, S., Kays, J., Wilkinson, R. H., and Murphy, G. E. The communication of suicidal intent. *Am. J. Psychiat., 115:*724–733, 1959.

Sainsbury, P. *Suicide in London.* Chapman and Hall, London, 1955.

Sainsbury, P. Suicide: Opinions and facts. *Proc. Royal Soc. Med., 66:*579–587, 1973.

Shneidman, E. S. Orientations toward death: A vital aspect of the study of lives. *Int. J. Psychiat., 2:*167–200, 1967.

Shneidman, E. S. *Encyclopaedia Britannica,* 14th ed. s.v., "Suicide," 1973.

Shneidman, E. S., and Farberow, N. L. *Clues to suicide.* McGraw-Hill, New York, 1957.

Stengel, E. *Suicide and attempt at suicide.* Penguin Books, Baltimore, 1964.

Swanson, W. C., and Breed, W. Black suicide in New Orleans. In *Suicidology: Contemporary developments,* ed. E. S. Shneidman. Grune and Stratton, New York, 1976, pp. 99–128.

Tenoche, A., Pugh, T. F., and MacMahon, B. Suicide rates among current and former mental institution patients. *J. Nerv. and Ment. Diseases, 138:*124–130, 1964.

Varah, C. *The Samaritans.* Macmillan, New York, 1966.

4. Schizophrenia: phenomenology

What is schizophrenia?

Schizophrenia, it has been argued, is a wastebasket term that stigmatizes people for the rest of their lives. Those who take this view contend that more damage may be done to patients by the label than by their original emotional disturbance. Karl Menninger has written:

The name and the naming of . . . an instance of schizophrenia implies a hopelessness of outcome which has a derogatory effect on the patient. To be told that one has cancer is discouraging, I concede, but the designation of cancer, the psychological effect of being told that one has it, does not in itself materially affect the disease (in most cases) and may lead to corrective steps. In a psychological disease, on the other hand, the individual is nearly always negatively affected by the knowledge and the tendency toward the establishment of a self-fulfilling prophecy develops. The name spells great knowledge and great pessimism, neither of which the doctor may have. But the patient, knowing the prevalent opinion about such a disease, begins to feel pessimistic. So do those about him and all begin to fulfull these expectations (Menninger, 1970).

The Scottish psychiatrist R. D. Laing takes the more extreme position that schizophrenia may be a legitimate and productive means of dealing with the chaos of modern life. Laing has described many cases in which the harrowing experience of a schizophrenic breakdown was followed by rebirth to a fruitful, enhanced existence. In his view, treating schizophrenics with drugs aborts the rejuvenating experience of the psychosis and confines the patients to a stifling existence lacking in meaning.

The success of Laing's books is an indication of how intriguing the problem of understanding the experience of schizophrenia is. Schizophrenics often speak of explosive feelings concretely perceived within their minds. They seem to experience a disintegration of their sense of self, their feeling of personal unity. This crisis of identity is shattering, and it confronts them with basic existential questions such as, Who am I? What is the meaning of life? What is reality? Laing has not been the only writer to speculate that schizophrenics, in their grandiose ideation, are reporting back from a world of deeper emotional reality than we enter in ordinary life.

Whatever lies behind the label, schizophrenia accounts for more extensive debility than any other form of mental disorder. About 1 percent of the population in most countries suffers from schizophrenia, as defined by fairly rigorous criteria. Because schizophrenia usually begins at an early age, its victims are apt to lose most of their productive years. In addition to its early onset, schizophrenia follows a chronic, unremitting course in many patients, unlike other emotional disorders such as manic-depressive illness, which is almost invariably episodic with many prolonged remissions.

The varied symptoms that are lumped together under the rubric of schizophrenia raise questions about the existence of a distinct category of illness. Some schizophrenics have florid hallucinations and delusions; others do not. Some schizophrenics display grotesque motor symptoms, such as rigid catatonic posturing or extreme hyperactivity. Some even go about naked and smear themselves with their feces. Others are neat and orderly in appearance and manner. Do they have anything in common?

Despite the difficulty of defining schizophrenia, clinicians do have a "feel" for the bizarrely disorganized thought processes, feelings, and behavior that are typical of schizophrenics. The nature of these abnormalities can be grasped in the self-descriptions of recovered patients. One such individual became a psychiatric nurse after her recovery from an acute schizophrenic episode lasting about a year and published an account of her illness in a medical journal (McDonald, 1960). As with many schizophrenics, she was never quite right emotionally even in childhood and adolescence, though she functioned reasonably well at school.

I lived with constant fear . . . , making it impossible for me to make friends unless they were younger or in some respect inferior or unless they were so extroverted they could take me under their social wings and brighten my life a little. Intellectual pursuits were my only strength, and fear of failing at these kept me in a state of continual anxiety.

As her acute schizophrenic illness developed, she lost the ability that permits us to screen out much of the environment and focus only on what is most immediately relevant: "What I do want to explain is the exaggerated state of awareness in which I lived before, during and after my acute illness. . . . The walk of a stranger on the street could be a 'sign' to me which I must interpret. Every face in the windows of a passing streetcar would be engraved on my mind, all of them concentrating on me and trying to pass me some sort of message.'' Years later she concluded that more central to her illness than her hallucinations and delusions was the loss of this perceptual filtering mechanism, which helps keep the mental life of the sane tidily systematic: ''I had very little ability to sort the relevant from the irrelevant. The filter has broken down. Completely unrelated events became intricately connected in my mind.''

Experiences of others on psychedelic drugs reminded her of her own illness: ''I could talk to normal people who had the experience of taking mescaline or lysergic acid and they would accept the things I told them about my adventures in mind without asking stupid questions or withdrawing into a safe, smug world of disbelief.''

Clinicians often notice that the emotional perceptions of schizophrenics are quite accurate, that they can sense the subliminal feelings of others. Unfortunately, schizophrenics misjudge the meaning of such feelings, ascribing too much importance to them. McDonald writes of this experience: ''To feel that the stranger passing on the street knows your innermost soul is disconcerting. I was sure that the girl in the office on my right was jealous of me. . . . It's quite likely that these impressions were valid, but the intensity with which I felt them made the air fairly crackle when the stenographer in question came into my office.''

The concept of schizophrenia

Although the emotional disorders which we now call schizophrenia have been described in detail since the early eighteenth century, it was only around the beginning of the twentieth century that the unitary entity of dementia praecox or schizophrenia was delineated. The Belgian psychiatrist Morel first used the term *demence precoce,* defined as a ''mental deterioration of youth,'' to describe a process of intellectual deterioration in a patient whose symptoms had begun at the age of fourteen. However, Morel failed to identify unifying clinical features which would enable one to readily diagnose the condition without waiting for ultimate deterioration. In 1871 the German psychiatrist Heckel introduced the term *hebephrenia* to denote an illness that began in puberty and led to marked deterioration, with a loss of conceptual functioning that made the patients appear ''silly.'' In 1874 Kahlbaum reported his observation that certain psychotic patients exhibit striking motor symptoms ranging from stupor to pronounced hyperactivity. He called this illness *catatonia,* which means ''tension (muscular) insanity.'' In 1891 Pick described a group of patients who underwent a "simple deterioration" of the thinking process but displayed few of the florid hallucinations and delusions that characterized patients with catatonia and hebephrenia.

The primary credit (or blame) for bringing together all the disorders which are now known as schizophrenia under a single rubric, *dementia praecox,* belongs to Emil Kraepelin. One of his criteria for linking the disorders was that they generally commenced at a young age and had a poor prognosis. He discriminated dementia praecox from the other major psychosis, manic-depressive illness, which had a good prognosis. Together with hebephrenia and catatonia, Kraepelin included "dementia paranoides" in the dementia praecox syndrome. This decision to include some paranoid disorders in the spectrum of schizophrenia is still debated. What is called *paranoid schizophrenia* has a later onset than most other types of schizophrenia. Moreover, patients with paranoid schizophrenia undergo much less deterioration of personality than patients with severe cases of other forms of schizophrenia. In these two ways, paranoid schizophrenia does not conform to the concept of dementia praecox.

The Swiss psychiatrist Eugen Bleuler was disturbed by the rigid way psychiatrists adhered to the concept of dementia praecox in making diagnoses. He thought they were placing too much emphasis on the idea of deterioration: "There is hardly a single psychiatrist who has not heard the argument that the whole concept of dementia praecox must be false because there are many catatonic and other types who, symptomatologically, should be included in Kraepelin's dementia praecox, and who do not go on to complete deterioration" (Bleuler, 1950).

Nonetheless, Bleuler agreed with Kraepelin that the diverse symptom complexes represented a single disease entity, and he sought an underlying psychological disturbance. Bleuler was impressed with Freud's writings about the ways that unconscious thoughts are distorted into varied behavioral expressions. He concluded that the dramatic hallucinations and delusions were not primary to schizophrenia, since they were not present in some patients. Instead, what schizophrenics have in common, according to Bleuler, is a peculiar disturbance of mental associations, a loosening of the links between thoughts.

Bleuler's definition of schizophrenia, with relatively few alterations, reflects the broadest consensus among psychopathologists today. Emphasizing the inclusion of "patients whom we would neither call demented nor exclusively victims of deterioration early in life," Bleuler based the diagnosis on symptoms rather than clinical course: "By the term 'dementia praecox' or 'schizophrenia' we designate a group of psychoses whose course is at times chronic, at times marked by intermittent attacks, and which can stop or retrogress at any stage, but does not permit a full *restitutio ad integrum.* The disease is characterized by a specific type of alteration of thinking, feeling and relation to the external which appears nowhere else in this particular fashion.'' Bleuler made the important point that organic brain disease, which can produce all the symptoms of schizophrenia, must be excluded from the diagnosis. The term *schizophrenia* is reserved for cases in which ''primary disturbances of perception, orientation or memory are not demonstrable.'' Bleuler described this alteration in explaining how he derived the term: ''I call dementia praecox 'schizophrenia' because (as I hope to demonstrate) the splitting of the different psychic functions is one of its most important characteristics . . . the process of association often works with mere fragments of ideas and concepts. This results in associations which normal individuals will regard as incorrect, bizarre and utterly unpredictable.''

Though he thought that all schizophrenics have something in common, Bleuler, unlike some of his successors, acknowledged that there was no evidence to demonstrate that it is actually a single disease: ''For the sake of convenience I use the word in the singular, although it is apparent that the group includes several diseases.'' Indeed, the title of his book is *Dementia Praecox or the Group of Schizophrenias*.

Bleuler felt that the peculiar thought disorder of schizophrenia could give rise to all the other manifestations of the illness, including abnormalities in affect, delusions, and hallucinations. Others believe that emotional disturbance, such as loss of the ability to experience pleasure, produces the thought disorder rather than the reverse. Another theory is that an abnormality in perception causes schizophrenics to view the world differently, which then leads to abnormal thought patterns. Still another is that delusional thinking is primary and impaired associations follow. In the absence of conclusive studies, it is difficult to choose among these views of the fundamental disturbance in schizophrenia. However, there is more of a consensus about the clinical picture that most schizophrenics present.

Symptoms

In general, American psychiatrists tend to employ looser criteria for the diagnosis of schizophrenia than European psychiatrists (Carpenter et al., 1973). Many studies point to the failure of psychiatrists to agree among themselves on the diagnosis of individual patients (Robins, 1977; Spitzer and Fleiss, 1974).

One universally accepted criterion for diagnosing schizophrenia is to eliminate the presence of organic mental disturbance and affective disorder. If a patient displays clearcut mental disorientation for place, time, or person or has severe defects in memory, the diagnosis of schizophrenia should be questioned. Patients who have had major episodes of mania or severe depression preceding an apparent schizophrenic break are usually not suffering from a classic form of schizophrenia, though the best approach to classifying such *schizoaffective* disturbances is a matter of considerable debate.

Kraepelin, as we have seen, used the tendency for clinical deterioration to differentiate schizophrenic from affective disorders. If, by careful diagnosis, one could predict which patients will deteriorate and which will recover, the evaluation of care of patients would benefit greatly. Despite some success in this effort, however, it is fraught with difficulties. Moreover, to follow Kraepelin's logic faithfully, one would have to wait a long time to determine the course of illness before making the diagnosis of schizophrenia, which is not usually practical.

Reacting against this view, Bleuler placed the emphasis on disturbances in thinking, particularly a "looseness of associations"; this emphasis remains today. Unfortunately, thought disturbances can be difficult to pinpoint and must be inferred indirectly.

Moreover, psychiatrists in different cultures, especially American versus European, often disagree strongly as to what constitutes aberrant thinking. To develop a working system for diagnosing schizophrenia, using symptoms about which there is general agreement, Schneider (1959) selected eleven "symptoms of the first rank" which he felt were sufficiently pathognomonic so that, in the absence of organic signs, if only one of them was present a diagnosis of schizophrenia would be virtually certain. Most of these eleven symptoms involve specific types of auditory hallucination, such as voices talking about the patient, describing his or her activities or projecting personal thoughts aloud. The others refer largely to feelings that the patient's actions or thoughts are being imposed from without or that thoughts are being removed from his or her brain or broadcast to the world. The greatest virtue of Schneider's system is that it deals with concrete symptoms, such as auditory hallucinations and specific delusions of external control. However, some workers have found that his first-rank symptoms are present in as few as 28 percent of schizophrenics diagnosed by other fairly rigorous criteria (Taylor, 1972), while Carpenter et al. (1973) noted that as much as 23 percent of manic-depressive patients also display these symptoms.

In recent years, many researchers have been trying to improve the specificity and reliability of psychiatric diagnosis, especially for schizophrenia. Their studies suggest that there are subgroups of schizophrenics with different degrees of genetic component, different prognoses, and different responses to treatment (Gurland et al., 1970). These studies have culminated in the development of a set of more specific and reliable diagnostic criteria (Astrachan et al., 1972; Spitzer and Fleiss, 1974; Wing et al., 1974), many of which have been incorporated in the new edition of the Diagnostic and Statistical Manual of the

American Psychiatric Association (DSM-III). The following description and grouping of schizophrenic symptoms derives primarily from DSM-III.

According to this official diagnostic guide, schizophrenia is a disorder or group of disorders involving severe disorganization of social functioning as well as certain characteristic disturbances of thinking, feeling, and behavior. Because the disorder is viewed as chronic, the diagnosis is not made unless symptoms have been present continuously for at least six months. Abundant evidence indicates that short-lived schizophreniclike disturbances have a different genetic component and a better prognosis.

Formal thought disorder

For many psychiatrists, especially in the United States, a disturbance in the form rather than the content of thought is a hallmark of schizophrenia. Patients speak in ways which do not follow conventional semantic rules so that a listener cannot understand what is being said. In extreme cases patients are incoherent and will invent new words (neologisms). Typically, there is a loosening of associations so that the connections between statements are tangential or sometimes nonexistent. Even when the connections are superficially reasonable, there may be a poverty of content. A patient may speak at length but in such a vague, abstract, or stereotyped way that little if any information is conveyed. Schizophrenics often display "thought blocking," their flow of speech stopping abruptly as if the thinking processes had been paralyzed.

Delusions

While the classic schizophrenic thought disorder involves the form of thinking, *delusions* are disturbances in the content of thought. Specifically, delusions are false beliefs. Most of us are familiar with typical persecutory delusions such as, "The FBI is out to get me." These are most prominent in paranoid schizophrenics. Especially characteristic are the feeling that one's thoughts are being broadcast to the external world, that thoughts which are not one's own are being inserted into one's mind (thought insertion), or that thoughts are being removed from one's mind (thought withdrawal). In addition, patients often have a sense that their feelings and actions are not their own but are imposed from without (delusions of being controlled or of passivity). These delusions of thought insertion, thought withdrawal, and pasivity were proposed by Schneider (1959) as first-rank symptoms, assuring a diagnosis of schizophrenia.

Hallucinations

Hallucinations are disturbances in perception; they frequently but not invariably occur in schizophrenia. Auditory hallucinations are most common and typically involve hearing voices. The voices usually speak directly to the patient and comment on his or her ongoing behavior, often in a derogatory fashion. Patients may also have hallucinations of pure sounds, though these are much less frequent. Tactile, visual, taste, and olfactory hallucinations may occur, but they are more characteristic of organic brain syndromes. Though many psychiatrists regard hearing voices as being absolutely diagnostic of schizophrenia, careful studies have indicated that patients with affective disorders may also experience auditory hallucinations (Goodwin et al., 1971).

Affect and relationship to the external world
Schizophrenics commonly have "blunted" or inappropriate affective responses. Those with blunted or flattened affect may show no overt signs of emotion when told, for instance, that their parents have been killed. Those with inappropriate affect may laugh when given the same news. These abnormalities of affect, however, are not specific diagnostic signs. Depressed persons may also have a flattened affect. Moreover, the antipsychotic drugs may have the effect of reducing emotional highs and lows.

Schizophrenics are withdrawn emotionally and often physically from the external world, largely preoccupied with their own delusions, hallucinations, or other feelings and thoughts. Bleuler labeled this behavior *autism* and regarded it as one of the cardinal signs of schizophrenia. Schizophrenics also have difficulty describing just what they want. Many seem apathetic, devoid of any will, while others are markedly ambivalent. Though present in most schizophrenics, these signs are not unique to the illness.

Onset and course of illness
Schizophrenia typically makes its appearance during adolescence or early adult life. Patients with a good premorbid history, an acute onset with clear-cut precipitating factors, and a relatively short course of illness with relatively florid symptoms have the best prognosis for full recovery (Astrup and Noreik, 1966; Sartorius et al., 1978; Stephens, 1970). Since several studies indicate that six months of symptoms are one of the strongest prognostic indicators, DSM-III requires a six-month duration of illness for a diagnosis of schizophrenia.

One important distinction between schizophrenia and affective disturbance which was emphasized by Kraepelin is that most schizophrenics fail to return fully to normal premorbid functioning. By contrast, patients with affective disorders usually do return to their normal functioning between acute episodes.

The difficulty in judging the nature of a patient's mental illness by his or her outcome is that a patient's fate is affected by many factors besides the inherent features of the disease. When environmental conditions are carefully matched, patients with an acute onset and good premorbid history generally fare better than those with an insidious onset and aberrant behavior since early childhood. However, living conditions are rarely the same for any two individuals. Patients with the "good prognosis" type of acute schizophrenia, if sent to the back wards of a primitive state mental hospital, may proceed to deteriorate and remain hospitalized for the rest of their lives. Numerous studies have confirmed that much of the disordered behavior of schizophrenics in such hospitals is attributable to the effects of chronic institutionalization. Still, a substantial number of schizophrenics will deteriorate and will never be able to return to society despite application of the best available drug and psychosocial therapy.

Subtypes

Since the symptoms of schizophrenia are so varied, several systems of classification are feasible. The classic types of schizophrenia described by Kraepelin and Bleuler, mainly hebephrenic, catatonic, and paranoid, are based on clusters of symptoms present during the acute psychosis. These groupings probably do not represent distinct subtypes of the illness, since a given individual can display different symptom clusters at different times.

The behavior of hebephrenic schizophrenics is extremely disorganized. Their conversation is markedly incoherent and their affect is flat, incongruous, or silly. The word "hebephrenia" derives from Hebe, the mythological daughter of Zeus who was cup bearer to the gods, and then she would do some clowning. Hebephrenics generally have a poor premorbid personality and an insidious onset of illness, and they deteriorate more than other schizophrenics.

Catatonia is one of the most dramatic forms of schizophrenia. In catatonic stupor the patient seems totally out of contact with reality, adopting strange, statue-like postures and maintaining them for long periods of time. When an examiner moves the patient's limbs to a new position, he or she will follow along, a pattern referred to as "waxy flexibility." Patients in catatonic stupor may remain mute for periods of up to many months.

Catatonic excitement is essentially the opposite of stupor. Patients run about, jump over furniture, bang on the wall frantically. Their hyperactivity is so extreme that they sometimes die of exhaustion, heart failure, and hyperpyrexia (excessively high body temperature). Patients frequently alternate between periods of stupor and excitement. Catatonia was once frequently observed but now is rare.

Paranoid schizophrenia is dominated by delusions of persecution or grandiosity. Paranoid schizophrenics tend to be better organized in their behavior than most other schizophrenics. Their affective responses may seem fairly normal, and their speech is relatively coherent. The illness usually develops later in life than other forms of schizophrenia and does not tend to merge with them. Several investigators have suggested that paranoid schizophrenia is a distinct disease entity because relatives of paranoid patients more often develop paranoid schizophrenia than other subtypes.

The most useful classifications are probably those based on premorbid history and the onset of symptoms. Patients referred to as *process* schizophrenics have never had a normal relationship with other people. Even in their first years, they seem withdrawn or inappropriate in their behavior. Symptoms usually develop slowly and insidiously; the family often can't pinpoint when the patient passed from sanity to psychosis. Process schizophrenics tend to have recurrent acute psychotic episodes and to deteriorate gradually. Their families have a relatively high incidence of schizophrenia. By contrast, *reactive* schizophrenics have a relatively normal premorbid adjustment and experience a sudden psychotic breakdown with identifiable precipitating factors. The psychotic episode tends to be more florid, with vivid hallucinations and delusions. Reactive schizophrenics have little, if any, family history of schizophrenia; instead, there is an increased incidence of affective disorder among their relatives. The prognosis is much better for reactive than process schizophrenics.

Schizophreniform and schizoaffective disorders

Patients with both affective and schizophrenic symptoms are classified in DSM-III as having a distinct disorder, *schizoaffective disturbance*. If their psychosis lasts less than six months but longer than a week, they receive the diagnosis of *schizophreniform disorder*.

In considering a diagnosis of schizoaffective disturbance, the timing of the affective symptoms is critical. Most schizophrenics are depressed when they recover from an acute schizophrenic episode, as if their return to sanity brings them face to face with the depressing reality of what they have just experienced. To qualify for a diagnosis of schizoaffective illness, however, depressive or manic symptoms of at least a week's duration should have preceded or coincided with the schizophrenic symptoms. Ever since Kasanin introduced the term *schizoaffective* in 1933, there has been controversy as to whether this disorder relates more to schizophrenia or to affective disorder, or is in fact an intermediate type of psychosis. Relatives of schizoaffective patients have a much higher incidence of affective disorder than relatives of schizophrenics do (Clayton, et al., 1971; Procci, 1976; Vaillant, 1962), and this favors the idea that schizoaffective disorders are part of the affective group (Pope and Lipinski, 1978).

Patients with schizophreniform disorders, like those with schizoaffective disturbances, usually have a relatively good premorbid level of functioning, an acute onset of illness, good prognosis, florid symptoms, and very little family history of schizophrenia. In contrast to schizoaffective patients, they do not suffer depression or mania before or along with their psychosis.

DSM-III also includes a category of *brief reactive psychosis*. These are individuals with schizophreniclike symptoms lasting less than one week. Such individuals invariably have a better premorbid history and prognosis than those with schizophrenic disorders of longer duration. As the term indicates, brief reactive psychosis often represents a reaction to overwhelming environmental stress.

Paranoid disorders

Some persons have delusions of persecution or jealousy without any symptoms of schizophrenia. They are diagnosed, according to DSM-III, as having paranoid disorders. Most often their behavior at work and in other everyday situations is fairly normal. But they tend to have serious difficulties in social and marital relationships, usually because of their paranoid thoughts. Such individuals have not been studied extensively since they rarely seek psychiatric treatment on their own. Their encounters with the mental health professions often stem from confrontations with the law since they are prone to become involved in lawsuits.

At least two forms of paranoid disorders are distinguished. One, referred to as *paranoia,* is characterized by a remarkably isolated delusional system which is virtually permanent and unshakable despite the presence of rather normal behavior in other spheres of life. The other, *paranoid state,* disrupts the patient's life more, so that it may become chaotic. Sometimes, paranoid delusional systems are shared by two close individuals, often husband and wife. This *folie à deux* is distinguished as a separate entity in DSM-III.

References

Astrachan, B. M., Harrown, M., Adler, D., Brauer, L., Schwartz, C., and Tucker, G. A checklist for the diagnosis of schizophrenia. *Br. J. Psychiat, 121:*529–539, 1972.

Astrup, C., and Noreik, K. Functional psychoses: Diagnostic and prognostic models. C. C. Thomas, Springfield, Ill. 1966.

Bleuler, E. *Dementia praecox or the group of schizophrenias.* Trans. by J. Zinkin. International University Press, New York, 1950, p. 8.

Cameron, N. Experimental analysis of schizophrenic thinking. In *Language and thought in schizophrenia,* ed. J. Kassenin. University of California Press, Berkeley, 1944.

Carpenter, W. T., Strauss, J. S., and Bartko, J. J. A flexible system for the diagnosis of schizophrenia report from the WHO international pilot study of schizophrania. *Science, 182:*1275–1278, 1973.

Carpenter, W. T., Strauss, J. S., and Mulek, I. Are there pathognomic symptoms in schizophrenia? *Arch. Gen. Psychiat., 28:*847–852, 1973.

Chapman, J. The early symptoms of schizophrenia. *Br. J. Psychiat., 112:225–*251, 1966.

Clayton, P. J., Rodin, L., and Winokur, G. Family history studies III: Schizoaffective disorder, clinical and genetic factors including a one to two year follow up. *Psychol. Med., 1:*326–332, 1971.

Goldstein, K. Methodological approach to the study of schizophrenic thought disorder. In *Language and thought in schizophrenia,* ed. J. Kassenin. University of California Press, Berkeley, 1944.

Goldstein, K., and Schurer, M. Abstract and concrete behavior, an experimental study with special tests. *Psychol. Monographs, 53:*239, 1941.

Goodwin, D. W., Alderson, P., and Rosenthal, R. Clinical significance of hallucinations in psychiatric disorders. *Arch. Gen. Psychiat., 24:*76–80, 1971.

Gurland, B. J., Fleiss, G. L., Cooper, J. E., Sharpe, L., Kendell, R. E., and Roberts, P. Cross national study of diagnosis on mental disorders: Hospital diagnosis and hospital patients in New York and London. *Comp. Psychiat., 11:* 18–25, 1970.

Kasanin, J. The acute schizo-affective psychoses. *Am. J. Psychiat., 13:*97–126, 1933.

McDonald, N. Living with schizophrenia. *Canad. Med. Assoc. J., 82:*218–221, 1960.

Menninger, K. Syndrome, yes: Disease entity, no. In *The schizophrenic reactions,* ed. R. Cancro. Brunner/Mazel, New York, 1970, pp. 71–78.

Pope, H. G., Jr., and Lipinski, J. F. Diagnosis of schizophrenia and manic depressive illness is a reassessment of the specificity of "schizophrenic": Symptoms in the light of current research. *Arch. Gen. Psychiat., 35:*811–828, 1978.

Procci, W. R. Schizoaffective psychosis: Fact or fiction? A survey of the literature. *Arch. Gen. Psychiat., 33:1167–*1178, 1976.

Robins, E. New concepts in the diagnosis of psychiatric disorders. *Ann. Rev. Med., 28:*67–73, 1977.

Sartorius, N., Aablensky, A., and Shapiro, R. Cross cultural differences in the short term prognosis of schizophrenic psychoses. *Schizophrenia Bull., 4:*102–113, 1978.

Schneider, K. *Clinical psychopathology.* Trans. by M. W. Hamilton. Grune and Stratton, New York, 1959.

Spitzer, R. L., and Fleiss, J. L. Renanalysis of the reliability of psychiatric diagnosis. *Br. J. Psychiat., 125:*341–347, 1974.

Stephens, J. H. Long-term course and prognosis of schizophrenia. *Seminars in Psychiatry, 2:*464–485, 1970.

Szasz, T. S. *Ideology and insanity.* Anchor Books, New York, 1970, p. 216.

Taylor, M. Schneiderian first rank symptoms and clinical prognostic features in schizophrenia. *Arch. Gen. Psychiat., 26:*64–67, 1972.

Vaillant, G. E. The prediction of recovery in schizophrenia. *J. Nerv. and Ment. Diseases, 135:*534–543, 1962.

Vigotsky, L. S. *Thought and language,* eds. E. Hanfam and G. Vakar. Wiley and Sons, New York, 1962.

Wing, J. K., Cooper, J. E., and Sartorius, N. *Description and classification of psychiatric symptoms: An instruction manual for the P.S.E. and CATEGO symptoms.* Cambridge University Press, London, 1974.

5. Schizophrenia: etiology and treatment

Etiology

There has been much controversy over the relative influence of psychological and biological factors in the development of schizophrenia. The question has not been answered, but investigators now agree that both kinds of factors are involved. Family studies demonstrate a high incidence of communication disorders in the families of schizophrenics. From a psychological viewpoint, if parents deal with their children in a convoluted, "double-binding" manner, their behavior alone might suffice to generate schizophrenia in the children. Proponents of a genetic point of view would argue that the parents' behavior merely reflects their own generic component of schizophrenia. Twin studies reveal that if one member of a pair of monozygotic (identical) twins develops schizophrenia, the other has a much higher chance of becoming schizophrenic than if the pair were dizygotic (fraternal) twins or merely siblings. Such evidence argues strongly for a genetic determinant of schizophrenia. Theorists of a nongenetic persuasion, however, correctly point out that the concordance rate for schizophrenia in identical twins is only 50 percent, which indicates that environmental factors must also be involved.

Of course, the environmental factors need not be psychological. For instance, the schizophrenic twin of a pair may have experienced intrauterine difficulties which the other was spared. Indeed, among monozygotic twins discordant for schizophrenia, the schizophrenic twin generally has a lower birth weight (Pollin and Stabenau, 1968). On the other hand, in such discordant twin pairs the schizophrenic member displays aberrant relationships with parents and other siblings from earliest childhood (Mosher et al., 1971). Let us see how far this nature-nurture controversy can be resolved by examining some of the relevant research findings.

The earliest genetic studies explored rates of schizophrenia in relatives of schizophrenics. Virtually all of these studies demonstrated a higher rate in relatives of schizophrenics than in the general population (Rosenthal, 1971). The risk of developing definite schizophrenia is five to fifteen times higher in siblings than in the general population. Interestingly, the risk for parents of schizophrenics is not as great as for siblings. Since parents and siblings both share about half their genes with schizophrenics, one might have expected the same rate of illness in these two groups. In any event, the finding that schizophrenia runs in families is consistent with psychogenic as well as genetic theories. Thus, attendance at Harvard University also runs in families but would hardly be considered a genetic trait.

The risk of developing schizophrenia in relatives of schizophrenics varies with the closeness of biological relationship. For the general population the risk is about 1 percent. For parents, siblings, and children of schizophrenics the risk averages 5, 10, and 14 percent, respectively. For half-siblings, uncles and aunts, nephews and nieces, and grandchildren who share only one quarter of the genes, the risk is greater than that of the general population but less than that of first-degree relatives. The risk of developing schizophrenia is highest of all for children whose father and mother are both schizophrenic; about half these children become schizophrenic.

Evidence that schizophrenia and affective psychosis are separate genetic entities has been found in the diagnoses of relatives. Affective disorders predominate in the kin of patients with manic-depressive psychoses, while schizophrenia is most frequent in the relatives of schizophrenics, especially in those with the most severe forms of schizophrenia (Odegaard, 1972).

Numerous twin studies of schizophrenia carried out since the 1930s address the nature-nurture issue more directly. The rationale is simply that identical twins share all their genes, while fraternal twins are no closer genetically than non-twin siblings; since both identical and fraternal twins are raised during the same time span by the same parents, they may be assumed to share common psychosocial influences to about the same degree. In virtually all these studies, the concordance rate has been substantially higher in identical than in fraternal twins. While there is considerable variability among studies, the mean concordance rate for monozygotic twins is about 50 to 60 percent, and for dizygotic twins it averages about 10 to 15 percent (Rosenthal, 1971).

Since environmental factors are presumably the same for monozygotic and dizygotic twins, one would think that these studies clearly demonstrate the role of genetic influences. Still, the studies were criticized on the grounds that identical twins surely must have more nearly identical psychological environments than fraternal twins (Jackson, 1960). The thrust of this argument is countered by results from studies of monozygotic twins raised in separate households with no knowledge of each other; concordance for schizophrenia is still 50 percent or more in these twins. The number of subjects in these few studies, however, was limited (for obvious reasons, considering the difficulty of finding identical twins raised separately, where at least one has developed schizophrenia).

A different approach has been to study the offspring of severely schizophrenic mothers removed from their children during the first three days of life (Heston, 1966). These children still grew up to develop schizophrenia at the same rate as children reared by their schizophrenic parents.

In a more elaborate study in Copenhagen, where detailed population records of mental illness are available, the biological and adoptive relatives of adopted children who later developed schizophrenic or schizophreniclike disorders were compared for the presence of psychiatric disturbance (Kety et al., 1968). As a control, biological and adoptive relatives of nonschizophrenic adoptees were also evaluated. There was a much higher incidence of definite, severe schizophrenia in the biological relatives of schizophrenic adoptees than among those of control adoptees. By contrast, schizophreniclike disorders, such as *schizoid personality*, had about the same frequency in the two groups of relatives. This indicates that definite schizophrenia has a genetic basis which the other disorders lack.

This initial study done in the Greater Copenhagen area was extended to the entire country of Denmark so that a total of 74 schizophrenic adoptees and more than 1,000 relatives were evaluated. Besides corroborating the results of the initial study, the second investigation identified subtypes in the relatives with greater certainty. Biological relatives of adoptees with definite schizophrenia had a high incidence of chronic but not of acute schizophrenia. Strikingly, biological relatives of acute schizophrenics showed very little evidence of schizophrenia-related disorders. Again, therefore, we have evidence that chronic schizophrenia has genetic determinants which acute schizophrenia does not share (Kety et al., 1978; Rosenthal et al., 1971; Wender et al., 1971, 1977).

These conclusions were further strengthened by detailed comparisons of biological and adoptive parents of schizophrenics with adoptive parents of normal persons. Clinical interviews and psychological tests revealed more disturbance among the biological parents of schizophrenics than in the other two groups (Wender et al., 1977).

Adoption studies have been instrumental in changing concepts about the development of schizophrenia; however, even the most avid proponents of the role of genetics agree that environmental factors are important. Kinney and Jacobsen (1978) reasoned that for any group of schizophrenics, those with the least genetic vulnerability should exhibit the highest incidence of environmental precipitants. Using the Copenhagen group of schizophrenic adoptees studied by Kety et al., they compared the frequency of environmental factors in schizo-phrenics thought to have a high genetic risk with those thought to have a rela-tively low genetic risk. Genetic risk was rated as high as if the schizophrenic adoptee had a biological parent, sibling, or half sibling who was schizophrenic.

Psychiatric interviews with the adoptive parents indicated greater apparent psychopathology among the parents in the low-risk group. Patterns of abnor-mality in these parents included reports of being shy and reserved as an adult, teased as a child, lacking in spontaneity and experiencing phobias during adulthood. Also, a higher incidence of brain abnormalities, such as seizures and EEG aberrations, among the low-risk schizophrenics indicated that some of the environmental factors predisposing to schizophrenia could be biological.

Another way to examine environmental factors in schizophrenia is to com-pare identical twins discordant for schizophrenia. In 100 discordant monozygo-tic twins studied by Pollin and Stabenau (1968), the schizophrenic co-twins on the average had a lighter birth weight and experienced more difficulty breathing at birth. This again suggests the possibility of a role for neurological damage occurring during fetal life or at birth.

Psychotherapy

There is a long tradition of psychotherapy in the treatment of schizophrenia. Eminent clinicians such as Harry Stack Sullivan and Freida Fromm-Reichmann devoted much thought and effort to the difficult task of conducting psychody-namic psychotherapy with schizophrenics, but rarely did they carry out con-trolled studies. More recently there have been several controlled comparisons of psychotherapy and drug therapy. May (1968) divided newly hospitalized schizophrenics into four groups receiving no therapy, psychoanalytic psycho-therapy, phenothiazines alone, or phenothiazines plus psychoanalytic psycho-therapy. Improvement in the group receiving psychotherapy alone was no greater than in the control group which received no therapy. Patients receiving drugs alone showed substantial improvement, and 90 percent of the patients were discharged during the study period. The combination of psychotherapy and drugs resulted in no greater improvement than drug treatment alone.

In another study performed at the Massachusetts Mental Health Center, the major psychiatric teaching hospital of Harvard Medical School, Grinspoon et al. (1968, 1972) addressed the criticism that in some studies comparing psycho-therapy with drug treatment of schizophrenia, the psychotherapy was adminis-tered by relatively junior personnel. In this investigation, senior members of the Harvard psychiatry faculty provided intensive, psychoanalytically oriented psy-chotherapy. Again, no greater improvement was observed with psychotherapy plus drugs than with phenothiazine drugs alone. Indeed, when placebos were substituted for the phenothiazine in the group under psychoanalytic treatment, patients markedly deteriorated.

In another study conducted at the same institution, Greenblatt et al. (1965) compared the relatively intensive psychosocial therapies offered at the Mas-sachusetts Mental Health Center (psychotherapy, social work, occupational therapy, psychodrama) with the less intensive psychosocial therapy at a nearby state hospital. All the patients in the study received social therapy; some re-ceived phenothiazines while others were given matching placebos.

Patients receiving drugs in both institutions showed substantial improvement, and whether or not they received intensive or limited psychosocial therapy made no difference. The patients who did not receive drugs tended to deterio-rate regardless of the intensity of the psychosocial therapy. Though these and other studies raise a question about the value of psychotherapy for schizo-phrenia in relieving psychotic symptoms, psychosocial therapies do help schiz-ophrenics in remission readjust to the outside world, and many clinicians feel that they may act synergistically with drug therapy (Gorham and Bokorny, 1964).

Drug treatment

The antipsychotic drugs, also called *neuroleptics,* are unquestionably the most effective treatment for schizophrenia. Introduced in France about 1952, these drugs have been used widely in the United States since 1956. Chlorpromazine, the parent neuroleptic drug, was first synthesized as an antihistamine but proved so sedating in animals that it was considered unlikely to have clinical application as an antihistamine. Henri Laborit, a French surgeon, had been using the antihistamine promethazine for its sedating effect as an adjunct to relax patients before surgical anesthesia. Hearing that chlorpromazine was even more sedating than its close relative promethazine, Laborit tried it. He found that the drug seemed to detach patients from their environment.

The French psychiatrists Jean Delay and Pierre Deniker reasoned that such a drug might be effective in calming schizophrenics (Delay and Deniker, 1952). They were struck by the fact that besides quieting hyperactive patients, the drug activated withdrawn patients. In their initial relatively uncontrolled study, they felt certain that chlorpromazine was truly reducing schizophrenic symptoms. Though chlorpromazine usage spread rapidly through Europe and the United States, several years passed before controlled research established that chlorpromazine and related neuroleptic drugs exert fundamental actions against the symptoms of schizophrenia.

The discovery of chlorpromazine radically altered the prospects of schizophrenics. Patients who would have been hospitalized for a lifetime were now being discharged early and could maintain relatively independent lives in the community. Public mental institutions, which had been largely custodial centers, could now make use of social counseling and psychotherapy. Before the drugs were available, many patients had been so disturbed that psychotherapy was impractical.

One important outcome of drug therapy has been a drastic reduction in the number of hospitalized schizophrenics. Between the mid-1940s and the mid-1950s the number of hospitalized mental patients in the United States had been increasing steadily, from 462,000 in 1946 to 560,000 in 1955. In the next decade, it fell to 426,000, largely because of the introduction of neuroleptic drugs.

Since chlorpromazine is sedating, the first question was whether its efficacy merely reflected sedation. The effects of chlorpromazine were compared with those of standard sedatives such as phenobarbital in several controlled studies. None of the sedatives had antischizophrenic actions, while the neuroleptics clearly relieved the patients' psychotic symptoms. Moreover, newer neuroleptic drugs that are not sedating have proved to be as effective as chlorpromazine in treating schizophrenia.

A second question was: Which types of symptoms respond best to neuroleptics? It has been found that the neuroleptics substantially reduce the primary symptoms of schizophrenia, such as thought disorder, hallucinations, and delusions, and have less effect on symptoms that are not characteristically schizophrenic, such as anxiety and hostility (Davis and Garver, 1978). Neuroleptics have been compared with benzodiazepine drugs, the class which includes Valium and Librium, in numerous studies. With anxious patients, Valium and Librium are much more effective than neuroleptics in relieving anxiety. In treating the specific symptoms of schizophrenia, however, neuroleptics are consistently more effective than the benzodiazepines. For the symptoms of schizophrenia, benzodiazepines are no more efficacious than placebos.

The neuroleptics usually do not cure schizophrenics. After treatment most patients continue to appear somewhat aberrant in their thought processes, though often the disturbance is minimal. The best evidence that neuroleptics can't fully cure schizophrenia is the high incidence of relapse when treatment is stopped. Maintenance therapy with neuroleptics is required for continued relief of symptoms. In well-controlled studies, patients relieved of their symptoms with neuroleptics have been either maintained on drug therapy or switched to placebos. The incidence of relapse at six months was about 60 percent in the placebo group and about 30 percent in the group continuing with drug treatment (Hogarty and Goldberg, 1973; Leff and Wing, 1971).

Side effects of neuroleptics

Neuroleptics have serious side effects whose incidence varies with the different drugs. Since all the neuroleptics are of approximately equal efficacy in treating schizophrenia, the choice often depends on the patient's susceptibility to the various side effects.

Some drugs are quite sedating and can cause orthostatic hypotension, a condition in which blood pressure falls abruptly when a sitting patient stands. Most patients become tolerant to both the sedative and hypotensive effects of the neuroleptics, but in others these effects are so severe that the clinician must switch to a different drug.

The most troublesome side effects of the neuroleptics involve the movement-regulating systems of the brain. These are called *extrapyramidal* side effects, because the extrapyramidal areas of the brain, especially the corpus striatum, regulate motor behavior. Some extrapyramidal effects resemble the symptoms of Parkinson's disease: reduced spontaneous motor behavior, rigidity of the limbs and facial muscles, and tremor. Sometimes abrupt and bizarre movements take place. An even more common extrapyramidal symptom is *akathisia*. Patients with akathisia are unable to sit still, impelled to move about. Their incessant movement may be mistaken for emotional agitation, and the nurse may administer another neuroleptic dose to control the condition, instead exacerbating it.

All of these acute extrapyramidal side effects diminish as the dose of the drug is reduced. They can be counteracted with anticholinergic drugs used to treat Parkinson's disease.

One of the most serious side effects of neuroleptics is *tardive dyskinesia*. In contrast to the rigidity and reduced spontaneous movement associated with extrapyramidal effects, patients with tardive dyskinesia display an excess of motor activity, especially of the facial muscles and tongue. Although the major disability associated with tardive dyskinesia is the disfiguring appearance of the patient's face, sometimes the symptoms are so severe that they interfere with eating. While extrapyramidal side effects tend to occur shortly after drug therapy begins, tardive dyskinesia usually does not appear until patients have been taking large doses of a neuroleptic for months or years. Paradoxically, reducing the dose generally worsens the symptoms of tardive dyskinesia while raising it tends to lessen them. Thus, they are difficult symptoms to relieve. In some patients they are virtually irreversible.

Neuroleptic drugs exert hormonal influences via the pituitary gland, particularly by increasing the secretion of prolactin from the pituitary. The normal function of prolactin is to stimulate the mammary glands to form and secrete milk, and it also inhibits ovulation, which accounts for the infertility of nursing mothers. By raising prolactin levels in the blood, neuroleptics frequently cause amenorrhea, infertility, and abnormal milk secretion.

Neurotransmitters, neuroleptics, and schizophrenia

For many years biochemists have searched for a specific abnormality in the body fluids of schizophrenics, and many false leads have been pursued. So far no biochemical defect has been demonstrated in schizophrenic tissue and verified in other studies. Yet evidence for a genetic factor in the vulnerability to develop schizophrenia implies some biochemical abnormality.

More fruitful than the "looking for a needle in the haystack" approach of screening body fluids of schizophrenics have been indirect pharmacological studies. We know that neuroleptics exert selective actions against the symptoms of schizophrenia. Perhaps if we knew the specific locus in the brain where these drugs act, this site might bear some relationship to the biochemical aberration in schizophrenia. Neuroleptics are chemically reactive substances which can interact with a variety of biochemical systems in the brain. Chlorpromazine, for example, has numerous effects in brain tissue. How does one distinguish biochemical actions that are merely incidental from those that account for the therapeutic actions of the drug?

One strategy available to the pharmacologist is to study a series of drugs. If their clinical potency parallels their ability to produce a special biochemical action, than that action may well be the therapeutic one. Among the various biochemical actions of neuroleptics, the only kind that correlates closely with the drugs' clinical potency are their effects upon dopamine, a neurotransmitter described in Chapter 6.

The fact that neuroleptics increase dopamine metabolites suggests that the drugs accelerate the firing of dopamine neurons (Carlsson and Lindquist, 1963). Carlsson and Lindquist speculated that dopamine neurons fire more rapidly because the neuroleptics are blocking receptor sites for dopamine located on adjacent neurons. Somehow a feedback message informs the dopamine neurons that the receptors for dopamine are "starved" of the chemical and request an increase in production. A variety of indirect evidence consistent with this hypothesis has accumulated over the years, but it received much stronger support after researchers acquired the ability to identify biochemically the post-synaptic receptor sites for dopamine (Creese et al., 1978). Dopamine receptors can be measured by monitoring the binding to neuronal membranes of radioactive forms of the neuroleptic drugs under carefully specified conditions. To determine whether a drug blocks dopamine receptors, one finds out if it will reduce the amount of radioactive neuroleptic bound to these receptors. The relative potency of neuroleptics in blocking dopamine receptors measured this way closely parallels their clinical potency. By contrast, the action of neuroleptics on receptors for other neurotransmitters does not correlate at all with their antischizophrenic activity. Furthermore, no drugs other than neuroleptics block dopamine receptors in doses used clinically.

Thus, it is now fairly well established that neuroleptic drugs exert their therapeutic actions against schizophrenia by blocking receptor sites for dopamine in the brain. These drugs also produce their extrapyramidal side effects by blocking dopamine receptors, specifically in the corpus striatum, thereby creating a functional deficiency of dopamine. And the increased plasma levels of prolactin produced by the neuroleptic drugs are secondary to a blockade of dopamine receptors in the pituitary gland. At what site in the brain might the antischizophrenic actions of neuroleptics be exerted? Likely possibilities are the dopamine tracts in the limbic system and frontal cerebral cortex, since these areas regulate emotions and certain types of thought.

Actions of neuroleptics at dopamine receptors are also involved in tardive dyskinesia. After chronic blockade of dopamine receptors by high doses of drugs for long periods of time, the receptors seem to fight back, becoming hypersensitive to dopamine. This accounts for the resemblance between tardive dyskinesia and the symptoms of an excess of dopamine. Direct studies in rats treated chronically with neuroleptics have revealed an actual increase in the number of dopamine receptors associated with a behavioral hypersensitivity to dopamine in these animals (Creese et al., 1978).

The selective blockade of dopamine receptors by neuroleptics has led many investigators to ask if an abnormality in dopamine disposition might underlie schizophrenia. Other drug-related evidence favors this possibility. In large doses, amphetamines produce a psychosis which is clinically indistinguishable from acute paranoid schizophrenia (see Chapter 4). There have been many reports of patients with amphetamine psychosis mistakenly diagnosed as schizophrenics (Snyder, 1974). Amphetamine psychosis is widely viewed as a more valid drug model of psychosis than the psychoses produced by any other drugs. Moreover, in low intravenous doses, amphetamines sharply exacerbate the symptoms of schizophrenics. In these cases the drug does not produce a drug psychosis of its own; rather it worsens whatever symptoms the patient may be experiencing: a paranoid patient becomes more paranoid, a catatonic individual more catatonic. These low doses of amphetamines do not affect the symptoms of manic, depressed, or neurotic patients (Janowsky and Davis, 1976).

How do amphetamines exert their effects? Because of their chemical similarity to the catecholamines, norepinephrine, and dopamine, it is generally accepted that amphetamines facilitate the actions of catecholamines in the brain. They cause a release of norepinephrine and dopamine from nerve endings into the synaptic cleft. A variety of pharmacological evidence suggests that amphetamines worsen schizophrenic symptoms at low doses and elicit psychosis at high doses primarily through the release of dopamine.

Thus, enhancing the actions of dopamine worsens schizophrenic symptoms, while blocking dopamine receptors alleviates them. These findings provide strong evidence that dopamine plays a crucial role in the abnormal brain function of schizophrenics. They do not, however, establish that dopamine systems are the locus of schizophrenic disturbance. It could be that fundamental abnormality is several steps removed, and that by altering dopamine activity we indirectly affect that abnormal system.

References

Carlsson, A., and Lindquist, M. Effect of chorpromazine and haloperidol on formation of 3-methanytyramine and mormetanephrine in mouse brain. *Acta Pharmacologica Toxicologica, 20:*140–144, 1963.

Creese, I., Burt, D. R., and Snyder, S. H. Biochemical actions of neuroleptic drugs. In *Handbook of psychopharmacology,* vol. 10, eds. L. L. Iversen, S. D. Iversen, and S. H. Snyder, Plenum Press, New York, 1978, pp. 37–89.

Davis, J. M., and Garver, D. L. Neuroleptics: Clinical use in psychiatry. In *Handbook of Psychopharmacology,* vol. 10, eds. L. L. Iversen et al., 1978.

Delay, J., and Deniker, P. Le Troitement des psychoses par une methode neurolytique deriver de l'hibernotherapi. In *Congress de Medecins Alienistes et Neurologistes de France,* Eds. P. Cossa Maisson Editeurs, Libraires de L'Academic de Medicine, Paris, 1952, pp. 497–502.

Gorham, D. R. and Pokorny, A. D. Effects of phenothiazines and/or group psychotherapy with schizophrenics. *Dis. Nerv. Sys., 25:*77–87, 1964.

Greenblatt, M., Salomon, M. H., Evans, A. S., and Brooks, G. W. *Drug and social therapy in chronic schizophrenia.* C. Thomas, Springfield, Ill., 1965.

Grinspoon, L., Ewalt, J. R., and Shader, R. I. Psychotherapy and pharmacotherapy and chronic schizophrenia. *Am. J. Psychiat., 124:*1645–1652, 1968.

Grinspoon, L., Ewalt, J. R., and Shader, R. I. *Schizophrenia: Pharmacotherapy and psychotherapy,* Williams and Wilkins, Baltimore, 1972.

Heston, L. L. Psychiatric disorders in foster home reared children of schizophrenic mothers. *Br. J. Psychiat., 112:*812–825, 1966.

Hogarty, G. E., and Goldberg, I. C. Drugs and social therapy in the after care of schizophrenic patients. *Arch. Gen. Psychiat., 28:*54–64, 1973.

Jackson, D. D. A critique of the literature on the genetics of schizophrenia. In *The idealogy of schizophrenia,* ed. D. D. Jackson. Basic Books, New York, 1960, pp. 37–87.

Janowsky, D. S., and Davis, J. M. Methylpheidate, dextroampetamine, levamphetamine effects on shizophrenic symptoms. *Arch. Gen. Psychiat., 33:*304–308, 1976.

Kety, S. S., Rosenthal, D., Wender, P. H., and Schulsinger, F. The types and prevalence of mental illness in the biological and adoptive families of adopted schizophrenics. In *The transmission of schizophrenia,* eds. D. Rosenthal and S. S. Kety. Pergamon Press, Oxford, 1968, pp. 345–362.

Kety, S. S., Rosenthal, D., Wender, P. H., Schulsinger, F., and Jacobsen, B. The biologic and adoptive families of adopted individuals who became schizophrenic: Prevalence of mental illness and other characteristics. In *The nature of schizophrenia,* eds. L. C. Wynne, R. L. Cromwell, and S. Matthysse. Wiley and Sons, New York, 1978, pp. 25–37.

Kinney, D. K. and Jacobsen, B. Environmental factors in schizophrenia: new adoption study evidence. In *The nature of schizophrenia,* eds. L. C. Wynne, R. L. Cromwell and S. Matthyse, Wiley and Sons, New York, 1978, pp. 38–51.

Leff, J., and Wing, J. Trial of maintenance therapy and schizophrenia. *Br. Med. J., 2:*599–605, 1971.

May, P. R. A. *Treatment of schizophrenia.* Science House, New York, 1968.

Mosher, L. R., Pollin, W., and Stabenau, J. R. Families with identical twins discordant for schizophrenia: Some relationships between identification, thinking styles, psychopathology and dominance-submissiveness. *Br. J. Psychiat., 118:*29–42, 1971.

Odegaard, O. The multi-factorial theory of inheritance in predisposition to schizophrenia. In *Genetic factors in schizophrenia,* ed. R. Kaplin. C. C. Thomas, Springfield, Ill., 1972, p. 256.

Pollin, W., and Stabenau, J. R. Biological psychological and historical differences in a series of monozygotic twins discordant for schizophrenia. In *The transmission of schizophrenia,* eds. D. Rosenthal and S. S. Kety, Pergamon Press, Oxford, 1968, pp. 317–332.

Rosenthal, D. *Genetics of psychopathology.* McGraw-Hill, New York, 1971.

Rosenthal, D., Wender, P., Kety, S., Welner, J., and Schulsinger, F. The adopted-away offspring of schizophrenics. *Am. J. Psychiat., 128:*307–311, 1971.

Snyder, S. H. *Madness and the brain.* McGraw-Hill, New York, 1974.

Wender, P. H., Rosenthal, D., Rainer, J. D., Greenhill, L., and Sarlin, M. B. Schizophrenics adopting parents psychiatric status. *Arch. Gen. Psychiat., 34:*777–784, 1977.

Wender, P. H., Rosenthal, D., Zahn, T. P., and Kety, S. S. The psychiatric adjustment of the adopting parents of schizophrenics. *Am. J. Psychiat., 127:*1013–1018, 1971.

6. Chemical messengers in the brain

It is a truism that all our thoughts and feelings emanate from information-processing events in the brain. Less well appreciated is the fact that virtually all this information processing seems to involve communications between nerve cells (which are called *neurons*) via chemicals known as *neurotransmitters*.

In the nineteenth century it was thought that all neurons were continuous with each other rather than separate cells. At the turn of the century, the great Spanish neuroanatomist Ramon y Cajal showed that neurons were discrete structural entities with many processes impinging on other neurons. The complex network formed by these processes distinguishes neurons from cells in other parts of the body, and it was this that had caused the confusion. The place where neurons meet is the synapse (Figure 6.1). For many years, scientists debated whether the electricity of nerve impulses literally "jumped" across the synaptic gap or whether chemicals released by one neuron diffused through the synaptic cleft to the adjacent neuron. It is now well established that almost all synaptic transmission in the brain involves the release of neurotransmitters from nerve cell endings, which then act at specific receptor sites of other neurons located on the membrane of their cell body or one of its processes, called *dendrites*. Any given neuron may, through its branching axons, send information to several thousand other neurons and, at the same time, receive input via its dendrites from thousands of other neurons. Such complex interactions underlie the richness of human brain function.

Thus, an understanding of how the brain operates, of what biological processes underlie thinking and feeling, demands an appreciation of neurotransmit-

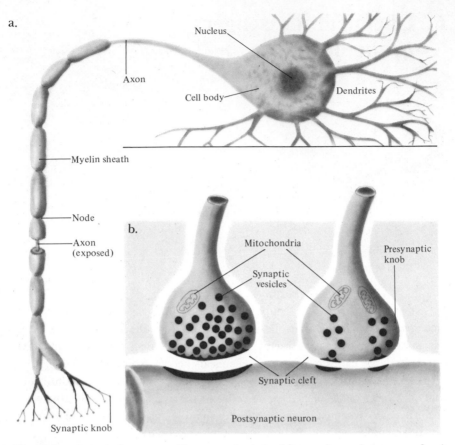

Fig. 6-1a. A typical neuron with many short dendrites and one long axon. **b.** A schematic example of a synapse.

ters, including their formation, release, action at receptors, and subsequent destruction. Synaptic transmission is also important in clarifying how drugs affect mental activity. Essentially every psychoactive drug known is thought to act primarily by altering some aspect of neurotransmitter disposition. Accordingly, this chapter will deal with neurotransmitters, the neuronal systems containing them, and their interactions with drugs.

Neurotransmitters

Acetylcholine has the longest history of investigation as a neurotransmitter, followed closely by norepinephrine (see Figure 6.2). Acetylcholine was the first discovered of all neurotransmitters and established firmly the notion that nerves communicate with each other by releasing chemicals and not by an electric current "jumping the gap" between adjacent neurons. *Norepinephrine* and *dopamine* are two catecholamine neurotransmitters. "Catechol" refers to the benzene ring structure containing two adjacent OH groups, while "amine" refers to the nitrogen group of the side chain. Interactions of psychotropic drugs with these two catecholamine neurotransmitters have been demonstrated in many studies, and a misconception arose that the catecholamines and acetylcholine, along with *serotonin,* another transmitter relevant to psychotropic drug action, account for the bulk of synaptic transmission in the brain. Quantitatively, these compounds are only minor transmitters in the brain, though they may have particular importance in the brain regions concerned with emotional behavior. Even in the corpus striatum, the area of the brain with the highest concentration of *dopamine,* only about 15 percent of the nerve terminals use dopamine as their transmitter. In the hypothalamus, the brain region richest in norepinephrine, only about 5 percent of the nerve terminals use that neurotransmitter. In the brain as a whole, the two catecholamines probably account for transmission at no more than about 1 to 2 percent of synapses. Serotonin is the transmitter at considerably fewer synapses than the catecholamines. Although such es-

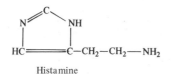

Histamine

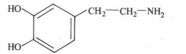

Dopamine

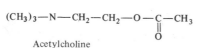

Acetylcholine

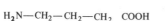

GABA (gamma–aminobutyric acid)

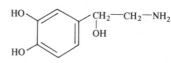

Norepinephrine

$H_2N—CH_2—COOH$

Glycine

$HOOC—CH_2—CH_2—CH—COOH$
                                $|$
                               NH_2

Glutamic acid

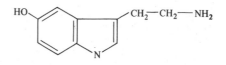

Serotonin (5–hydroxytryptamine)

Fig. 6-2. Structures of amine and amino acid neurotransmitters.

timates are more difficult to obtain for acetylcholine, it is unlikely that more than 5 to 10 percent of the synapses in the brain utilize acetylcholine. There is now considerable evidence that *histamine* is a neurotransmitter in "emotional" areas of the brain, such as the hypothalamus, but its levels in the brain are substantially lower than those of serotonin and the catecholamines.

What, then, are the major neurotransmitters in the central nervous system? Most likely they are a variety of amino acids. In certain brain regions *gamma-aminobutyric acid (GABA)* probably accounts for transmission at between 25 and 40 percent of synapses. GABA inhibits the firing of neurons and is therefore a major inhibitory transmitter. In the spinal cord and brain stem the amino acid glycine, in addition to its other metabolic functions, seems to be a prominent inhibitory transmitter at about the same percentage of synapses as GABA. It should be borne in mind that, with only rare exceptions, a given neuron uses only a single neurotransmitter. Thus, GABA and glycine are transmitters at distinct synapses. The identity of the major excitatory neurotransmitters which stimulate the firing of neurons is somewhat less certain. However, *glutamic* and *aspartic acids,* which uniformly excite neurons, satisfy many requirements of prominent excitatory neurotransmitters.

Table 6-1 Some prominent neurotransmitters in the brain

Acetylcholine	The first known neurotransmitter, discovered in the 1920s. It is the neurotransmitter at nerve-muscle connections for all the voluntary muscles of the body as well as at many of the involuntary (autonomic) nervous system synapses. Despite its long history, the exact role of acetylcholine neurons in the brain is unclear.
Norepinephrine	One of the two catecholamine neurotransmitters and the second known transmitter, having been characterized in the 1930s. It was discovered as the transmitter of the sympathetic nerves of the autonomic nervous system which mediate emergency responses, such as acceleration of the heart, dilatation of the bronchi, and elevation of blood pressure.
Dopamine	Another catecholamine neurotransmitter, discovered in 1958 as a major transmitter in the corpus striatum, a part of the brain regulating motor behavior. Destruction of the dopamine neurons in the corpus striatum is responsible for the symptoms of Parkinson's disease, such as rigidity and tremor. Blockade of the actions of dopamine in other brain regions accounts for the therapeutic activities of antischizophrenic drugs (see Chapter 5).
Serotonin	The transmitter of a discrete group of neurons that all have cell bodies located in the raphe nuclei of the brain stem. Changes in the activity of serotonin neurons are related to the actions of psychedelic drugs.
Enkephalins	Composed of two peptides, each containing five amino acids. The enkephalins are neurotransmitters that were discovered as the normally occurring substances which act upon opiate receptors. Thus, enkephalins can mimic the effects of opiates. Enkephalin neurons are localized to areas of the brain which regulate functions that are influenced by opiate drugs.

Substance P	A peptide containing eleven amino acids. It is a major transmitter of sensory neurons which convey pain sensation from the periphery, especially the skin, into the spinal cord. Opiates relieve pain in part by blocking the release of substance P. Substance P is also found in numerous brain regions.
GABA (*Gamma-amino-butyric acid*)	This is one of the amino acid transmitters in the brain. It has no known function besides serving as a neurotransmitter and occurs almost exclusively in the brain. GABA reduces the firing of neurons and so is an inhibitory neurotransmitter. It is the transmitter at 25 to 40 percent of all synapses in the brain, and so, quantitatively, it may be the predominant transmitter of the brain.
Glycine	Besides its roles as a conventional amino acid in protein synthesis and general metabolism, glycine serves as an inhibitory neurotransmitter in small neurons in the spinal cord and brain stem. Here it is a transmitter at 30 to 40 percent of synapses and quantitatively is more prominent than GABA, which in turn predominates in higher centers such as the cerebral cortex.
Glutamic acid	One of the major amino acids in general metabolism and protein synthesis, glutamic acid is also a neurotransmitter. It stimulates neurons to fire and is probably the principal excitatory neurotransmitter in the brain. Glutamic acid appears to be the neurotransmitter of the major neuronal pathway that connects the cerebral cortex and the corpus striatum. It is also the transmitter of the granule cells, which are the most numerous neurons in the cerebellum. There is some evidence that glutamic acid is the principal neurotransmitter of the visual pathway. No drugs are yet known to exert their effects via interactions with glutamic acid.
Histamine	In addition to its roles in the periphery in allergic conditions and in regulating acid secretion by the stomach, histamine is a neurotransmitter in the brain. It is most highly concentrated in areas of the brain that regulate emotional behavior, and its localization is roughly similar to that of norepinephrine. It is unclear whether the central effects of antihistamine drugs, such as somnolence, relate to actions at brain histamine receptors.

A major recent development has been the discovery that numerous *peptides* may also be neurotransmitters. Peptides consist of amino acids linked together, and many of them are hormones, such as insulin. Proteins are merely very large peptides. The most intensively studied peptide transmitters are the opiatelike peptides called *enkephalins*. Their discovery stemmed from fundamental investigations of opiate receptors, the sites at which opiate drugs such as morphine and heroin exert their effects. By monitoring the binding of radioactive opiates to brain membranes, it was possible to identify specific binding sites which represent the opiate receptors (Snyder, 1978). The location of opiate receptors is highly circumscribed in parts of the central nervous system that mediate pain perception and emotional regulation as well as a limited number of other areas not classically associated with opiate actions. As a general rule, the precise microscopic localizations of opiate receptors explain the major pharmacologic effects of opiates.

The dramatic properties of the opiate receptor suggested that it is not an evolutionary vestige but may serve to interact with a normally occurring morphinelike substance. Such a substance was indeed isolated from the brain by Hughes et al. (1975) and confirmed soon thereafter (Simantov and Snyder, 1976). It is a mixture of two peptides, each five amino acids in length and differing only in one amino acid (Figure 6.3). These are referred to as *methionine-enkephalin (met-enkephalin)* and *leucine-enkephalin (leu-enkephalin)*. The five amino acids of met-enkephalin, together with twenty-six others, make up an opioid peptide called *β-endorphin,* which is found in large concentrations in the pituitary gland.

Using immunohistochemical techniques that label antibodies to peptides fluorescently, it is possible to visualize peptides such as enkephalin and map their microscopic localization. Enkephalins are highly concentrated in the same brain regions as those where opiate receptors are localized. In the spinal cord, enkephalin and opiate receptors are concentrated in a dense, narrow band just where sensory nerves enter the spinal cord. Here, enkephalin appears to act upon opiate receptors on the surface of sensory nerve terminals, conveying information about pain perception. At these sites it inhibits the release of the peptide neurotransmitter *substance P,* which normally conveys pain sensation. This peptide, which consists of eleven amino acids, is found in some of the same brain areas as enkephalin. Besides functioning as a neurotransmitter of pain pathways, substance P is also localized in parts of the limbic system in areas regulating emotion. Its exact function in these parts of the brain is unclear.

By identifying areas of the brain which are richest in opiate receptors and enkephalin neurons, one can explain most of the effects of opiate drugs. For instance, while some of the analgesic effects of opiates are mediated at a spinal cord level, opiates also affect the subjective appreciation of pain, which means they must act on the brain as well. The periaqueductal gray area in the brain stem is a site where electrical stimulation produces analgesia, so it is assumed to be involved in integrating information about pain. Opiate receptors and enkephalin neurons are enriched in the periaqueductal gray. Injection of morphine directly into this area produces analgesia.

When people die of opiate overdose, the primary cause of death is depression of respiration. The victims simply stop breathing because sites in the brain which maintain respiration involuntarily, even when we are asleep, are depressed by opiates. One of these respiratory centers is in the nucleus of the "solitary tract" in the brain stem. This nucleus possesses an extremely dense cluster of opiate receptors and enkephalin neurons.

How do opiates cause euphoria? A group of structures in the brain collectively referred to as the *limbic system* are well known for their involvement in the regulation of emotional behavior. Opiate receptors and enkephalin neurons are highly concentrated in several structures of the limbic system. Additionally,

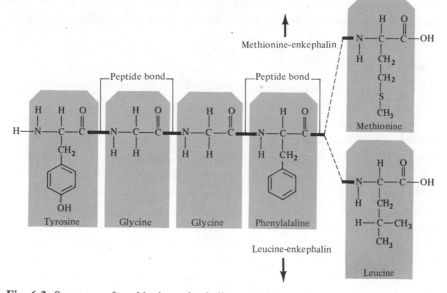

Fig. 6-3. Structures of methionine-enkephalin and leucine-enkaphalin, which share identical amino acid sequences except for their terminal units.

the major norepinephrine pathway in the brain has its cell bodies in the *locus coeruleus,* a small nucleus in the brain stem (see below). The locus coeruleus has one of the heaviest concentrations of enkephalin neurons and opiate receptors in the brain. Since norepinephrine is accepted by most researchers as a neurotransmitter of emotional behavior, the locus coeruleus may also be an important site of opiate action.

Interestingly, though the enkephalins are recently discovered neurotransmitters, we probably know more about their behavioral roles than we do with other neurotransmitters. For instance, scientists have not yet even mapped out the localization of acetylcholine neurons in the brain, much less discerned their function, despite the fact that acetylcholine was already well known in the 1920s.

Neurotensin is a peptide of thirteen amino acids (Carraway and Leeman, 1975), with a distribution in the brain closely similar to that of enkephalin (Uhl et al., 1977). The possibility that neurotensin is involved in pain perception is supported by findings that when injected into ventricles of the mouse brain, neurotensin is more potent as an analgesic than enkephalin (Clineschmidt and McGuffin, 1977).

Despite the quantitative predominance of amino acid transmitters in the brain, little is currently known about their interactions with psychotropic drugs.

The most detailed information is available for the biogenic amines norepinephrine, dopamine, and serotonin, and for the opioid peptide enkephalin.

Amine tracts

A major advance in understanding the functions of the amines in the brain occurred when histochemical techniques were developed to localize neurons containing norepinephrine, dopamine, and serotonin. In the histochemical fluorescence method, serotonin can be distinguished from the catecholamines by the
wave length of fluorescence, which varies in such a way that serotonin appears
bright yellow and the catecholamines appear bright green. Although both dopamine and norepinephrine flruoesce green, they can be differentiated by their
response to drugs. What are the pathways of these neuronal systems? The cell
bodies of all of them lie within the brain stem. Axons ascend or descend
throughout the brain and into the spinal cord. For each of the amines, there are
several separate tracts (see Figure 6.4).

Norepinephrine

There are two major norepinephrine tracts. The *ventral* (*anterior*) *pathway* has
cell bodies in several locations in the brain stem and axons that ascend in the
medial forebrain bundle and terminate at synapses mainly· in the hypothalamus
and limbic system. The cell bodies of the *dorsal pathway* are discretely localized in a single nucleus of the brain stem, the locus coeruleus. Its axons also
ascend in the medial forebrain bundle but more dorsally (toward the back surface of the brain) than those of the ventral pathway. Terminals of the dorsal
pathway are located predominantly in the cerebral cortex and hippocampus.
Some axons from the locus coeruleus descend to form synapses with the large
Purkinje cells of the cerebellum. Certain cells from the locus coeruleus give off
axons that bifurcate, sending one branch to the cerebral cortex and another to
the cerebellum. In this way a single neuron can influence widespread parts of
the brain.

Knowing the course of these neurons, one can readily speculate as to their
function. It is likely that the ventral norepinephrine pathway, with terminals in
the pleasure centers of the lateral hypothalamus, may subserve such affective
behaviors as euphoria and depression. The dorsal norepinephrine pathway to
the cerebral cortex may be associated with the control of alertness.

Other norepinephrine pathways with cell bodies in the brain stem send axons
down the lateral sympathetic columns of the spinal cord, terminating at various
levels. These neurons influence a variety of spinal cord reflexes. Conceivably,
these pathways may mediate emotional influences on muscle tone in conditions
such as anxiety and tension.

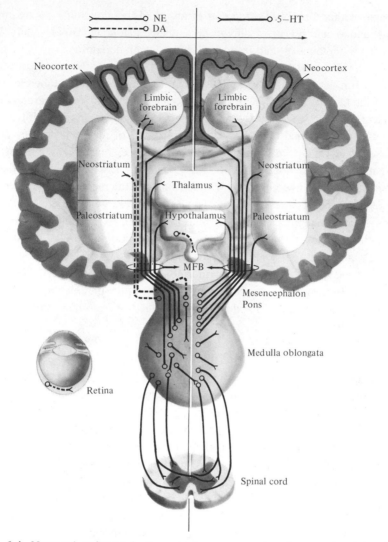

Fig. 6-4. Neuronal pathways in the central nervous system for norepinephrine (NE), dopamine (DA), and serotonin (5-HT). In this diagram, the serotonin pathways are shown on the right, the norepinephrine pathways on the left.

Dopamine

There are several discrete dopamine pathways. The most prominent one has cell bodies in the substantia nigra area of the brain stem and axons that terminate in the caudate nucleus and putamen, two structures of the corpus striatum, which is involved in coordinating motor activity. This pathway deteriorates in Parkinson's disease, accounting for the inability to move and the tremor which characterize this disease. Restoration of the depleted dopamine by treatment with its amino acid precursor dihydroxy-L-phenylalanine (L-dopa) greatly alleviates the symptoms of Parkinson's disease. Other dopamine pathways have cell bodies close to the substantia nigra, just dorsal to the interpeduncular nucleus, with terminals in the nucleus accumbens and olfactory tubercle, both parts of the limbic system. There are also dopamine neurons in the cerebral cortex. The functions of these dopamine pathways are poorly understood, but they may relate to emotional behavior. Indeed, blockade of receptors for dopamine in these brain regions is thought to underlie the therapeutic actions of antischizophrenic drugs (for the details, see Chapter 5). Dopamine cells in the arcuate nucleus of the hypothalamus with terminals in the median eminence probably regulate the release of hypothalamic hormones, which then act on the pituitary gland to regulate release of pituitary hormones. Dopamine appears to inhibit the release of the pituitary hormone prolactin in normal physiologic doses. Drugs used to treat schizophrenia, by blocking dopamine receptors, elevate plasma levels of prolactin. This hormone normally acts on the breasts to provoke mild secretions and on the gonads. Thus, schizophrenic women treated with these drugs may be troubled by the side effects of abnormal milk secretion and amenorrhea.

Serotonin

All cell bodies of the serotonin-containing neurons are localized in a series of nuclei in the lower midbrain and upper pons that are called the *raphe nuclei*. Serotonin is so highly concentrated in raphe nuclei that probably almost all their cells are serotonergic. Axons of these cells ascend primarily in the medial forebrain bundle and give off terminals in all brain regions, but with the majority in the hypothalamus and the fewest in the cerebral cortex and cerebellum. Selective destruction of the raphe nuclei in animals results in insomnia and some agitated peculiar behavior. Restoring the depleted serotonin with tryptophan or 5-hydroxytryptophan, the amino acid precursor of serotonin, puts such insomniac animals to sleep. Similarly, stimulation of the raphe nuclei at physiological frequencies makes animals somnolent. Thus, the serotonin neurons play some role in regulating sleep-wakefulness cycles. Psychedelic drugs appear to exert their behavioral effects by inhibiting the firing of serotonin neurons (for details, see Chapter 9).

Amine metabolism

Understanding the metabolic pathways of the biogenic amines is important in appreciating the interactions of psychoactive drugs with them. The amino acid

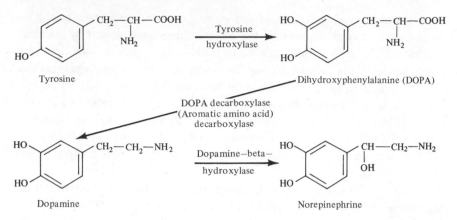

Fig. 6-5. Metabolic pathway for the conversion of tyrosine to dopa, dopa to dopamine, and dopamine to norepinephrine. The enzymes that catalyze these three reactions are tyrosine hydroxylase, dopa decarboxylase, and dopamine-beta-hydroxylase, respectively.

tyrosine is the dietary precursor of the catecholamines (see Figure 6.5). The first enzyme in the biosynthetic pathway of the catecholamines is tyrosine hydroxylase, which converts tyrosine into dihydroxyphenylalanine, referred to usually as *dopa*. Tyrosine hydroxylase is considered to be the major rate-limiting enzyme in catecholamine biosynthesis because increasing or decreasing its activity produces corresponding changes in the levels of the catecholamines. Experimental drugs that block this enzyme, such as α-methyltyrosine, deplete the brain of catecholamines, and this causes apparent sedation in animals and depressionlike symptoms in human beings. Dopa is decarboxylated by the enzyme dopa-decarboxylase to dopamine. Decarboxylation denotes removal of the carboxy (COOH) group, which is the "acid" moiety of an amino acid. The product of decarboxylation of an amino acid is an *amine*.

In norepinephrine neurons, dopamine is converted to norepinephrine by the addition of a hydroxyl (OH) group by the enzyme dopamine-β-hydroxylase. Dopamine neurons do not contain any dopamine-β-hydroxylase, so dopamine remains the major catecholamine in these neurons.

Knowledge of catecholamine metabolism has provided a biochemical measure of the firing rate of catecholamine neurons. Under normal conditions, when a neuron fires and releases a molecule of a catecholamine, the neuron must synthesize a new catecholamine molecule to replace the one just released. Accordingly, when the firing rate of catecholamine neurons is accelerated, there is a parallel increase in the conversion of tyrosine to new catecholamines. Pharmacologists have applied this principle with great success to an analysis of the influence of psychotropic drugs and varying environmental states on the firing rate of catecholamine neurons. For instance, amphetamine acts by releasing catecholamines from their nerve terminals. To replace the released catecholamine, the neuron accelerates its synthesis, which pharmacologists can measure as a reflection of the effects of the drug. Similarly, a role for norepinephrine neurons in stress situations was elucidated by these biochemical techniques. When rats are stressed by being placed in a cold room, restrained, or forced to swim, the synthesis of norepinephrine is selectively speeded up, indicating that the stressful stimulus provoked firing of the norepinephrine neurons.

Catecholamines can be metabolically degraded primarily by two enzymes, *monoamine oxidase* and *catechol-O-methyltransferase (COMT)* (see Figure 6.6). Monoamine oxidase removes the amine or nitrogen-containing group from dopamine and norepinephrine, converting them to the corresponding aldehydes, with structures that are intermediate between an alcohol and an acid. These, in turn, can be converted by aldehyde dedrogenase to the corresponding acids, or they may be reduced to form alcohols. Dietary factors, such as the ingestion of ethanol, can determine the relative amounts of catechol acids or alcohols formed from the catecholamines because ethanol competes with the aldehyde derivatives for aldehyde dehydrogenase.

Catecholamines can be modified by the enzyme COMT, which adds a methyl (CH_3) group to the meta hydroxyl of the catecholamines. Adding such a methyl group inactivates the catecholamines, so that COMT activity is one way of terminating the actions of dopamine and norepinephrine after they are released. Reuptake inactivation, a more important process, will be discussed below. COMT acts on any catechol compound, including the aldehydes and acids formed from the actions of monoamine oxidase on the catecholamines. When norepinephrine is methylated by this enzyme, the product is called *normetanephrine*. There is no corresponding name for the methylated derivative of dopamine, which is simply referred to as *3-0-methyl-dopamine*.

Like COMT, the enzyme monoamine oxidase is relatively nonspecific and acts on all monoamines—including serotonin, normetanephrine, and 3-0-methyl-dopamine—converting them first into their respective aldehydes and then into acids or alcohols. Thus, alcohol or acid possessing a methyl group on its catechol ring results from the actions of both monoamine oxidase and COMT. In the peripheral sympathetic nervous system, the 0-methylated acid product of norepinephrine degradation is called *vanillylmandelic acid* and is often referred to as *VMA*. Its levels are measured in clinical laboratories to monitor sympathetic nervous function and to diagnose tumors that produce norepinephrine or epinephrine, such as pheochromocytomas and neuroblas-

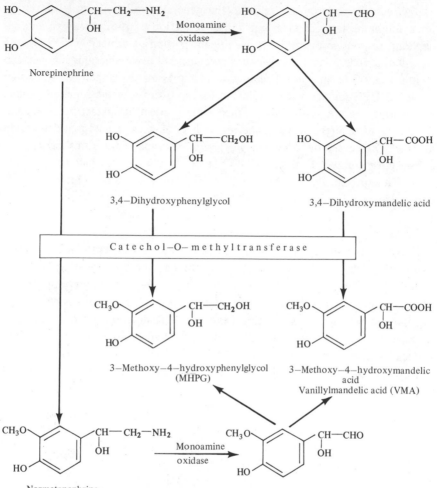

Fig. 6-6. Metabolic degradation of the catecholamines, norepinephrine, and normeta-nephrine, by monoamine oxidase and catechol-O-methyltransferase.

tomas. The corresponding end product of dopamine metabolism is called *homovanillic acid*. The more frequently dopamine neurons fire, the more homovanillic acid is formed. Thus, pharmacologists often measure the brain's content of homovanillic acid to estimate the activity of dopamine receptors.

In the brain, reduction to an alcohol of the aldehyde formed from the action of monoamine oxidase on norepinephrine or normetanephrine is more frequent than its oxidation to an acid, so that the major metabolite in the brain is an alcohol derivative called *3-methoxy-4-hydroxylphenylglycol (MHPG)*. Because

MHPG can diffuse from the brain to the general circulation, its levels in the urine might be thought to give a direct reflection of the activity of norepinephrine neurons in the brain. A significant portion of urinary MHPG derives from the peripheral nervous system, however, and a variable amount, perhaps as much as 60 to 80 percent, comes from the brain. Nonetheless, measuring urinary MHPG may become a valuable tool in estimating the function of norepinephrine neurons in the brain. Since antidepressant drugs act by enhancing the effects of norepinephrine, some researchers have suggested that depression itself may be caused by a deficiency of norepinephrine. To test this theory, scientists have compared urinary MHPG levels in depressives and normal subjects. Though the average MHPG levels in depressives are normal, a subpopulation may have extremely low levels.

Serotonin

Tryptophan, the dietary amino acid that is the precursor of serotonin, receives a hydroxyl group in a reaction catalyzed by the enzyme tryptophan hydroxylase to form *5-hydroxytryptophan* (see Figure 6.7). Then 5-hydroxytryptophan has its acid carboxyl group removed by 5-hydroxytryptophan decarboxylase, forming the neurotransmitter serotonin. Serotonin is destroyed by monoamine oxidase, which converts the transmitter to its aldehyde, just as it does with the catecholamines. The aldehyde formed from serotonin is mainly oxidized to *5-hydroxyindoleacetic acid,* although a limited amount is reduced to the alcohol *5-hydroxytryptophol.*

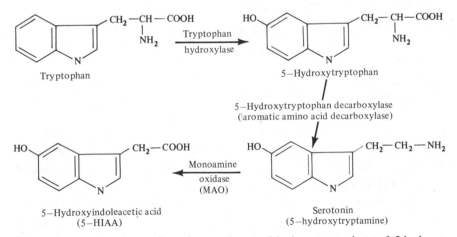

Fig. 6-7. Metabolic conversion of tryptophan to 5-hydroxytryptophan, of 5-hydroxytryptophan to serotonin, and of serotonin to 5-hydroxy-indoleacetic acid.

Reuptake inactivation of neurotransmitters

After discharge at synapses, acetylcholine is inactivated by being destroyed by the enzyme acetylcholinesterase. In contrast, none of the enzymes that degrade serotonin or the catecholamines appear to be responsible for their inactivation after release at synapses. Instead, these amines are predominantly inactivated by reuptake into the nerve terminals that released them. This process was discovered and shown to be responsible for synaptic inactivation of norepinephrine in the peripheral sympathetic nervous system by Axelrod (1965). Since then, highly efficient and specific uptake systems have been demonstrated for all the neurotransmitter candidates in the central nervous system—norepinephrine, dopamine, serotonin, GABA, glutamic and aspartic acids, and glycine. It appears likely that reuptake inactivation is a fundamental mechanism for neurotransmitter inactivation and that the enzymatic degradation of acetylcholine is an exception to the rule. Interference with the reuptake system of inactivation is a major mechanism of action of several psychotropic drugs. For instance, the tricyclic antidepressants appear to act by inhibiting the reuptake of norepinephrine and serotonin (for detailed discussion, see Chapter 2).

References

Anden, N. E., Dahlstrom, A., Fuxe, K., Larrson, K., Olson, L., and Ungerstedt, U. Ascending monoamine neurons to the telencephalon and diencephalon. *Acta Physiol. Scand., 67:*313, 1966.

Axelrod, J. The metabolism, storage and release of catecholamines. *Progr. Horm. Res., 21:*497, 1965.

Carraway, R., and Leeman, S. The amino acid sequence of a hypothalamic peptide, neurotensin. *J. Biol. Chem., 250:*1907, 1975.

Clineschmidt, B. V., and McGuffin, J. Neurotensin administered intracisternally inhibits responsiveness of mice to noxious stimuli. *Eur. J. Pharmacol., 46:*395, 1977.

Hughes, J. T., Smith, T. W., Kosterlitz, H. W., Fothergill, L., Morgan, B. A., and Morris, H. R. Identification of two related pentapeptides from the brain with potent opiate agonist activity. *Nature, 258:*577, 1975.

Simantov, R., and Snyder, S. H. Morphine-like factors in mammalian brain: Structure elucidation and interactions with the opiate receptor. *Proc. Natal. Acad. Sci., USA, 73:*2515, 1976.

Snyder, S. H. Catecholamines and serotonin. In *Basic neurochemistry,* eds. R. W. Albers, G. J. Siegel, R. Katzman, and B. W. Agranoff. Little, Brown, Boston, 1972, pp. 89–104.

Snyder, S. H. The opiate receptor and morphine-like peptides in the brain. *Am. J. Psychiat., 135:*645, 1978.

Uhl, G. R., Kuhar, M. J., and Snyder, S. H. Neurotensin: Immunohistochemical localization in rat central nervous system. *Proc. Natl. Acad. Sci., USA, 74:*4059, 1977.

7. Drug abuse: definitions

Defining drug abuse is a highly subjective matter which varies widely in different cultures. Medical terminology describing the misuse of drugs is often as misleading as lay terminology. There is no consensus as to the precise meaning of words such as "addiction," "habituation," and "drug dependence." Historically, "drug addiction" has denoted the repeated use of a socially disapproved drug. The World Health Organization defined *drug addiction* in 1950 as:

A state of periodic or chronic intoxication, detrimental to the individual and society, produced by the repeated consumption of a drug (natural or synthetic). Its characteristics include:

1. An overwhelming desire or need (compulsion) to continue taking the drug and to obtain it by any means.
2. A tendency to increase the dose.
3. A psychic (psychological) and sometimes a physical dependence on the drug.

Two aspects of this definition can be readily demonstrated in animal models: tolerance and physical dependence. *Tolerance* means that with repeated administration of a drug, a larger dose is required to produce effects which earlier were apparent at smaller doses. One can be tolerant to a drug without being addicted at all. There are two forms of tolerance, *metabolic* and *cellular*. Metabolic tolerance refers to the greater efficiency of enzymes in the body, usually in the liver, at degrading a drug upon repeated exposure, so that with a given dose a chronic user of the drug will have lower blood and brain levels than a novice. Cellular tolerance occurs as target cells in the brain become less sensitive to the effects of the drug when it is administered chronically. With cellular tolerance to a drug, diminished responses are observed even when blood and brain levels are just as high in an experienced user as in an individual receiving the drug for the first time.

Physical dependence refers to a state in which pronounced "abstinence" symptoms will appear when a chronically administered drug is terminated. Abstinence symptoms following withdrawal of opiates, alcohol, barbiturates, and amphetamines are readily demonstrated in both animals and human beings. One can be physically dependent on a drug without being a self-administering addict. Hospital patients treated with opiates often experience withdrawal symptoms when the prescription is terminated.

A primary characteristic of addiction, according to the World Health Organization definition, is *compulsive use*. This irresistible craving is difficult to quantify. In experimental studies, one can measure the number of times an animal presses a lever to activate intravenous self-administration of a drug. Rats and monkeys will self-administer opiates, cocaine, amphetamines, barbiturates, and alcohol with great avidity.

To distinguish degrees of drug abuse, the World Health Organization attempted to differentiate *drug habituation* from addiction with the following definition:

Drug habituation is a condition resulting from the repeated consumption of a drug. Its characteristics include:

1. A desire (but not a compulsion) to continue taking the drug for the sense of improved well-being which it engenders.
2. Little or no tendency to increase the dose.
3. Some degree of psychic dependence on the effect of the drug, but absence of physical dependence and hence of an abstinence syndrome.
4. Detrimental effects, if any, primarily on the individual.

A *habit-forming* drug is regarded as less dangerous than an addicting one. This distinction, however, involves difficult value judgments. Since chronic amphetamine use is not as clearly associated with physical dependence as opiates and barbiturates, amphetamines have been regarded as habit-forming but not addicting. Yet heavy amphetamine use can be more harmful than opiate addiction.

Because of continued semantic difficulties such as these and the lack of general acceptance of any definitions of drug abuse, the World Health Organization in 1964 replaced "addiction" and "habituation" with the term *drug dependence,* which simply means "a state arising from repeated administration of a drug on a periodic or continuous basis.'' To differentiate drug abuse, one simply specifies the particular drug being used—for example, drug dependence of the morphine type—and so on. Rather than taking this reductionist approach, however, many clinicians and researchers still use the terms *addiction* and *habituation*.

Opiate refers to a drug of the morphine class either extracted directly from the opium poppy or synthesized chemically. A large number of opiates are marketed, mostly as *analgesics,* to relieve pain, but also as antidiarrheal compounds. Some opiates, such as diphenoxylate (Lomotil), do not enter the brain readily and therefore are used to treat diarrhea without producing euphoria or analgesia. Propoxyphene (Darvon), one of the most widely used drugs in the United States, is employed like aspirin for mild or moderate pain, but it is a weak opiate and retains all the addictive properties of other opiates.

Narcotic is a vague term which has been widely misused with derogatory connotation to describe any psychotropic drug that is abusable, especially "downers." Technically, it is *synonymous* with *opiate*. However, the very misuses of the word, which has been applied to substances as diverse as marijuana, cocaine, morphine, and even caffeine, emphasizes the importance of learning specifics about each class of psychoactive drugs.

8. Opiates

Though the problems of heroin addiction have made many opiates seem a menace to the public, these drugs have had major therapeutic uses for a very long time. Aspirin and other agents relieve mild to moderate pain, but opiates are the only drugs that can alleviate severe pain. They are also the only powerful antidiarrheal agents available. Until the present century, opiates were one of the few genuinely effective classes of drugs in the physician's armamentarium. In the days before tranquilizers and sleeping pills, they were used to promote sleep and to relieve anxiety. The important place of opiates in medicine was well characterized by the eminent seventeenth century physician Thomas Sydenham, who wrote, "I cannot forebear mentioning with gratitude the goodness of the Supreme Being who has supplied afflicted mankind with opiates for their relief; no other remedy being equally powerful to overcome a great number of diseases or to eradicate them effectually" (quoted by Ray, 1972).

Until the nineteenth century, the only opiates available were extracts of the opium poppy plant. In the early 1800s the chemist Frederich Serturner isolated the active ingredient of the poppy and named it morphine after Morpheus, the Greek god of dreams. The only other naturally occurring opiate is codeine, which is present in the poppy at about $1/20$th the concentration of morphine.

The subjective effects of opium were known to several ancient civilizations, including the Sumerian (about 4000 B.C.), while the addictive properties of the drug were recognized by Greek physicians at the time of Hippocrates. However, opium smoking became popular only in the eighteenth century in the Orient.

The oral use of crude opium extracts produced a mild form of addiction which did not represent a serious public health problem. Widespread concern about severe opiate addiction originated in the second half of the nineteenth century with the invention of the hypodermic needle and the ready availability of pure morphine. Intravenous morphine to relieve severe pain rapidly was a medical breakthrough that had wide application in the Civil War, but it created so many addicts among Civil War veterans that opiate addiction came to be known as the "soldiers disease."

Heroin addiction in twentieth-century America

Drug addiction is largely a social disorder and has been likened to an infectious disease. When asked why they started injecting heroin, addicts often say that their friends were doing it and speak of the macho quality of the behavior. Much of the personality disintegration accompanying heroin addiction does not stem from the effects of the drug itself but from its association with an underworld culture.

In the late nineteenth century, many drug companies searched actively for a new opiate with all the good but none of the bad properties of morphine. The Bayer Drug Company in Elberfeld, Germany, introduced aspirin in 1900. Two years before, in 1898, the Bayer chemist Dreser had added two acetyl groups to morphine, thereby creating heroin. The acetyl groups facilitate the passage of heroin from the blood into the brain. Thus, heroin is more potent than morphine, acts more rapidly, and can produce more euphoria.

Physicians adopted heroin as a miracle cure for morphine addiction. And indeed, heroin was quite effective in weaning morphine addicts away from their former drug. Surprisingly, it took about five to ten years before heroin addiction itself was widely recognized. By 1915 heroin had fully supplanted morphine as the drug of choice for opiate addicts. Besides its greater euphoric properties, heroin was desirable because it was readily available as a cough suppressant without a prescription, while stiff regulations governed accessibility to morphine or crude opium extracts.

In the early twentieth century, the greatest number of morphine and heroin addicts resided in New York City. The Boylan Act of 1914, passed by the New York State legislature, controlled the prescribing of most opiates and also established guidelines regulating the maintenance administration of opiates to addicts. Numerous opiate maintenance clinics were established to contain "the problem of heroin addiction." The rationale was very much like that of the British system of regulating addicts by providing them with drugs at no expense but under strict medical supervision. In this way the underworld trafficking in opiates could be suppressed. Addicts had no need for a life of crime to secure their drug and would be less liable to develop hepatitis from dirty needles or to die from overdoses.

Entry of the United States into World War I seems to have provided an impetus for a major change (Musto, 1974). To "strengthen" young men for war, alcohol and all drugs were banned from army training camps. At the same time, there was a movement to rid American cities of "degenerates," including drug addicts. Though there were in fact only a few thousand heroin addicts in New York state, exaggerated claims were made of up to 200,000 addicts in New York City alone. It was argued erroneously that heroin use led to violent behavior and that three-quarters of crimes would be eliminated if drugs were controlled.

In this atmosphere it seemed inappropriate to be providing addicts with their drugs in public clinics. Accordingly, the U.S. Treasury Department issued regulations which in effect closed all the drug maintenance clinics. This endeavor to eliminate opiate addiction may have been responsible in large part for its perpetuation in a more pernicious form associated with widespread theft to pay for illicit drugs and organized crime networks to provide street supplies of heroin.

In the mid 1960s a major heroin "epidemic" spread throughout the United States, predominantly in the black community. At about the same time, heroin was being used extensively by U.S. troops in Vietnam, where the drug was freely available in a highly potent form. Differences between heroin addicts in the United States and addicted American soldiers in Vietnam illustrate the role of social factors in drug abuse. Typical heroin addicts in black ghettos do not respond well to most rehabilitation efforts and continue abusing drugs for prolonged periods. By contrast, after they had been detoxified from their addiction and had come back to the United States, Vietnam veterans rarely returned to heroin (Bourne, 1974). The difference probably reflects the important role of the environment in drug abuse. Even when attending a drug abuse clinic, the ghetto addict remains in his demoralizing neighborhood environment, close to friends who are still addicts and close to sources of illicit heroin. By contrast, the soldiers in Vietnam learned about heroin addiction while in an unusual environment and extinguished this learning upon their return to a familiar one.

Effects of opiates on the body

Opiates affect many systems in the body. Their major medical role is to induce *analgesia,* which means relief of pain. Unlike local anesthetics, opiates do not abolish pain directly at the sensory nerve endings in the skin or body organs. Instead, they act on the brain to diminish the affective or feeling component of pain. Patients in severe pain treated with morphine report that pain is still present but that it doesn't bother them any longer.

Perhaps related to the influence of opiates on the feeling aspect of pain is their ability to elicit euphoria. Most, but not all, individuals treated with these drugs report a relaxed sense of well-being and an indifference to anxiety-provoking stresses. Whereas amphetamines produce an energized, hyperactive, exuberant euphoria, opiates elicit a feeling of quiet peacefulness and somnolence.

The immediate effects of an intravenous injection of heroin provide much of the reinforcement that "hooks" a user. The *rush* is a sensation of extreme pleasure, with a tingling, pervasive warmth in the abdomen that is likened by many addicts to a sexual orgasm, but better. At the same time, the body itches and the eyes become red because morphine releases histamine throughout the body. Within minutes after the injection, a brief period of sedation and sometimes light sleep ensues. During this "nodding" the user has vivid and usually pleasant dreams. In one of these dreams, Samuel Taylor Coleridge perceived the intense imagery which he later expressed in the poem *Kubla Khan*. During the rush and nodding, anxieties and worries vanish together with all sexual desire and appetite for food.

The act of injecting the drug itself becomes an important part of the addict's life. "Needle freaks" will insert the needle, withdraw and reinject blood again and again sometimes without ever administering a drug. Psychoanalysts emphasize the passive aspect of this behavior and equate the insertion of the needle in the vein with penile penetration. Though the heroin user may be nauseous and even vomit, euphoric sensations override the misery of nausea, which addicts accordingly label a "good sick."

The most unfortunate sequel to heroin injection is sudden death. About 1 percent of all heroin users die each year from apparent overdose. Deaths often take place shortly after the users have been released from jail, where they may have lost their tolerance to heroin. But many of these deaths may not be due to heroin. Opiates kill by depressing respiration, which takes many minutes or hours, whereas heroin addicts often die instantaneously, with the needle still in their vein. Because autopsy reveals their lungs to be congested with fluid, many of these deaths may represent a massive allergic reaction to the chemicals such as quinine mixed with the heroin.

Through its effects on the chemoreceptor trigger zone in the brain stem, morphine can elicit nausea and vomiting, which may be a particularly troublesome side effect in patients with advanced cancer who are greatly malnourished and who can therefore ill afford to vomit. The most serious adverse effect is depression of the respiratory centers in the brain stem. Normally these centers are stimulated by high levels of carbon dioxide in the blood to accelerate breathing. This feedback control is lost when opiate levels in the blood are sufficiently high. Breathing remains under conscious control, so that an individual suffering from an opiate overdose will breathe if instructed to do so but will stop breathing after falling asleep. Respiratory depression is the major cause of death from opiate overdose. In treating such overdoses, one must keep the victim awake and demand that he or she follow orders to breathe.

Opiates constrict the pupils of the eyes. The "pinpoint" pupils of an addict are a simple and fairly reliable indication of opiate addiction. Opiates also cause constipation by decreasing the frequency of the peristaltic contractions of the intestines, which normally propel food from stomach to anus. This constipating effect does not involve the central nervous system so that diphenoxylate (lomotil), an opiate that does not readily penetrate from blood to brain, is an ideal antidiarrheal agent; it relieves diarrhea but does not produce somnolence, euphoria, or respiratory depression.

How opiates act

Opiates begin to exert their actions after binding to highly selective sites on the external membranes of specific nerve cells (Snyder, 1975). These sites are specific membrane proteins referred to as *receptors*. The opiate receptors are similar in their general features to receptors for neurotransmitters. Indeed, opiate receptors were designed by nature for naturally occurring opiatelike neurotransmitters (see below and Chapter 6). The clinical potencies of different opiates correlate well with their affinity for binding to the opiate receptors. These receptors can be revealed microscopically by autoradiography, a procedure in which the receptors are labeled with a highly radioactive opiate, after which the radioactive grains are "developed" and examined under the microscope. Opiate receptors are localized to specific areas of the central nervous system, whose functions are susceptible to the influence of morphine. In the spinal cord, for instance, opiate receptors are confined to a dense band in the dorsal gray matter, the first way station in the integration of sensory information. Opiate receptors are also localized to the central gray matter of the midbrain, where electrical stimulation can produce analgesia. Parts of the limbic system, which regulates affective behavior, contain high levels of opiate receptors. Opiate receptors in the pretectal part of the brainstem, which regulates pupillary diameter, account for the pinpoint pupils.

Because opiates act at specific receptors by a "lock and key" mechanism, it is possible to design opiate antagonists which occupy opiate receptors, preventing access of opiates such as morphine but not themselves eliciting euphoria or analgesia. Opiate antagonists such as naloxone have proved to be life-saving in treating patients with opiate overdoses. Victims in deep coma can be revived almost immediately by the intravenous injection of a small dose of naloxone, which "pulses" heroin off its receptor sites and wakens the patient. Long-acting opiate antagonists offer promise in treating heroin addiction. The rationale is similar to that for using disulfiram in alcoholism. With a long-acting antagonist in the circulation, the addict would feel nothing when administering heroin; after a while, the compulsive craving for heroin would be extinguished. Antagonists have been employed in treating heroin addiction only experimentally so that one cannot yet judge their efficacy.

For many years, it seemed impossible to separate the analgesic effects of opiates from their addictive propensity. By exploiting the concept of opiate antagonists, however, analgesics with less addicting potential have recently become available. These drugs are *mixed agonist-antagonists* which combine the agonist properties of morphine with the antagonist actions of naloxone. Apparently their agonist activity elicits analgesia, while their antagonist actions block any tendencies of the drug to provoke addiction. Because of their lesser addictive potential, mixed agonist-antagonist opiates such as pentazocine (Talwin) are not subject to the stringent legal regulations that govern the use of other opiates.

Since the human body was not created with morphine as a component, it is reasonable to ask whether the opiate receptor might normally interact with some naturally occurring substance. As we have seen, it has been shown recently that the brain possesses a morphinelike substance, enkephalin, which is a peptide composed of five amino acids (Chapter 6). The amounts of enkephalin in different parts of the brain parallel variations in the distribution of the opiate receptor. When delivered directly into animal brains, enkephalin produces analgesia. It is likely that enkephalin is a neurotransmitter of neuronal pathways in the brain that regulate pain and emotion. New drugs based on the enkephalin chemical structure might prove valuable as analgesics or as mood regulators.

The opiate addict

So many different types of individuals become opiate addicts that attempting to delineate a psychological profile of the addict is probably futile. Some investigators have described a specific addictive personality that combines immaturity with a low tolerance for frustration and strong oral needs and often with sociopathic impulses (Hekimian and Gershon, 1968). But the personality characteristics of long-term addicts may not reflect their preaddictive characteristics. Also, vast numbers of easily frustrated "oral" personalities are exposed to opiate use, but only a small proportion ever become addicts. Conversely, almost 100 percent of men in certain combat units in Vietnam became heroin addicts soon after first exposure (Bourne, 1974).

Sociocultural factors probably constitute a major determinant of addiction. Until the 1960s heroin addiction was confined to black inner-city ghettos; only recently has it spread to white middle-class youth. Physicians and nurses, with more access than most people to these drugs, have the highest addiction rate of any social grouping, an incidence of about fifty to a hundred times that of the general population.

The initial exposure to heroin is usually through a friend or acquaintance who is seeking a comrade-in-drugs and often a potential customer. The first injection often produces nausea and displeasure, but with repeated administrations over a period of a week or a month, the incipient addict comes to enjoy the drug. The initial motivation for experimenting with heroin may be no stronger than a desire to participate in a forbidden activity with one's friends coupled with an urge to bring novelty and pleasure into an otherwise depressing life. Regardless of the first inducement, the drug user is soon obliged to continue opiate use simply to prevent withdrawal symptoms. From then on, economic factors play a major role in the addict's life. Securing money to support a habit, often $100 a day or more, may require thievery, prostitution, selling drugs, or recruiting new users.

Abstinence

Withdrawal symptoms vary with the amount of drug being used. Since the concentration of pure chemical in street drugs is often very low, many users are less strongly addicted than they believe. Many can be withdrawn from opiates "cold turkey" with no substitute medication.

The first signs of abstinence appear about four hours after the last heroin injection and are heralded by a vague feeling of anxiety and an enormous craving for the drug. By eight hours after the last dose, persistent yawning is evident as well as profuse perspiration, teary eyes, and a runny nose. At about twelve hours, the pupils become dilated and the victim's body hair almost literally "stands on end" with prominent goose flesh. This piloerection accounts for the label "cold turkey" applied to the abrupt withdrawal process. Muscle twitches of the calves and feet, which appear after twelve hours, are so characteristic that they have prompted the slang term "kicking the habit." Bones and muscles throughout the body ache constantly, and between eighteen and twenty-four hours, blood pressure, pulse, breathing rate, and body temperature begin to rise. The patient now begins to vomit and have profuse diarrhea. Men ejaculate spontaneously and women experience orgasms, though these are not at all pleasurable. After about thirty-six hours the symptoms subside.

Treatment

For many years the Public Health Service Hospital in Lexington, Kentucky, was the country's leading treatment facility for heroin addicts. Careful follow-up studies revealed that more than 90 percent of addicts returned to heroin use upon release from the hospital. This disappointing outcome prompted the pessimistic conclusion that "once an addict always an addict."

Whether or not opiate use produces a permanent need for the drug, this reasoning led to a promising method of treatment, the use of methadone. Drug-free residential community treatment programs and narcotic antagonists are the other approaches to treatment.

Methadone maintenance

Vincent Dole and Marie Nyswander initiated methadone maintenance programs on the premise that opiate addiction is a metabolic disease whose victims require a daily dose of opiates much as diabetics require insulin (Dole and Nyswander, 1965, 1967). They tried to replace addiction to heroin with addiction to methadone, a synthetic opiate. Pharmacologically, methadone is not very different from morphine or heroin. However, differences in the way it is absorbed from the intestines and metabolized in the body result in two characteristics which make it ideally suited for an opiate maintenance program. While heroin is essentially inactive when taken by mouth, methadone is just as effective orally as intravenously, so that the undesirable effects of "shooting up," such as hepatitis from infected needles, can be avoided. Methadone is three to six times as long-acting as heroin so that a single dose each day may be all the addict needs to prevent withdrawal symptoms. In the pioneering Dole-Nyswander program, addicts were treated each day with gradually escalating doses of methadone. Whereas 10 to 20 milligrams of the drug might have sufficed to replace the amount of heroin formerly used by the addict, doses of methadone were escalated to levels of 100 to 140 milligrams daily. At these very high doses, Dole hoped that all the sites where opiates act in the brain might be saturated with the drug so that the addict would feel nothing when he or she injected opiates and, therefore, would have no motivation to return to heroin.

Their success was striking. In Dole's own words, "The most dramatic effect of this treatment has been the disappearance of narcotic hunger. All of the patients previously had made efforts to remain drug-free after withdrawal, but were unable to resist the craving. Drug hunger became intolerable for most of them shortly after discharge from a withdrawal unit and return to their neighborhood. It became especially severe when they were exposed to emotional stress. With methadone maintenance, however, patients found that they could meet addict friends, and even watch them inject heroin without great difficulty. . . . They have stopped dreaming about drugs, and seldom talk about drugs when together'' (Dole and Nyswander, 1965).

A little emphasized but very important feature of the Dole-Nyswander program was the intense effort devoted to vocational and social rehabilitation. Every patient was placed in steady, meaningful employment with frequent monitoring of work performance. Patients' urine was screened routinely for the presence of heroin.

Because theirs was an experimental program, Dole and Nyswander treated only older, long-term heroin addicts who had failed in numerous other treatment programs. Despite "stacking the cards against themselves," they reported astonishing results, with 80 to 100 percent success and very few relapses in follow-up studies for several years.

Following this great success, the federal and state governments have financed many methadone programs throughout the United States. By the mid-1970s between 100,000 and 200,000 addicts, representing one-third to one-half of all the heroin addicts in the United States, were enrolled in these treatment programs. On this large scale, therapeutic results have been less impressive, though control of the addiction is still obtained in about 50 percent of cases. Administering methadone poses few problems. Difficulties arise instead in providing adequate emotional support and vocational rehabilitation for thousands of addicts. Diversion of the clinics' methadone supplies into illicit street traffic in several cities has converted heroin addicts into intravenous methadone addicts. Indeed, in New York City in 1975 the number of deaths from methadone overdose exceeded those associated with heroin. Some people seem to prefer the life of the drug community, stealing, and pushing to the less exciting enrollment in a drug clinic.

Narcotic antagonists

Many oppose the use of methadone on the grounds that the "cured" patient is still addicted to an opiate. Accordingly, researchers have used narcotic antagonists such as naltrexone to treat addiction. Patients are first maintained on methadone for a few months and then slowly withdrawn. Once drug-free, they receive long-acting opiate antagonists. While under the influence of the antagonist, the former addict should experience no euphoria regardless of how high a dose of heroin he or she self-administers.

This approach is still experimental. Some investigators think that the success of treatment with methadone depends on its opiate properties satisfying a profound need which cannot be met by antagonists. Advocates of antagonists argue that these agents may actually cure the compulsive craving for narcotics. When the drug user cheats and injects heroin, the absence of euphoria would tend to extinguish further craving.

Psychosocial treatment

The concept that a heroin addict can be rehabilitated without any drugs was put into practice in the United States in 1958 when an ex-alcoholic founded Synanon, a group with a philosophy like that of Alcoholics Anonymous. Based on the rationale that narcotic addicts suffer from an incurable disease, Synanon was designed as a residential center where former addicts would live together in close contact for the rest of their lives. Synanon communities are organized as communes in which ex-addicts work in various business enterprieses and share the proceeds. A crucial therapeutic tool is "the game," a psychologically violent group encounter that takes place several times each week. New members are attacked again and again for their failure to be honest with themselves, especially in their drug-seeking behavior. The communal living conditions and the game have attracted many nonaddicts into Synanon societies. The vigorous reorientation of life style prompts some addicts to become permanently drug-free. Success seems to depend in large part on wreching the addict away from former "drug" associates and a previously meaningless life. The increasingly bizarre behavior of Charles Diederich, the founder of Synanon, caused a corresponding deterioration in the functioning of Synanon in the late 1970s.

Numerous other residential drug-free treatment centers have been patterned after Synanon. Most of these are not as stringent in demanding that the addict devote his or her entire life to the group. Instead, these programs are looked upon as way stations for rehabilitation after which the ex-addict returns to the general community.

For addicts who stay in Synanon and other similar programs, the outcome is usually promising. But dropout rates are as high as 80 percent. Moreover, a residential facility is much more expensive than a methadone clinic. Partly because of cost effectiveness, methadone maintenance programs have become the major mode of rehabilitating heroin addicts.

Is addiction irreversible?

Even with modern therapies, opiate addicts are notoriously resistant to treatment. Methadone maintenance, currently the most effective approach, isn't a cure at all; the patient is still addicted to opiates. Therefore, numerous researchers have theorized that administration of opiates for a long enough period elicits permanent changes in the body. According to this view, an addict has a marked propensity to succumb to opiate addiction if ever exposed to drugs, even many years after terminating the use of heroin. This idea is reminiscent of traditional Alcoholics Anonymous philosophy. Direct evidence favoring such a hypothesis has been obtained in behavioral studies with rats (Cochin and Kornetsky, 1964). Cochin and Kornetsky found evidence for an extraordinarily long-lasting influence of opiates. One year after morphine administration, a long interval in a rat's life, the animals were still tolerant to morphine. Critics argued that the rats were not pharmacologically tolerant to the drug for an entire year. Instead, they had learned a behavioral repertoire associated with morphine administration and were able to remember this state-dependent learning a year later.

Methadone maintenance was developed according to the rationale that addicts require opiates the way most people need vitamins. As Dole emphasizes, "rather than assuming with the older clinicians that the pharmacologic drive for narcotics is terminated by detoxification, and therefore that the relapse is a psychogenic or a purely conditioned phenomenon, Marie Nyswander and I think it more likely that the psychologic factors are only triggers for relapse, the underlying cause of which is a persistent neurochemical disturbance. In this sense addiction is a metabolic, rather than a psychologic disease" (Dole, 1972). One could speculate that an abnormality, perhaps a deficiency, of enkephalins in the brain causes the future addict to suffer chronic emotional pain which is best relieved with heroin. Dole has advocated that some addicts should be maintained on methadone for the rest of their lives.

The very success of the methadone program lends some weight to this argument. However, there is already evidence that many addicts can be withdrawn gradually from methadone after a few years and will remain in a drug-free state. The experience with American soldiers who became addicted to heroin in Vietnam is also illuminating. These individuals were not maintained on methadone at all. Instead, they were gradually withdrawn from heroin, discharged from the army, and returned to the United States. When reevaluated a year later, only 7 percent of them had returned to heroin use. Thus, in this case, opiate addiction certainly did not produce a permanent craving for the drug (Robins, 1974).

References

Bourne, P. G. *Addiction*. Academic Press, New York, 1974.
Cochin, J., and Kornetsky, C. Development and loss of tolerance to morphine in the

rate after single and multiple injections. *J. Pharmacol. and Exp. Ther.*, *145:*1–10, 1964.

Dole, V. P. Narcotic addiction, physical dependence and relapse. *N.Eng. J. Med.*, *286:*988–992, 1972.

Dole, V. P., and Nyswander, M. A medical treatment for diacetylmorphine (heroin) addiction. *J. Am. Med. Assoc.*, *193:*646–650, 1965.

Dole V. P., and Nyswander, M. Heroin addiction, a metabolic disease. *Arch. Int. Med.*, *120:*19–24, 1967.

Hekimian, L. J., and Gershon, S. Characteristics of drug abusers admitted to a psychiatric hospital. *J. Am. Med. Assoc.*, *205:*125–130, 1968.

Hughes, J., Smith, T. W., Kosterlitz, H. W., Fothergill, L. A., Morgan, B. A., and Morris H. R. Identification of two related pentapeptides from the brain with potent opiate agonist activity. *Nature*, *258:*577–579, 1975.

Musto, D. F. *The american disease*. Yale University Press, New Haven, 1974.

Ray, O. S. *Drug society and human behavior*. C. B. Mosby Co., St. Louis, 1972, p. 180.

Robins, L. *The Vietnam drug user returns*. McGraw-Hill, New York, 1974.

Snyder, S. H. The opiate receptor in normal and drug altered brain function. *Nature*, *257:*185–189, 1975.

9. Psychedelic drugs

The psychedelic drugs have widely varying chemical structures but all share the ability to elicit a similar constellation of profound subjective experiences. The drugs are also known as *hallucinogenic* or *psychotomimetic* compounds. They rarely produce frank hallucinations—namely, seeing or hearing something which is not present in the environment. Instead, they bring about distortions of what is perceived visually. *Psychotomimetic* is not an altogether appropriate term either, because drugs of many different classes can precipitate psychoses. The term *psychedelic* derives from Greek words meaning "mind manifesting" and was introduced by Humphrey Osmond to denote the drug-induced changes in consciousness which give a subjective sense of mind expansion: "I have tried to find an appropriate name for the agents under discussion: a name that will include the concepts of enriching the mind and enlarging the vision . . . my choice, because it is clear, euphonious, and uncontaminated by other associations, is psychedelic, mind manifesting" (Osmond, 1957).

The psychedelic experience

Because the effects of psychedelic drugs are greatly dependent upon the psychological makeup of the drug taker, his or her mood, and the setting, the variety of psychedelic experiences is enormous. Some people experience nothing even at high doses, while many others describe overwhelming sensations. Nonetheless, there are certain typical experiences, particularly changes in perception and the sense of self.

With moderate doses of LSD ingested orally, about 100 to 200 micrograms, few effects are discernible for thirty to sixty minutes. There may be slight nausea, though not enough to cause vomiting. The first changes are sensory. Objects in the visual field may take on a purplish tinge. Everything perceived is enhanced. Perception seems to be so incisive that users feel they can discern individual pores in the skin. Contours of objects become distorted in accordance with viewers' feelings so that, by focusing upon an object, they may see it proceed to swell and undulate. The sense of time changes dramatically so that a minute may seem like an hour. The few hours under the influence of the drug may feel like a lifetime. This change in time perception results from an internal "speeding up" of mental processes. With the intensive recording of every instant, more events seem to transpire per unit of time, conveying the impression that time has slowed down. Distances expand as well, so that walking across the room may feel like an interminable journey.

All of these sensory changes contribute to the phenomenon of *synesthesia,* a seeming transmutation of the sense in which a stimulus is perceived. The subject may *see* sounds or *hear* colors. Upon exposure to a loud noise, for example, some subjects have reported seeing the sound waves undulating before them.

After spending a day under the influence of mescaline, Aldous Huxley described his experience in *The Doors of Perception:* "I was not now looking at an unusual flower arrangement. I was seeing what Adam had seen on the morning of his creation—the miracle, moment by moment, of naked existence. . . . The legs, for example, of that chair—how miraculous their tubularity, how supernatural their polished smoothness! I spent several minutes—or was it several centuries—not merely gazing at those bamboo legs, but actually *being* them" (Huxley, 1954).

Emotional changes usually commence shortly after the sensory alterations, though this order is not constant and some drug experiences can be either sensory-oriented or feeling-oriented. One drug effect is the emergence into conscious awareness of presumably forgotten or repressed thoughts and feelings. More dramatic are changes in the sense of self, notably the feeling that one is merging with the totality of the universe, that all is one. This transcendental state resembles the experiences of mystics, and it is the aim of many psychedelic drug users, with its profound sense of serenity and contemplation.

Unfortunately, these same mental changes, essentially a loss of self-identity, a dissolving of ego boundaries, may be responsible for panic states which are the most adverse effects of the drugs. Problems arise particularly with individuals whose sense of self is already tenuous and with obsessive, rigid people who demand that their environment be predictable and well ordered. The drug-elicited loss of self-identity can cause overwhelming terror. In such states, drug users have leaped to their death from windows, set themselves aflame, or killed others.

Researchers have attempted to analyze the nature of the psychedelic experience, but this has proven to be a difficult task. There seems to be a change in filtering mechanisms so that normally screened-out features of the external environment and repressed internal feelings now penetrate to awareness. The profound impact of these new perceptions may derive from the alerting, stimulant actions of the drugs. Psychedelic drug users are intensely alert and can usually recall every aspect of their drug experience. This feature differs somewhat from the effects of marijuana, which also enhances sensory perception but at the same time is sedating.

Psychedelic drugs are psychotomimetic only insofar as the changes in perception and self-identity are so great that the individual appears to have "lost contact" with reality. Unlike other drugs which can be psychotomimetic at certain doses, such as atropine, bromides, and alcohol, psychedelic drugs do not produce organic changes such as disorientation. Even with high doses, users generally are able to speak coherently and are well oriented to time, place, and person.

Varieties of psychedelic drugs

Though LSD is the best known of the psychedelic drugs, a large number of chemical compounds can produce very similar effects. Two traditional ones are mescaline, the active ingredient of the peyote plant, and psilocybin, derived from the mushroom *Psilocybe Mexicana*. Dimethyltryptamine (DMT) is a synthetic compound closely related in structure to psilocybin. DOM, also known as STP, is a synthetic psychedelic drug related chemically both to mescaline and the amphetamine derivative MDA (3,4-Methylenedioxy-amphetamine).

Nuances of the drug experience vary among different psychedelic drugs. The effects of a moderate dose of LSD last about eight hours. Mescaline is somewhat longer acting, its effects persisting for about twelve hours. The quality of the drug experience is somewhat different with mescaline than with LSD. There is a predominance of sensory effects that are generally pleasant and fascinating to the user, and less drug-induced introspection. DOM is metabolized more slowly in the body than LSD or mescaline, and its effects may last for twenty-four to forty-eight hours. Correspondingly, it has a greater tendency to elicit "bad trips." By contrast, DMT is the shortest-acting psychedelic drug.

Because it is destroyed in the gastrointestinal tract, DMT is usually injected or "snorted." Since its effects last only forty-five to sixty minutes, DMT is advocated as "the businessman's luncheon psychedelic."

Model psychosis

One of the first questions addressed in research on psychedelic drugs was whether they may provide a drug model of schizophrenia. Investigators reasoned that if LSD or mescaline induce symptoms which meaningfully resemble those of schizophrenia, then elucidating the biochemical actions of the drugs might lead to an understanding of brain malfunctions in schizophrenia. Another rationale holds that if a drug can produce psychotic symptoms resembling schizophrenia, perhaps there is a "schizophrenogenic toxin" in the blood or brain of schizophrenics chemically related to the drug. Over a hundred years ago, the French psychiatrist Jacques-Joseph Moreau proposed that the psychotomimetic effects of hashish, then fashionable among Parisian writers, might provide a valuable tool for elucidating the mechanisms of mental illness (Moreau, 1973). In this century, Stockings (1940) proposed that mescaline psychosis mimics aspects of schizophrenia.

The largest body of model psychosis research was initiated with the discovery of the potent actions of LSD. After initial enthusiasm about how the absence of confusion and disorientation in psychoses induced by psychedelic drugs resembles functional psychoses such as schizophrenia, researchers became more skeptical. They noted that psychedelic drugs don't typically elicit hallucinations, only perceptual distortions. Moreover, while schizophrenic hallucinations are auditory, visual changes predominate with psychedelic drugs. Even when schizophrenics do experience visual hallucinations, these differ in important ways from those induced by psychedelic drugs. In schizophrenia, for instance, visual hallucinations appear suddenly and without warning, while those of mescaline and LSD are preceded by unformed visual sensations and alterations of color, size, and shape. Moreover, whereas schizophrenic hallucinations are superimposed on a normal visual environment, psychedelic drugs produce diffuse distortions of the existing visual world. Schizophrenic hallucinations are apparent with eyes open, while those of psychedelic drugs are more readily seen with eyes closed (Feinberg, 1962).

Hollister (1962) showed that tape-recorded interviews with schizophrenics and with normal subjects under the influence of psychedelic drugs, edited to eliminate identifying clues, could be readily distinguished on the grounds that "In the schizophrenics the primary disturbance was in thinking, while the drug subjects' disturbance was in perceptions."

If LSD mimics schizophrenic symptoms, it would be expected to worsen those of schizophrenic patients. When administered to schizophrenics, however, the drug fails to accentuate their symptoms. Instead, it produces the typical spectrum of psychedelic actions which are distinguished by both the patients and the investigators from the underlying schizophrenic illness.

Though the psychedelic drug experience differs in many ways from the symptoms of advanced schizophrenics, there may be similarities between the early acute phases of schizophrenic breakdown and drug effects. Bowers and Freedman (1966) emphasized how the uncanny sensation of extraordinary clarity, of seeing into the essence of objects, which is characteristic of psychedelic drug effects, is also evident in the mental life of incipient schizophrenics. Direct quotations from schizophrenics early in the course of their disease or after an acute episode illustrate this state: "My senses were sharpened, sounds were more intense and I could see with greater clarity. Everything seemed very clear to me . . . my sense of taste seemed more acute" (Bowers and Freedman, 1966). "What I do want to explain, if I can, is the exaggerated state of awareness in which I lived before, during, and after my acute illness. At first it was as if parts of my brain 'awoke' which had been dormant, and I became interested in a wide assortment of people, events, places and ideas which normally would make no impression on me" (McDonald, 1960).

How psychedelic drugs act in the brain

Though it is difficult to specify exactly how any drug produces its behavioral effects, researchers have been more successful in elucidating actions of the psychedelic drugs than with most other psychotropic agents. In minute doses, LSD and other psychedelic drugs selectively inhibit the firing of the serotonin-containing neurons of the brain (Aghajanian, et al., 1973). These cells lie in the raphe nuclei a small area in the brain stem (see Chapter 6). Their axons ascend and branch extensively, sending terminals to impinge upon neurons throughout the brain, but with greatest densities in the limbic system, which appears to be the key area of the brain for regulating emotion. Stimulation of the raphe cells at normal physiological frequencies produces somnolence, while lesions of the raphe cells bring about a state of hyperalertness resembling the behavioral effects of LSD in animals.

The ability of psychedelic drugs to stop raphe cells from firing is highly selective. No drugs other than psychedelics influence raphe cell firing in this way. Moreover, raphe cells are the only neurons affected; cells only a fraction of a millimeter from the raphe nuclei do not respond to LSD.

Serotonin neurons are thought to be part of the filtering system of the brain.

They fire in response to sensory stimulation and exert an inhibitory effect on other neurons throughout the brain. Presumably the blockade of their firing by psychedelic drugs accounts for the drug-induced mental and emotional "flooding" of perceptual input.

Adverse effects

One cannot become addicted to psychedelic drugs. They do induce a mild degree of tolerance, but this is short lived. Thus, if one takes a fixed dose of LSD on four consecutive days, it will produce fewer effects on the fourth than on the first day. After drug use stops for two or three days, however, an individual's sensitivity will return to baseline levels.

Numerous physical dangers of LSD use have been reported, including chromosome breakage and brain atrophy. These have not been substantiated in careful investigations.

The major harmful consequences of LSD ingestion are panic reactions or "bad trips." Some individuals have literally cut out their eyes while under the influence of the drug. Others have committed murder, and some have jumped to their deaths from high places. While there is evidence that panic reactions occur most frequently in those with underlying emotional disturbances, perfectly normal individuals may also have bad trips (Ungerleider and Fisher, 1967). Moreover, a given individual can have many consecutive pleasant drug experiences and then, for no apparent reason, suffer a severe panic reaction.

Flashbacks are recurrences of the psychedelic experience after a drug-free period. Flashbacks may occur a day, or a week, or many months after use of the drug. They are notoriously unpredictable, though some evidence suggests that they occur most frequently before an individual falls asleep, while driving, or during psychological stress (Shick and Smith, 1970). Some drug users have reported multiple flashbacks after taking a psychedelic drug only once. Flashbacks become less severe with the passage of time and gradually vanish. Though it has been speculated that they may be brought about by traces of the drug remaining in the body, studies of blood levels indicate that LSD almost certainly has completely disappeared from the body by the time the flashback takes place.

Almost all the tranquilizers have been tried in the treatment of panic reactions and flashbacks. The present consensus is that drugs should be used sparingly in treating these reactions. Calm reassurance generally suffices to carry the patient through the worst of the crisis, which usually last less than a day.

References

Aghajanian, G. K., Foote, W. E., and Sheard, M. H. Lysergic acid diethylamide: sensitive units in the midbrain raphe. *Science, 161:*706–708, 1973.

Bowers, M. G., Jr., and Freedman, D. X. Psychedelic experiences in acute psychosis. *Arch. Gen. Psychiat. 15:*240–248, 1966.

Feinberg, I. A comparison of the visual hallucinations in schizophrenia with those induced by mescaline and LSD-25. In *Hallucinations,* ed. L. J. West. Grune and Stratton, New York, 1962, pp. 64–76.

Hollister, L. E. Drug induced psychosis and schizophrenic reactions: A critical comparison. *Ann. N.Y. Acad. Sci., 96:*80–88, 1962.

Huxley, A. *The doors of perception.* Perennial Library, Harper & Row, New York, 1954, pp. 17, 22.

McDonald, N. Living with schizophrenia. *Canad. Med. Assoc. J. 82:*218–221, 678–681, 1960.

Moreau, J. J. *Hashish and mental illness.* Trans. by G. J. Barnett, Raven Press, New York, 1973.

Osmond, H. A review of the clinical effects of psychotomimetic agents. *Ann. N. Y. Acad. Sci.,* March 14, 1957.

Shick, J. F. E., and Smith, D. E. Analysis of the LSD flashback. *J. Psychedel. Drugs, 3:*13–19, 1970.

Smith, D. E. LSD, its use, abuse and suggested treatment. *J. Psychedel. Drugs, 1:*120, 1967.

Stockings, G. T. Clinical study of the mescaline psychosis with special reference to the mechanisms of the genesis of schizophrenia and other psychotic states. *J. Ment. Sci., 86:*29–47, 1940.

Ungerleider, J. T., and Fisher, D. D. The problems of LSD-25, and emotional disorder. *Calif. Med., 106:*49:–55, 1967.

10. Stimulants

Cocaine and the group of drugs collectively referred to as the amphetamines are the major abusable stimulants. They have a long and colorful history of both medical and recreational use.

Coca leaves, whose active ingredient is cocaine, have been chewed by South American Indians since before recorded history of that continent and were used widely by the Incas. The coca plant, according to Inca traditions, was a gift of the Sun God to their people. Originally the drug was reserved for Inca nobility, but after the Spanish conquest, its use spread through Indian society and had a special purpose in helping Indian workers endure the hardships of the Spanish mines. A history of this period contains an early allusion to the drug's withdrawal symptoms: "This herb is so nutritious and envigorating that the Indians labor whole days without anything else, and on the want of it, they find a decay in their strength (Pinkerton, quoted in Angrist and Sudilovsky, 1977).

Cocaine was isolated from coca leaves in 1865 by a German chemist, A. Niemann. However, major credit for bringing its stimulant properties to public attention belongs to Sigmund Freud, who conducted one of the first investigations of the drug's subjective effects. His enthusiastic papers alerted the European and American medical profession to the drug and probably delayed recognition of its abuse potential. Freud wrote, "Cocaine brings about an exhilaration and a euphoria which in no way differs from the normal euphoria of the healthy person. . . . You perceive an increase of self-control and possess more vitality and capacity for work. . . . In other words, you are simply normal and it is soon hard to believe that you are under the influence of any drug. . . . Long intensive mental or physical work is performed without any fatigue. . . . This result is enjoyed without any of the unpleasant after effects that follow exhilaration brought about by alcohol'' (Freud, 1885, 1970).

A few months after Freud's initial publication, his colleague Koller discovered that cocaine elicits local anesthesia when applied to the eyes of animals and human beings, a discovery which revolutionized all branches of surgery and virtually created ophthalmologic surgery. This genuinely important discovery helped to spread enthusiasm for cocaine, which soon became a favorite among the wealthy and numbered among its prominent users Thomas Edison, Pope Leo XIII, Queen Victoria, and Sarah Bernhardt. With extensive use the addicting properties of the drug soon became evident, and before long it was being called a "scourge of humanity." Medical uses of cocaine, except as a local anesthetic, quickly faded away.

Amphetamine is a generic term for a group of central nervous system stimulants that share a similar chemical structure. It also refers to a specific drug, the parent of the class. The amphetamine molecule was synthesized as an analogue of adrenaline to treat asthma. Its only other medical use has been in the treatment of narcolepsy, a condition in which patients spontaneously fall asleep during the day, even while vigorously active. College students deserve credit for noting its stimulant properties, as recorded in a 1937 editorial of the Journal of the American Medical Association: "Tablets (amphetamine) were used in the Department of Psychology at the University of Minnesota for the purpose of determining its effects in mental efficiency tests. It was noted that the drug prevented sleepiness and pepped up the person who was fatigued. Apparently, this information was disseminated to the student body by word of mouth and the drug has been and still is being obtained by the students from drug stores for the purpose of avoiding sleep and fatigue when preparing for examinations.''

During World War II amphetamines were used widely by troops of Japan, Germany, the United States, and Great Britain to prevent fatigue. In Japan after World War II ended, massive war stocks of amphetamines were dumped on the open market, where they were available without prescription. They were advertised to the demoralized population as providing "elimination of drowsiness and replenishing of the spirit." By 1954, at the peak of the epidemic that followed, about 1 percent of the Japanese population had become amphetamine addicts (Brill and Hirose, 1969). In Sweden amphetamine was strictly regulated as a dangerous drug, but other amphetaminelike drugs such as the dieting agent phenmetrazine (Preludin) were free of such control. Another epidemic occurred, and during this wave of phenmetrazine abuse in Sweden in the early 1960s, amphetaminelike agents were first used extensively by the intravenous route. In the United States the hippie movement, which first focused on psyche-delic drugs such as LSD, gradually turned toward amphetamines, "speed," in-jected intravenously.

Effects

In general, cocaine and the amphetamines produce similar effects. Cocaine may elicit more euphoria, but this could be more a function of dose and mode of ad-ministration than of anything intrinsic to the drug. Various amphetamine ana-logues have been synthesized with a view to facilitating one or another type of action, but the differences among these drugs tend to be nuances. Meth-amphetamine (Methedrine), favored by the drug culture, was publicized as more of a euphoriant than amphetamine itself. There were more likely reasons for its initial popularity, however: It was the only amphetamine available in dosage form for intravenous injection, and it was readily snythesized in un-derground laboratories. Phenmetrazine and diethylpropion (Tenuate) were in-troduced as weight-reducing pills, presumably with less of a central stimulant action. But the many cases of addiction to these drugs indicate that they do possess substantial stimulant properties. Methylphenidate (Ritalin), a stimulant with less appetite-suppressant effects than other amphetamines, has been used widely in treating hyperactive children, whose growth might be retarded by an appetite suppressant.

In low doses, cocaine and amphetamines behave just as Sigmund Freud re-ported, giving rise to feelings of energetic vitality, assertiveness, and alertness. Along with the absence of fatigue, there is a decrease of appetite. Many indi-viduals also feel tense, irritable, and, as the drug effects wear off, tired and somewhat depressed. At higher doses the alertness merges into a´ "driven" feeling, and thoughts move so rapidly that the individual has difficulty concen-trating and talks constantly, often irrelevantly.

Stimulants definitely enhance the performance of athletes, and not solely by preventing fatigue. In controlled, double-blind studies, highly trained college swimmers, runners, and weight throwers were tested both when rested and when fatigued taking either d-amphetamine or placebos. Improvement of per-formance ranged from 1 to 4 percent. Though this may seem small, it was sta-tistically significant for all types of athletic activity. Moreover, in competitive athletics, variations of this magnitude can spell the difference between a world record and trailing far behind the winner. That the drug influences motor coor-dination and strength rather than merely preventing fatigue is indicated by the fact that the greatest improvement occurred in shot-putting, a brief physical ac-tivity which is not likely to be strongly influenced by fatigue. Moreover, the ef-fects of amphetamine were more apparent in rested than in fatigued subjects

(Smith and Beecher, 1959). Not surprisingly, amphetamines are frequently used by professional and nonprofessional athletes despite vigorous efforts by regulatory bodies to prevent it.

Addiction

Individuals become addicted to stimulants because of their effects at high doses. The rush that follows a large intravenous dose is often described as a "full-body orgasm." The Swedish investigator Rylander (1969) wrote of an addict who reported that "at first he feels numbed and if he is standing he goes down on his knees. His heart starts beating at a terrible speed and his respiration is very rapid. And he feels as if he was ascending into the cosmos, every fiber of his body trembling with happiness." The desire for a more intense rush prompts users to inject progressively larger doses.

Sexuality is changed in amphetamine users. There is usually an increase in sexual pressure. Male amphetamine users often report delayed ejaculation accompanying an increase in libido, which leads to marathon sexual activities. Female users describe heightened sexuality with amphetamines more frequently than do males and may seek release in multiple sex partners and compulsive masturbation (Connell, 1958).

Along with their hyperalertness, amphetamine users become highly suspicious, and this may lead to violent behavior. Several murders have been reported by individuals under the influence of amphetamines. The suspicious, paranoid behavior of amphetamine addicts can lead to *amphetamine psychosis,* an acute paranoid disorder.

Amphetamine abusers often engage in stereotyped, compulsive behavior. The user "may sit in a tub and bathe all day long, clean up the home or a particular item, hold a note or phrase of music, or engage in nonejaculatory intercourse for extended periods" (Scher, 1966). This stereotyped behavior can be demonstrated in several animal species. In rats it is characterized by sniffing, licking, and gnawing, while cats show head and eye turning or sniffing. Monkeys and chimpanzees engage in repetitive manipulations of objects in their hands, resembling human amphetamine addicts who will sit for hours on end sorting small objects, endlessly dismantling clocks or radios, or doodling. In chronic users, the stereotyped behavior appears about the time that amphetamine psychosis develops.

Amphetamine psychosis: a model schizophrenia?

At one time or another almost every intravenous amphetamine addict experiences a drug-induced psychosis, an occupational hazard of "speed freaks."

The psychosis resembles acute paranoid schizophrenia closely enough that many amphetamine addicts have been admitted to a hospital with a diagnosis of schizophrenia before the drug history was obtained. A typical pattern of amphetamine psychosis is illustrated by the following case history (Angrist and Sudilovsky, 1978):

> This 18-year old male had been in a reformatory because of refractory truancy in the past and arrested for possession of marijuana and petty larceny. . . . He had sniffed glue and Carbona from ages 12 to 13, drank heavily from ages 13 to 15, and had used amphetamine orally and intravenously from age 16 onward. He had used heroin for three or four months between ages 17 and 18. He left high school in the eleventh grade. . . . In the two weeks prior to admission he stayed at his brother's and sister-in-law's apartment and had taken three to seven injections per day of a powder of unknown purity that he was told was methamphetamine. During this time he [thought] he heard his brother tell his sister-in-law that he had killed his mother and planned to kill him [the patient] as well. . . . In the hospital he was frightened, apprehensive, and felt that the staff and other patients were implying that ''he knew something'' that he refused to tell. . . . He became tearful, fearing that this was the place where patients were sent to be punished and perhaps even killed. His affect was blunt, constricted and, at times, incongruent. He showed a formal thought disorder. . . . When asked what ''a stitch in time save nine'' meant, he replied, ''Hurry up with that date and don't be late . . . make that first stitch right and the rest will follow''. . . . He responded to the proverb ''People who live in glass houses shouldn't throw stones'' thus: ''If you throw stones you risk your life. Living in a glass house would shatter your whole being.

Some investigators do not regularly observe such close parallels with schizophrenia in the disorders of thought and affect of amphetamine psychosis, and therefore they question whether amphetamine psychosis is a satisfactory drug model of schizophrenia. Others ask whether the drug merely precipitates latent schizophrenia. Since amphetamine addicts often go for days on end without sleeping, it has been suggested that the disorder is really a sleep deprivation psychosis. To resolve these questions, Griffith et al. (1970) attempted to demonstrate amphetamine psychosis experimentally in volunteers who were carefully screened by psychiatric interview and psychological testing to rule out schizophrenia or schizoid tendencies. The subjects received 5 to 10 milligrams of d-amphetamine by mouth every hour. They all developed a typical amphetamine-induced paranoid psychosis after ingesting between 100 and 800 milligrams, from one to four days after beginning to take the drug.

The ability to elicit the psychosis in subjects with no evidence of schizoid tendencies indicates that the condition is indeed drug-induced and not merely a precipitation of a latent psychosis. Moreover, the fact that some subjects became psychotic within twenty-four hours indicates that the condition is not due simply to sleep deprivation.

All the psychological effects of amphetamine, including euphoria, alertness, appetite suppression, and psychosis, are also elicited by cocaine.

Tolerance and dependence

Chronic users of stimulants develop pronounced tolerance. Whereas a normal dose of d-amphetamine is 10 milligrams, some addicts will take up to 2,000 milligrams. Addicts typically go on "runs" during which they remain awake for three or four days, injecting amphetamines every few hours. At a certain point they stop taking the drug and "crash." In this postamphetamine letdown, addicts are greatly fatigued and severely depressed. They typically enter a deep sleep which can last twenty-four to seventy-two hours. When they awake, they are ravenous and eat large quantities of food, as if to make up for the several days during which they ate little, if anything.

Formerly, some authorities in the area of drug dependence did not think that stimulants induced physical dependence because they could not detect a characteristic abstinence syndrome when the drug was discontinued. This was before the widespread use of amphetamines in large doses by intravenous injection. The profound postamphetamine state of depression appears to qualify as a withdrawal syndrome, so that "speed freaks" can be regarded as truly addicted.

Mechanism of action

Amphetamines and cocaine are thought to act by way of the catecholamine neurotransmitters in the brain, norepinephrine and dopamine (see Chapter 6). Chemically, amphetamine closely resembles norepinephrine and dopamine. An abundance of pharmacological evidence indicates that amphetamines displace the catecholamines from their storage sites in nerve terminals, thus releasing these neurotransmitters so that more of the molecules connect with receptor sites.

Cocaine also potentiates the actions of catecholamines, though its exact mechanism of action may not be identical to that of the amphetamines.

Medical uses

Dieting

The *anorectic* stimulants definitely decrease appetite and have been demonstrated in many studies to produce weight loss in obese patients. However, tolerance to the anorectic effects develops quite rapidly. The drugs facilitate weight loss over a four- to six-week period, but after two months or more they are no more effective than placebos.

Narcolepsy

This is a fairly rare, often incapacitating condition whose victims suffer from sudden and irresistible attacks of sleep. Patients will often fall asleep while standing, walking, or talking. When stimulated emotionally, they sometimes fall down suddenly, a phenomenon called *cataplexy*. Cataplexy involves a loss of tone in the muscles of the arms and legs, which relax during cataplectic attacks in the same way that these muscles relax during dreaming. Indeed, narcoleptic attacks appear to represent an intrusion into the waking state of a form of sleep, characterized by rapid eye movements and dreaming. When narcoleptics awake from their attacks, they invariably describe dreams.

Amphetamines are the only drugs known to be effective in treating narcolepsy. Patients often require large doses. Though some tolerance develops, it is usually possible to control the narcoleptic attacks with high but stable doses of the drugs.

Minimal brain dysfunction (MBD)

The condition of hyperactivity in children, also referred to as *hyperkinesis* or *minimal brain dysfunction (MBD)*, appears to be a valid category of psychopathology but one which is difficult to diagnose rigorously. Most normal children often seem hyperactive. Children with classic symptoms of MBD usually display normal intelligence but just can't sit still in class or at home. They appear to have difficulty focusing their attention on tasks at hand. Perhaps by enabling them to concentrate, amphetamines have a "paradoxical" calming effect on these children. MBD patients can tolerate large doses of d-amphetamine, up to 40 milligrams, which would be enough to cause marked agitation in an adult weighing twice as much.

Much controversy has arisen over the practice of administering amphetamines to misbehaving children who may or may not suffer from MBD. Because the symptoms of MBD are vague, it is difficult to be sure about the diagnosis. When a child displays marked symptoms of hyperactivity, a brief trial of amphetamine may be warranted and, if there is a rapid therapeutic response, the drug may be continued on the assumption that the child has MBD. If the child responds poorly, then the drug is discontinued and the diagnosis is presumed to be incorrect.

References

Angrist, B. M., and Sudilovsky, A. Central nervous stimulants. Historical aspects and clinical effects. In *Handbook of psychopharmacology,* vol. 11, eds. L. L. Iversen, S. Iversen, and S. H. Snyder. Plenum Press, New York, 1978, pp. 99–166.

Brill, H., and Hirose, T. The rise and fall of a methamphetamine epidemic. Japan, 1945–55. *Seminars in Psychiatry, 1:*179–192, 1969.

Connell, P. *Amphetamine psychosis.* Oxford University Press, London, 1958.

Editorial. Benedrine sukphate "pep pills." *J. Am. Med. Assoc., 108:*1973–1974, 1937.

Freud, S. On the general effects of cocaine medicinischirurgisches. *Central-Blatt, 20:*374–375, August 1885. Reprinted in *Drug Dependence, 5:*15, 1970.

Griffith, J., Cavanaugh, J. H., and Oates, J. Psychosis induced by the administration of d-amphetamine to human volunteers. In *Psychotomimetic Drugs,* ed. D. Efron. Raven Press, New York, 1970, pp. 287–294.

Pinkerton, quoted in Angrist, B. M., and Sudilovsky, A. Central nervous stimulants. Historical aspects and clinical effects. In *Handbook of psychopharmacology,* vol. 11, eds. L. L. Iversen, S. Iversen, and S. H. Snyder. Plenum Press, New York, 1978, pp. 99–166.

Rylander, G. Clinical and medico-criminalogic aspects of addiction to centrally stimulating drugs. In *Abuse of central stimulants,* eds. F. Sjoqvist and M. Tottie. Almqvist and Wiksel, Stockholm, 1969, pp. 251–273.

Scher, J. Patterns and profiles of addiction and drug abuse. *Arch. Gen. Psychiat., 15:*539–551, 1966.

Smith, G. M., and Beecher, H. K. Amphetamine sulfate and athletic performance. *J. Am. Med. Assoc., 170:*542–557, 1959.

Snyder, S. H. *Madness and the brain.* McGraw-Hill, New York, 1974.

11. Sedatives, hypnotics, and antianxiety drugs

Sedatives, anxiety-relieving agents, and sleeping pills are the most commonly used drugs in medical practice. Though they form a diverse group of drugs, most produce similar effects and probably share common sites of action in the brain. What might seem to be minor differences in the lag time before onset of action and the duration of effects, however, have major implications for clinical usefulness, susceptibility to abuse, and lethality. From early times, physicians have used a variety of sedating agents, including opium, cannabis, and barbiturates, to calm patients who have experienced severe physical or emotional trauma.

Only recently has the concept of specific "antianxiety agents" become popular. An *antianxiety drug* is supposed to relieve anxiety selectively at doses that do not produce drowsiness, relieving anxiety by different mechanisms than those which mediate sedative effects. Whether drugs prescribed as antianxiety agents indeed differ in a fundamental way from other sedatives is hotly debated.

The same drugs that are sedatives become *hypnotics* in higher doses, which means that they induce a state resembling normal sleep. An individual can be aroused from this state by sufficient stimulation. In still higher doses many of these drugs induce anesthesia, a profound sleep from which the patient cannot be roused until the blood level of the drug falls substantially. Some barbiturates are used in small doses as sedatives, in larger amounts as sleeping pills, and in high enough intravenous doses as surgical anesthetics.

Table 11-1 Sedative-hypnotics and antianxiety drugs

Barbiturates		
Thiopental	(Pentothal®)	Ultra-short-acting, used to induce general anesthesia
Secobarbital	(Seconal®)	Short- to intermediate-acting sedative-hypnotics
Amobarbital	(Amytal®)	
Phenobarbital	(Luminol®)	Long-acting sedative and anticonvulsant
Nonbarbiturates		
Meprobamate	(Miltown®)	Used to treat anxiety, though less effective and more dan-
	(Equanil®)	gerous than benzodiazepines
Methyprylon	(Noludar®)	Sleeping medication
Glutethimide	(Doriden®)	Sleeping medication
Thalidomide		Sleeping medication
Chloral hydrate	(Noctec®)	Sleeping medication
Paraldehyde		Sleeping medication
Methaqualone	(Quaalude®)	Sleeping medication
Benzodiazepines		
Diazepam	(Valium®)	Antianxiety, muscle relaxant, and anticonvulsant
Chlordiazepoxide	(Librium®)	Antianxiety
Oxazepam	(Serax®)	Antianxiety
Chlorazepate	(Tranxene®)	Antianxiety
Flurazepam	(Dalmane®)	Sleeping medication

Drug types

Bromides, a group of chemical substances whose active ingredient is the bromide ion, were used in the nineteenth century as sedatives and as antiepileptic drugs. It appears that they were almost as popular then as Valium and Librium are today. But bromides tend to accumulate in the body, and besides producing chronic intoxication, they can cause permanent neurological damage. Nonetheless, minute amounts of bromides are still employed in over-the-counter preparations such as Bromo-Seltzer.

Chloral hydrate and *paraldehyde* are sedatives that differ in structure from bromides and barbiturates but produce similar effects. They have been in use since the early twentieth century and are probably safer than barbiturates largely because their objectionable odor and the vile taste of paraldehyde are deterrents to suicidal overdosing.

Barbiturates began to be used widely as sedatives early in the twentieth century. Barbituric acid, the chemical precursor of the barbiturates, was synthesized in 1862 by the German chemist A. Bayer, whose company later introduced aspirin and heroin. Though instances of barbiturate addiction were noted as early as 1905, physicians were not convinced of the drugs' addictive properties until classic and severe withdrawal symptoms were demonstrated experimentally at the Narcotics Hospital in Lexington beginning in the 1950s

(Wikler, 1968). This prolonged medical acceptance of barbiturates and relative inattention to their dangers may explain in large part why barbiturate abuse is a serious problem today.

Once barbiturate abuse became well known, numerous nonbarbiturate sleeping pills were developed. However, while most of these differ chemically from barbiturates, their actions in the brain are quite similar and they are susceptible to the same degree of abuse. Among these drugs that were promoted as "safe" sleeping pills were methyprylon (Noludar®), glutethimide (Doriden®), and methaqualone (Quaalude®). Studies performed after they had been on the market for a while indicated that their addictive and lethal potential is very similar to that of the barbiturates. Because methaqualone was not strictly controlled by federal regulation at first, it became the favorite "downer" of the American drug culture in the late 1960s. Glutethimide is particularly dangerous because it is not readily removed from the circulation, even by vigorous hemodialysis with an artificial kidney. Thus, while lethal concentrations of barbiturates can be removed by hemodialysis, victims of glutethimide overdose must wait until the drug gradually disappears from the body through its own slow metabolism. Thalidomide is related chemically to glutethimide. Because it produced less of a hangover than most other hypnotics, thalidomide became the most popular sleeping medication in Germany before the discovery of its propensity to produce phocomelia, absence of arms or legs, in babies born to mothers who had been taking the drug.

The concept of selective antianxiety drugs was introduced in the early 1950s by the pharmacologist Frank Berger, who developed meprobamate (Miltown®, Equanil®), an agent that "tamed" aggressive laboratory animals. Meprobamate was advertised as a novel drug, a tranquilizer rather than a sedative. More than any other drug, meprobamate alerted the pharmaceutical industry to the vast commercial potential of drugs which selectively alter emotional behavior. Subsequent research has shown that meprobamate differs little from any of the other sedative-hypnotics that preceded it. However, meprobamate stimulated research to develop true antianxiety drugs, a goal which has apparently been attained in the benzodiazepines.

The best-known benzodiazepine is diazepam (Valium®), the most widely prescribed of all drugs in the world, with sales annually exceeding $350,000,000. The benzodiazepines are uniquely safe compared with other sedative-hypnotics. Five to ten times the normal sleep-inducing dose of a barbiturate is lethal. By contrast, people have consumed hundreds of benzodiazepine pills in suicide attempts with no adverse effect other than a prolonged sleep. Barbiturates kill by depressing the respiratory center in the brain, which apparently is much less sensitive to benzodiazepines. There is good evidence that one can relieve anxiety with doses of benzodiazepines which are not sedating, whereas comparable antianxiety effects are induced by barbiturates only at doses which produce drowsiness. While most benzodiazepines are advertised only as antianxiety drugs, in somewhat higher doses they are effective hypnotics. Largely because of marketing considerations, the benzodiazepine called flurazepam (Dalmane®) is advertised exclusively as a sleeping medication though it does not differ from other benzodiazepines. The major virtue of the benzodiazepines as hypnotics is their safety. Suicide is one of the leading causes of death in the United States, and overdose of sleeping pills is the most popular technique. Perhaps more distressing are the large number of individuals who accidentally take an overdose because of drug "automatism." Dazed from an already substantial dose of a hypnotic, often combined with alcohol, the still-awake victim does not remember that he or she has already taken several pills and proceeds to take the final, lethal dose.

Actions

Most sedative hypnotics act by similar mechanisms, which they share with alcohol. These drugs depress the firing activity of many cells in the brain, but much of the euphoria and relief from anxiety result from a lessening of the inhibition normally exerted by higher brain centers. Some researchers feel that all sedative-hypnotic drugs have distinct balances of antianxiety and sedating effects, barbiturates producing mainly sedation and benzodiazepines mainly antianxiety effects.

Through actions in the central nervous system, all of these drugs also produce muscle relaxation. Diazepam is currently the most widely used and most effective of all muscle relaxant drugs, being especially helpful in treating muscle spasm in stroke victims, children with cerebral palsy, and patients with back problems. It has been suggested that the capacity to relieve anxiety stems in part from muscle relaxation effects.

Benzodiazepines, barbiturates, and alcohol must share some sites of action, since cross-tolerance exists among them. Thus, the withdrawal symptoms of a barbiturate addict can be relieved by alcohol, benzodiazepines, or meprobamate, as well as by a barbiturate. Similarly, delirium tremens, the alcohol withdrawal syndrome, can be alleviated by a barbiturate, meprobamate, or benzodiazepine, as well as by alcohol itself. Besides these common actions, some researchers have argued that benzodiazepines exert unique antianxiety actions not displayed by other sedative-hypnotics.

Recent research clarifying the molecular mechanism of benzodiazepine action has greatly enhanced our understanding of how these drugs relieve anxiety and of ways in which they differ from barbiturates, alcohol, and meprobamate. Two groups of European researchers (Mohler and Okada, 1977; Squires and Braestrup, 1977) attempted to identify specific receptor sites in the brain for Valium, using a technique which earlier had resulted in the discovery of opiate receptors. They demonstrated that radioactive forms of Valium bind to brain membranes, and that the relative potencies of drugs in competing for these binding sites parallel their clinical effects. The detailed localization of these receptors has shed light on sites in the brain which mediate the various pharmacologic effects of the drugs (Young and Kuhar, 1979). Thus, the antianxiety effects of benzodiazepines may be explained by the high concentration of benzodiazepine receptors in portions of the limbic system, where benzodiazepines alter neuronal firing rates. Similarly, the ability of benzodiazepines to cause muscle relaxation may stem from effects on benzodiazepine receptors concentrated in portions of the spinal cord which control muscle tension.

Identification of benzodiazepine receptors has also clarified the relationship of these drugs to other sedative-hypnotics. Barbiturates, alcohol, and meprobamate do not bind to the benzodiazepine receptors. Accordingly, the common sedative-hypnotic effects of benzodiazepines and other agents must be exerted at some other site. Presumably, then, the benzodiazepine receptors are responsible for unique antianxiety effects of benzodiazepines.

What might be the normal role of benzodiazepine receptors? Might there exist a normally occurring neurotransmitter which acts at benzodiazepine receptors, much as enkephalin acts at opiate receptors? At the time of writing, numerous researchers are searching for such a chemical, but there are no clear conclusions. There is some evidence that the benzodiazepine receptor normally interacts with the inhibitory neurotransmitter GABA (see Chapter 6). Such a possibility would fit well with findings that benzodiazepines facilitate the effects of GABA on neuronal firing rates.

Abuse

Sedative-hypnotics are subject to abuse primarily because they produce a drowsy euphoria; hence the drugs are called "downers." If an individual is resting quietly, the drugs will simply make him sleepy. If he is engaged in animated conversation, they may produce a confused excitement and emotional lability. This difference, depending on setting, has a parallel with alcohol: People are more likely to become high at a cocktail party than when drinking alone at home.

If the brain level of a drug builds up slowly, one does not notice its effects and does not experience a subjective "high." Phenobarbital, a long-acting barbiturate, enters the brain quite slowly, fails to elicit euphoria, and thus is not abusable. The most popular barbiturates in the drug culture are the relatively short-acting agents secobarbital and pentobarbital. One of the virtues of the benzodiazepines is their slow onset of action, so that they produce very little euphoria.

When acutely intoxicated by sedative-hypnotics, people behave very much like someone drunk on alcohol. They are somewhat sluggish; they exhibit slurred speech, poor comprehension, faulty judgment, and emotional lability; and their natural personality traits are exaggerated.

One can develop clear-cut tolerance and physical dependence, hence physical addiction, to all sedative-hypnotics. Addicts to these drugs also demonstrate a compulsive craving for them, which, however, is not as strong as the compulsion for heroin. Tolerance is also less pronounced than with opiates, though many barbiturate addicts can remain alert with doses ten to twenty times those which would put a drug-naive individual to sleep. The most dangerous aspect of sedative-hypnotic addiction is that while individuals become markedly tolerant to sedating effects, the lethal dose is not much greater in addicts than in normal individuals. Thus, a barbiturate addict may die if he or she consumes less than twice the dose required to stay high.

Withdrawal symptoms from sedative-hypnotics are very much like those of alcohol withdrawal and accordingly are more serious than those that follow termination of opiate use. After a period of addiction to high doses of short-acting barbiturates and abrupt termination, the patient seems to feel well for twelve or more hours as blood levels fall and the intoxication clears. Soon, however, he or she becomes weak, tremulous, and restless, often with nausea, vomiting, and abdominal cramps. The peak of withdrawal occurs two to three days after stopping the drug, when delirium and convulsions appear. The delirium is very much like the delirium tremens of alcoholism. Individuals are confused and agitated, their body temperature rises, and they may die from heart failure. Visual hallucinations, frightening dreams, and confused disorientation are prominent. With longer-acting barbiturates such as phenobarbital or with benzodiazepines, withdrawal symptoms follow a slower course and don't peak until about a week after drug taking stops. Withdrawal symptoms can be minimized and convulsions and delirium prevented by administering barbiturates in gradually reduced doses.

Like most withdrawal symptoms, those associated with sedative-hypnotics are essentially the opposite of the effects produced by the drug itself. While barbiturates are sedating, during withdrawal patients are hyperexcited. Barbiturates are anticonvulsants, and convulsions may occur as part of the withdrawal syndrome.

References

Mohler, H., and Okada, T. Benzodiazepine receptor: Demonstration in the central nervous system. *Science, 198:*849–851, 1977.

Squires, R. F., and Braestrup, C. Benzodiazepine receptors in rat brain. *Nature, 266:*732–734, 1977.

Wikler, A. Diagnosis and treatment of drug dependence of the barbiturate type. *Am. J. Psychiat., 125:*758–765, 1968.

Young, S., and Kuhar, M. Autoradiographic localization of benzodiazepine receptors in the brains of humans and animals. *Nature, 280:*393–395, 1979.

12. Marijuana

The first report of the National Commission on Marijuana and Drug Abuse was entitled "Marijuana: A Signal of Misunderstanding." And with good cause. Marijuana has probably been the most controversial psychoactive drug in the United States, and much of the controversy has resulted from misunderstanding.

People have disputed, for instance, whether marijuana is a mild or powerful mind-altering drug. It is both. The potency of preparations is related to the content of $\Delta 9$-*tetrahydrocannabinol* (*THC*), the principal psychoactive ingredient. Different batches of marijuana and related preparations vary in their THC content from 0.1 to 10 percent, which can readily account for a hundredfold variation in subjective responses.

Though the term *marijuana* is used to refer to most druglike preparations of the cannabis or hemp plant, strictly speaking, it should be reserved for concoctions of the ground-up leaf which have a THC content of about 1 percent or less. This is the form of the drug used most frequently in the United States and Europe. A generic label for all psychoactive forms is *cannabis*. While cannabis extracts have been used as psychotropic agents for more than 300 years, the exact chemical structure of the active ingredient was established only in 1964 by the Israeli chemist Raphael Mechoulam. THC is secreted in a sticky resin by the flowering leaves of ripe male and female hemp plants. To obtain a highly potent cannabis preparation, one scrapes the THC-containing resin from the leaves of cultivated plants. Pressed into hard blocks and smoked, this material is known as *hashish* in the West and in India is *charas*. Because hashish has about ten times the THC content of average marijuana, it is more intoxicating and elicits hallucinogenic and psychotomimetic effects much more readily than does marijuana (see Table 12.1).

Though widely used as a mind-altering drug in India and the Middle East for centuries, cannabis was not introduced to Europe until the nineteenth century, when Napoleon's soldiers appear to have brought it back from Egypt. In the mid-nineteenth century, hashish became popular among literary circles in Paris and its effects were described with hyperbole. Alexander Dumas was greatly impressed by the ability of hashish to enhance sensory perceptions, including erotic sensations. He may have been the first to advocate cannabis as an aphrodisiac (Dumas, 1845): "And then followed a dream of passion like that promised by the Prophet to the Elect. Lips of stone turned to flame, breasts of ice became like heated lava, so that to Franz, yielding for the first time to the sway of the drug, love was a sorrow and voluptuousness a torture, as burning mouths were pressed to his thirsty lips, and he was held in cool serpent-like embraces."

Cannabis did not reach the United States until the twentieth century. In Mexico it was named *marijuana,* a term applied to a cheap form of tobacco. About 1910 Mexican laborers began bringing marijuana across the border into Texas. In New Orleans in the 1920s marijuana gained popularity as an illegal drug

Table 12-1 Cannabis preparations

Level of potency	Means of preparation and consumption
Mild Marijuana (American and European) Kif (North Africa), Dagga (South Africa) Bhang (An Indian term for a concoction utilizing leaves but not stems. The THC content tends to be higher than that of American-grown marijuana)	In preparing marijuana, the leaves or sometimes the stems, seeds, or entire plants are dried, ground, and smoked or sometimes baked into cookies. Bhang is often prepared as a liquid and consumed at social gatherings. Potencies vary greatly depending on THC content. Vietnamese marijuana may be five to ten times more potent than American varieties.
Intermediate Ganja (India): The dried flowering tops of cultivated plants, with a higher THC content than less cultivated plants, are employed	Ganja is baked into sweets, drunk, or smoked.
Potent Hashish Charas (India)	These are prepared by scraping the THC resin from the leaves of cultivated plants with high THC content. For hashish the resin is pressed into hard blocks and is usually smoked.

along with bootleg liquor. Its use was largely confined to poor blacks, a sociological feature that may account for the erroneous linking of marijuana to crime. Many newspaper articles in the 1920s and 1930s stated that the use of marijuana leads to aggressive criminal tendencies, though the evidence was merely that some people who committed crimes also smoked marijuana. A newspaper report from New Orleans provides an extreme example of this distortion: "The crime wave unquestionably was greatly aggravated by the influence of this drug [marijuana] habit. . . . Youngsters known to be 'muggleheads' fortified themselves with the narcotic [sic] and proceeded to shoot down police, bank clerks, and casual bystanders" (*Morning Tribune*, New Orleans, October 17, 19, 23 and 28, 1926). The U.S. Commissioner of Narcotics, Harry Anslinger, himself wrote: "An entire family was murdered by a youthful marijuana addict. . . . The boy said he had been in the habit of smoking something which youthful friends called 'muggles,' a childish name for marijuana" (Anslinger and Cooper, 1937).

In the charged atmosphere such publicity created, it was easy for Anslinger to secure passage in Congress of the Marijuana Tax Act of 1937, which outlawed the use of marijuana and made it essentially impossible to obtain samples for research.

Marijuana as medicine

In nineteenth century Europe and the United States, cannabis extracts were widely used to treat a number of medical conditions. In that period of more adventurous therapeutics, standard textbooks of pharmacology recommended: "Cannabis is very valuable for the relief of pain, particularly that depending on nervous disturbances: It produces sleep. . . . It is used in cough mixtures and does not constipate or depress the system as does morphine" (Hare and Christie, 1892). Extracts of opium and cannabis were prescribed for similar medical indications.

One difference between the two drugs noticed by nineteenth century physicians was that prolonged use of cannabis did not produce addiction. Nor was it as constipating as opiates. However, opiates were clearly more powerful in relieving pain.

Cannabis use declined in medical practice in the late nineteenth and early twentieth centuries. A crude plant extract, it was quite insoluble and could not be injected intravenously. Since the THC content of different cannabis batches varies enormously, the therapeutic effects of a given preparation were difficult to predict. In the late nineteenth century pure morphine, which could be readily quantified and injected, became available. Soon afterward aspirin and barbiturates were introduced. Thus, years before marijuana was outlawed (in 1937), physicians prescribed it less and less.

New scientific developments may revive cannabis as a therapeutic agent. Pure THC is now available, and analogues have been developed which are soluble in water and can be readily injected. Some of these produce a variety of medically useful effects at low doses which do not alter mental functioning. THC has been documented as an effective analgesic in cancer patients. It is also an antiemetic, preventing nausea and vomiting, especially in cancer patients receiving powerful nausea-inducing anticancer drugs (Sallan et al., 1975). The nineteenth century practice of treating asthma with cannabis has been supported in scientific studies which indicate that smoked or orally ingested marijuana causes bronchodilation, reversing the symptoms of asthma (Tashkin et al., 1974; Vachon et al., 1973). One effect of marijuana that could be of wide benefit is its ability to lower intraocular pressure, thus relieving the symptoms of glaucoma, the second leading cause of blindness in the United States (Hepler et al., 1976). Such studies have prompted the synthesis of THC analogues that have therapeutic but not psychotropic actions. None is yet available for clinical use.

Behavioral effects

Marijuana users get "high." What is the nature of this altered state of consciousness? How does it compare with the effects of psychedelic drugs, barbiturates, amphetamines, and other drugs? The closest parallel is probably with the effects of psychedelic drugs in low doses. Perceptual changes occur but are not so violent as with LSD. Frank hallucinations are rare with marijuana and uncommon even with high doses of hashish. Sensations of vision, sound, smell, taste, and touch are accentuated so that the drug user may become entranced with them. One marijuana smoker reported his sensations as follows:

When looking at pictures they may acquire an element of visual depth, a third dimensional aspect. Things are seen more sharply in that their edges, contours stand out more sharply against the background. My visual perception of the space around me is changed so that what I am looking at is very real and clear, but everything else I am not focusing on visually seems further away and otherwise less real or clear. . . . I can hear more subtle changes in sounds, for example the notes of music are purer, more distinct, the rhythm stands out more. I can understand the words of songs which are not clear when straight. . . . My sense of touch is more exciting, more sensual. Some surfaces feel much smoother, silkier, while some surfaces feel much rougher, irregular and the roughness or graininess forms interesting patterns. Smells become richer and more unique. Taste sensations take on new qualities, and if I try to imagine what something tastes like, I can do so very vividly (Tart, 1970).

The apparent enhancement of sensory perception, which accounts for much of the enthusiasm for marijuana, is often accompanied by other changes in space and time perception: "When I walk someplace my experience of the distance covered is quite changed so that distances seem to get greater, especially between me and the things or me and other people. Time passes very slowly; it's not just that things take longer, certain experiences seem outside of time, are timeless" (Tart, 1970).

There has been a lot of research on the effects of marijuana on memory and other mental processes. Even highly intoxicated users are able to perform a variety of memory tests quite well. When they try hard, they can compensate for their intoxication. Long-term memory does not seem to be impaired at all. When users are asked to recall something memorized after a delay, they do well, but their ability to remember things learned in the immediate past is impaired. Cannabis may interfere with short-term memory by causing the individual to "overload" his or her short-term memory stores: "The presentation of the word 'apple' to a subject under the influence of cannabis might cause information to enter short-term stores such as 'it's a fruit called an apple which is round, red, shiny and sweet tasting' whereas for a subject who has not taken cannabis, only the name of the stimulus might enter short term storage" (Tinklenberg and Darley, 1976). Besides explaining memory impairment with marijuana use, an inability to filter out unimportant information could also be related to the perceptual changes. The user might become so entranced by what he or she perceives as to lose the ability to screen any of it out of the intake into short-term memory. The increased flow of data into short-term stores may also account for changes in the sense of time passage as the individual's subjective tempo accelerates.

It is difficult to discern which drug effect is primary and which is secondary. One could argue that the greater attractiveness of sensory percepts causes the marijuana user to focus on them to an inordinate degree, which then impairs memory. On the other hand, a primary change in memory processing, with a flooding of short-term memory reservoirs by information that is ordinarily too insignificant for pickup, could enhance the subjective richness of sensory events.

Physical effects

Cannabis produces few definite physical effects. Those which are most easily measured and which occur reliably in all drug users are an engorgement of the conjuctival blood vessels of the eye, hence "red eyes" and an acceleration of heart rate. Appetite is stimulated, which may or may not be related to an enhancement of taste perception.

Marijuana also elicits somnolence. Some users consider the drug an ideal hypnotic: "I find it very easy to go to sleep at my usual bedtime when stoned. I get very drowsy even though it's not late. My sleep is particularly refreshing if I go to bed stoned" (Tart, 1970). There seems to be little of the hangover associated with most sleeping pills. The sleep-promoting effects of cannabis distinguish it from psychedelic drugs, which greatly enhance alertness.

Tolerance

Most drugs of abuse provoke tolerance. Some studies and reports of users have left the impression that marijuana is an exception. A "reverse" tolerance is described in which experienced users seem to be more sensitive to the subjective effects of the drug than naive subjects. This may, however, merely reflect the greater skill of experienced users in inhaling and thus delivering more drug to the brain or in detecting and responding to subtle cues of drug intoxication. When THC is administered both day and night in substantial doses, tolerance becomes readily evident; individuals show no greater response to 200 milligrams of the drug than they did to 20 to 40 milligrams before tolerance was induced (Jones and Benowitz, 1976). In these studies, abrupt termination of THC was followed within twelve hours by withdrawal symptoms such as "hot flashes," sweating, runny nose, loose stools, hiccups, and loss of appetite. Subjects compared these symptoms to a moderate case of the flu. The existence of withdrawal symptoms indicates that one can become physically dependent upon marijuana, at least with high enough doses. In the amounts most often used socially, however, it is unlikely that an appreciable degree of tolerance or physical dependence ever develops. The practical question facing society with a pleasure-giving drug such as marijuana is whether the user is in danger of becoming a compulsive addict. Compulsive craving, the socially crucial element in addiction, certainly exists for alcohol, opiates, barbiturates, and nicotine but apparently not for marijuana.

Dangers

A whole host of adverse medical effects have been described in marijuana users. There have been reports of brain atrophy, depressed immune responsiveness, chromosomal damage, and even allegations of fetal malformations in children of marijuana smokers. There have been claims that marijuana causes precancerous changes in the lungs (Nahas, 1973).

Careful studies have failed to reproduce the most alarming of these findings (National Commission, 1972). If such serious pathological changes occurred in American marijuana smokers consuming moderate amounts, they should be even more severe in cannabis users from cultures where the average consumption is higher than in the United States and where the THC content of the cannabis preparations is also usually higher than in the United States. Accordingly, the physical status of heavy cannabis users has been compared to that of nonusers in Greece, Jamaica, and Costa Rica (Coggins, 1976; Stefanis, 1976).

In these studies the users consumed an average of five to ten cigarettes daily for five to twenty years. The THC content of cigarettes was generally 2 to 5 percent, substantially higher than the 1 percent THC content of the marijuana smoked by most American users. The incidence of mental illness or abnormalities of mood, thought, and behavior was no different in chronic heavy marijuana smokers in Jamaica than in nonsmokers matched for socioeconomic status. In a study of long-term hashish users in Egypt, heavy users did show marked psychic dependence on the drug and appeared to be slow learners and to display a lessened work capacity (Soueif, 1971). However, a significant number of the users also employed other psychoactive drugs, especially opium, which makes it difficult to assess the relative contributions of cannabis and opium to the observed disabilities.

Among medical findings in the Jamaican and Greek studies, chest x-rays, chromosome analyses, electrocardiograms, blood and chemistry tests, and liver and kidney functions were no different in smokers and nonsmokers. The smokers consistently did show reduced pulmonary function quite similar to that observed in tobacco cigarette smokers.

Though marijuana rarely, if ever, precipitates a major psychosis by itself, it can provoke panic reactions. Panic states account for more than 75 percent of all adverse reactions to the drug and seem to depend generally on the user's expectations (Weil, 1970). In colleges where marijuana use is a common and casually accepted practice, less than 1 percent of users panic. In contrast, in a rural Southern college where marijuana smoking is a deviant behavior, one-fourth of first-time users develop panic reactions. In a typical panic state, the smoker is terrified by a sense of impending mental breakdown or suspicions of being pursued by the police. The reactions usually last two to six hours and infrequently as long as one or two days. Victims are best treated by simple reassurance, not by hospitalization or tranquilizing drugs.

There has been concern that marijuana elicits an "amotivational syndrome." In the hippie culture of the 1960s, many users of marijuana and other psychotropic drugs seemed to lose a desire to work and compete. West (1970) described this as follows:

The experienced clinician observes personality changes that may grow subtly over long periods of time: diminished drive, lessened ambition, decreased motivation, apathy, shortened attention span, distractibility, poor judgment, impaired communication skills, loss of effectiveness, introversion, magical thinking, derealization and depersonalization, diminished capacity to carry out complex plans or prepare realistically for the future, a peculiar fragmentation of thought, habit deteriorations and progressive loss of insight. There is a clinical impression of organicity to this syndrome that I simply cannot shake off or explain away.

Such observations raised the question of whether these individuals dropped out because of drug use or whether the drugs were mainly a matter of life style, a sign of their disinclination to adopt the conventional behavior patterns of "straight" society.

Mendelson et al. (1976) obtained direct experimental evidence that heavy marijuana use does not decrease motivation. Heavy and casual users of marijuana were maintained on a research ward where they were paid to perform a variety of psychomotor tasks. The subjects could use the money to purchase marijuana cigarettes. During periods of heavy marijuana use, even when subjects were intoxicated most of the day, there was no decrease in work output. This contrasted with the behavior of alcoholics maintained in the same research ward setting, who stopped performing the tasks during periods of heavy drinking.

Marijuana and driving

More than anyplace else, the conflict between drug use and social needs is apparent in automobile driving. Habitual smokers of marijuana maintain that their driving skills never suffer, even when they are "stoned out of their minds." Such statements seem dangerously reminiscent of alcoholics who, though grossly uncoordinated, still protest that they can drive reliably.

Several research studies have compared the influence of alcohol and marijuana on driving, usually utilizing simulators in which the subject is seated behind a console mock-up of an automobile facing a movie screen that projects a driver's-eye view of the road. In one of the first studies, by Crancer et al. (1969), experienced smokers consumed two marijuana cigarettes or enough alcohol mixed with orange juice to reach a blood level of 0.1 percent, the legal definition of intoxication. Though subjects appeared quite intoxicated on marijuana, their total score in the driving simulator was no different than when they were sober. In contrast, consuming the equivalent of six ounces of 86 proof whiskey produced marked impairment on all driving measures.

This apparent clean bill of health for marijuana has been disputed by others.

Since the Crancer et al. subjects were regular marijuana smokers, perhaps they were eager to prove that marijuana is safe and alcohol dangerous and accordingly pushed themselves to perform well on marijuana and to falter under the influence of alcohol. Even if the subjects were not cheating, their unimpaired performance on marijuana may reflect the often observed ability of marijuana smokers to compensate for their intoxication when they try hard enough.

Because of the altered perception of time and space, marijuana smokers usually report that slow rates, such as 20 miles per hour, seem like breakneck speed, so that they drive more cautiously and slowly than when sober and cling to the right-hand lane. This subjective impression has been borne out in experimental studies that show an increased cautiousness and more accurate judgment of risk for individuals under the influence of marijuana (Dott, 1972). Subjects under the influence of alcohol displayed more aggression and less adequate risk judgment. Alcohol, but not marijuana, seriously impaired responses to emergency signals.

Thus, marijuana seems to produce fewer detrimental influences on driving performance than alcohol. Marijuana is probably not totally innocuous, since a number of studies have demonstrated impairments in specific areas of driving performance, such as reaction time and monitoring the speedometer. It would be foolhardy to advocate driving while stoned. Nonetheless, of the potential dangers associated with marijuana use, automobile driving performance appears to be affected less than might be anticipated for a known intoxicant.

References

Anslinger, H. J., and Cooper, C. R. *American Magazine, 124:*150, 1937.

Coggins, W. J. The Costa Rica cannabis project: An interim report on the medical aspects. In *The pharmacology of marijuana,* eds. M. C. Braude and S. Szara. Raven Press, New York, 1976, pp. 667–670.

Crancer, A., Dille, J., Wallace, J., and Haykin, M. Comparison of the effects of marijuana and alcohol on simulated driving experience. *Science, 164:*851–854, 1969.

Dott, A. B. Effect of marijuana on risk acceptance in a simulated passing task. DHEW Publication No. HSM72-10010, U.S. Department of Health, Education and Welfare, Washington, D.C., 1972.

Dumas, A. *The Count of Monte Cristo,* chapter 31, "Sinbad the Sailor," English ed. Fred Defau and Co., New York, 1845.

Hare, H. A. and Christie, W. *A system of practical therapeutics,* vol. 3. Lee Brothers, Philadelphia, 1892.

Hepler, R. S., Frank, I. M., and Petrus, R. Ocular effects of marijuana smoking. In *The pharmacology of marijuana,* eds. M. C. Braude and S. Szara. Raven Press, New York, 1976, pp. 815–824.

Jones, R. T., and Benowitz, N. The thirty day trip—clinical studies of cannabis tolerance and dependence. In *The pharmacology of marijuana,* eds. M. C. Braude
   and S. Szara. Raven Press, New York, 1976, pp. 627–642.
Mendelson, J. H., Kuehnle, J. C., Greenberg, I., and Mello, N. K. The effects of
   marijuana use on human operant behavior: individual data. In *The pharmacology
   of marijuana,* eds. M. C. Braude and S. Szara. Raven Press, New York, 1976,
   pp. 643–653.
Nahas, G. G. *Marijuana, deceptive weed.* Raven Press, New York, 1973.
National Commission on Marijuana and Drug Abuse. *Marijuana a signal of misunderstanding.* Government Printing Office, Washington, D.C., 1972.
Sallan, S. E., Zinberg, N. E., and Frei, E., III. Antiemetic effect of Δ-9-tetrahydrocan-
   nabinol in patients receiving cancer chemotherapy. *N. Eng. J. Med., 293,* 1975,
   pp. 795–797.
Soueif, M. I. Long-term effects of cannabis. *Bull. Narcotics 23:*17–28, 1971.
Stefanis, C., Boulougouris, J., and Liakos, A. Clinical and psychophysiological effects
   of cannabis in long term users. In *The pharmacology of marijuana,* eds. M. C.
   Braude and S. Szara. Raven Press, New York, 1976, pp. 659–665.
Tart, C. T. Marijuana intoxication. Common experiences. *Nature 226:*704, 1970.
Tashkin, D. P., Shapiro, B. J., and Frank, I. M. Acute effects of smoked marijuana and
   oral Δ-9-tetrahydrocannabinol on specific airway conductants in asthmatic sub-
   jects. *Am. Rev. Resp. Diseases, 109:*420–428, 1974.
Tinklenberg, J. R., and Darley, C. F. A model of marijuana's cognitive effects. In *The
   pharmacology of marijuana,* eds. M. C. Braude and S. Szara. Raven Press, New
   York, 1976, pp. 429–439.
Vachon, L., Fitzgerald, M. X., Solliday, M. H., Gould, I. A., and Gaensler, E. A.
   Single dose effect of marijuana smoke. Bronchial dynamics and respiratory
   center sensitivity in normal subject. *N. Eng. J. Med., 288:*985–989, 1973.
Weil, A. T. Adverse reaction to marijuana. *N. Eng. J. Med., 282:*997–1000, 1970.
West, L. J. In *Psychotomimetic drugs,* ed. D. H. Efron. Raven Press, New York, 1970,
   pp. 325–328.

13. Alcoholism

In 1970, the President of the United States, Richard Nixon, declared heroin addiction to be America's number one social problem. This was clearly an overstatement. Considering only the problem of drug abuse, alcohol affects by far the greatest number of people, and it is the third leading cause of death in the United States. About 250,000 heroin addicts live in the United States, while, depending on one's definition, there are between 10 and 15 million alcoholics. Since alcoholics often disrupt the lives of their spouses and children, another 40 to 60 million individuals might be considered victims of alcoholism. Strangers are also victimized in automobile accidents, in which about half of all fatalities and serious injuries result from excessive drinking. Since alcohol-related accidents occur most often at night, the odds are 8 to 1 that a driver killed in a single vehicle crash between 9 and 12 P.M. has been drinking heavily. Fully 70 percent of males killed in auto accidents have blood alcohol levels of 0.1 percent or higher within fifteen minutes of the crash (Ray, 1972). A blood alcohol level of 0.1 percent would normally be produced by ingesting five ounces of whiskey.

Though crimes committed by heroin addicts to pay for their drugs have been given more attention in the news media and have aroused more fear, alcoholism is in fact more widely associated with crime. In almost half of all assaults and murders, either the assailant or the victim, or both, have been drinking heavily (Chafetz, 1975). About 30 percent of all arrests in the United States are for public drunkenness.

Alcohol plays a major economic role in the United States. Sales of alcoholic beverages amount to $25 billion each year, and $300 million per year are spent advertising them. About 100,000,000 people in the United States drink alcoholic beverages, the average adult consuming nine quarts of pure alcohol annually. About 90 percent do not suffer lasting adverse consequences. The great prevalence of alcohol use may well account for the failure of our society to devote adequate attention to alcoholism as a problem of drug abuse. Because most of us drink, we have trouble detecting that fine point at which the consumption of alcohol becomes abuse.

This distinction varies among societies. The average adult Italian, for instance, consumes fifteen quarts of pure alcohol each year, yet drunkenness is uncommon in Italy. With little more than half that per capita alcohol consumption, the United States has a higher incidence of alcoholism. The explanation is apparently related to differences in the pattern of drinking. Italians tend to drink wine at meals and family gatherings without inebriation, while Americans favor cocktails with a high alcohol content designed for rapid effect. The French consume four times more alcohol each year per capita than Americans and may well be world leaders in the incidence of alcoholism.

What is alcoholism?

Many definitions and classifications of alcoholism have been formulated over the years, none of them altogether satisfactory. One of the most widely used was hammered out by a World Health Organization expert committee in 1952:

Alcoholics are those excessive drinkers whose dependence on alcohol has attained such a degree that it shows a noticeable mental disturbance or interference with their bodily or mental health, their interpersonal relations, and their smooth social and economic functioning; or who show the prodromal signs of such developments. They therefore require treatment (Glatt, 1961).

According to the DSM-II, people suffer from alcoholism whenever their "alcohol intake is great enough to damage their physical health, or their personal social functioning, or when it has become a prerequisite to normal functioning" (Diagnostic and Statistical Manual of Mental Disorders, 1968). The DSM-II distinguishes three degrees of alcoholic disturbance. An individual suffers from "episodic excessive drinking" if he or she "becomes intoxicated as frequently as four times a year." Those "who either become intoxicated more than twelve times a year or are recognizably under the influence of alcohol more than once a week even though not intoxicated are considered to display habitual excessive drinking." The most severe level of disturbance is "alcohol addiction" in which "there is direct or strong presumptive evidence that the patient is dependent on alcohol.'' If available, the best direct evidence of such dependence is the appearance of withdrawal symptoms. A person's inability to go one day without drinking is presumptive evidence. When heavy drinking continues for three months or more, it is reasonable to presume that he or she has become addicted to alcohol. Withdrawal symptoms are the clearest sign of physical dependence and are seen most dramatically in delirium tremens.

Physical effects of alcohol

Knowing how the body disposes of alcohol helps in understanding how it acts and which drinking patterns bring about the greatest intoxication. Alcohol is absorbed mostly from the stomach and small intestine. Absorption from the small intestine is much more rapid and complete than from the stomach, which explains why drinking during a meal will decrease the likelihood of rapid absorption and intoxication. The food slows digestive movements which propel the stomach contents into the intestine so that alcohol remains in the stomach longer, adsorbed to the protein content of the food. Milk slows the absorption of alcohol more than most other foods, and the alcohol in beer is also slowly absorbed. Carbonated water accelerates the absorption of alcohol because it speeds up peristalsis and accelerates the passage of alcohol from the stomach to the small intestine. On the other hand, plain water simply lowers the alcohol concentration in the stomach and intestine and thus slows its absorption. Thus, Scotch-and-soda is more inebriating than Scotch-and-water, and champagne intoxicates more readily than wine of the same alcoholic content.

After being absorbed, alcohol is distributed throughout the body fluids. Since heavier persons have more body fluid, they develop a correspondingly lower concentration of blood alcohol. On a percentage basis, women have more fat than men and hence less fluid per unit of weight. Thus, they will generally develop a higher blood concentration of alcohol than men of the same weight who have had the same amount to drink.

Alcohol penetrates membranes throughout the body, including the membranes of the placenta, so that a mother's blood alcohol level is reflected in her unborn child. The behavior of children born to severely alcoholic women is impaired, a condition called the *fetal alcohol syndrome,* which was not widely appreciated until the mid-1970s.

Alcohol is almost completely metabolized by the enzyme alcohol dehydrogenase, producing about 200 calories of energy per ounce. Alcohol is not a very nutritious dietary substance, but it can supply quick calories without making the drinker fat. Since alcohol is rapidly absorbed and metabolized, it provides a ready source of energy. It is not stored in the body or converted into any sort of storage form, so that alcohol itself does not contribute to obesity; instead, it is the food eaten with the alcohol which increases body weight.Alcohol is metabolized at a fixed rate that does not vary as the concentration in the blood increases. The average rate at which alcohol is degraded, primarily by the liver, is about 10 milliliters (a third of an ounce) each hour. If one drinks more rapidly, the blood alcohol level will rise as alcohol accumulates.

Besides changing behavior, alcohol has a number of effects throughout the body which are readily apparent to most drinkers. It inhibits the secretion of the antidiuretic hormone of the pituitary gland so that one is disposed to urinate, which causes a certain amount of dehydration. In addition, alcohol causes fluid inside cells to move outside, which dehydrates most cells of the body and probably accounts for the thirst most people experience after a bout of drinking. Hangover symptoms include thirst, an upset stomach, and a headache. Alcohol can cause stomach troubles because it directly irritates the stomach lining. Headache may not be attributable to alcohol but rather to congeners, which are alcohol-related substances produced during fermentation. Vodka, which is almost pure ethanol, has a very low congener content of about 0.10 percent and so is less likely to produce hangover headaches. Beer has an equally low level of congeners, about a fourth the level of wine. Most whiskeys have about 0.2 percent of congeners. Aging whiskey increases congeners to about 0.4 percent so that well-aged brandy and Scotch probably have the highest level of congeners and can provoke the worst hangover headaches.

Behavioral effects

Alcohol is a central nervous system depressant. It affects the brain much like barbiturates and other anesthetics. Until the advent of nitrous oxide and ether in the early 1900s, it was the major anesthetic used for surgery. No one knows exactly how alcohol acts. However, it is generally thought that its first effect on the brain is to depress the reticular activating system of the brain stem, which normally suppresses higher centers such as the cerebral cortex. The cortex is thereby released from restraint and one feels "uninhibited." Individuals lose their critical faculties, becoming expansive in speech and vulnerable to uncontrolled emotional outbursts. Because of their facility in speech while under the influence of alcohol, many people have thought that alcohol, in low or moderate doses, is a stimulant. There is no firm evidence for this belief.

It is also a popular belief that alcohol enhances sexual functioning. Again, it is the release from mental inhibitions that gives this impression. In fact, alcohol reduces sexual performance, decreasing a man's capacity for erection. Shakespeare gave this a classic statement in *Macbeth* (Act II, Scene 3):

Macduff: What three things does drink especially provoke?

Porter: Marry, sir, nose-painting, sleep and urine. Lechery, sir, it provokes and unprovokes: it provokes the desire but it takes away the performance. Therefore, much drink may be said to be an equivocator with lechery: it makes him cometh and it mars him; it sets him on, and it takes him off.''

Efficiency in performing complex or newly learned psychomotor tasks is uniformly decreased even by relatively low amounts of alcohol, while familiar and simple tasks are less affected. Alcohol in low doses does improve performance of tasks for which anxiety or general inhibition while sober impedes performance.

Disruption of behavior is closely related to blood levels, which are calculated according to the percentage of the blood volume accounted for by alcohol. Since a gram is equivalent in volume to a millimeter, 100 grams of alcohol in 100 millimeters would represent a blood level of 100 percent. Also, 100 milligrams (a milligram is one-thousandth of a gram) in 100 millimeters of blood represents 0.10 percent. A rough relationship between blood alcohol levels and behavior is described by the tale of D's (Ray, 1972):

At less than .03% the individual is dull and dignified.
At 0.05%, he is dashing and debonair.
At 0.1%, he may become dangerous and devilish.
At 0.20%, he is likely to be dizzy and disturbing.
At 0.25%, he may be disgusting and disheveled.
At 0.30%, he is delirious and disoriented and surely drunk.
At 0.35%, he is dead drunk.
At 0.60%, the chances are that he is dead.

Most legal authorities consider an individual to be intoxicated when his blood level exceeds 0.15 percent, that is, 150 milligrams of alcohol per 100 millimeters of blood. An adult man weighing about 150 pounds attains a blood level of about 0.15 percent alcohol by drinking on an empty stomach, in a one-hour period, about five cans of beer, five glasses of unfortified wine, or 5 ounces of whiskey. To reach the same blood level would require more ethanol for someone heavier and less for someone who is lighter or for a woman of the same weight.

The natural history of alcoholism

It is the task of clinical medicine to describe the natural history of a disease process, that is, the course of its progression if unaltered by any form of treatment. If alcoholism is a disease, then one might expect it to possess a distinctive natural history. The most widely accepted model description of the course of events in alcohol dependence was proposed by Jellinek, who felt that in most if not all cases alcoholism has four phases (Jellinek, 1952).

Phase I

For most alcoholics there is a long latency period between the first drink and the beginning of serious drinking problems. Most persons are introduced to drinking during adolescence and slowly build up to a problem drinking stage in their mid or late twenties (Cahalan and Cisin, 1968a). There are some exceptions to this rule, however, and the pace of events can be much quicker (Glatt, 1961).

The first phase is a prealcoholic one, during which drinking progresses from a pleasant social activity to a panacea for everyday tensions, an antianxiety drug. In some cases, drinking at this stage is unrelated to tensions or emotional distress but arises from occupational temptation, as with newspaper reporters or diplomats, who confront drinking opportunities several times each day. This phase is paralleled in addiction to drugs such as barbiturates or amphetamines, first taken respectively for insomnia or dieting but then used more and more for their psychotropic effects.

A tolerance for alcohol soon appears, with more drinking at more frequent intervals required to attain psychotropic effects. In a perverse way this tolerance can make a person feel more powerful since he can "hold his liquor" and drink a partner "under the table."

Phase II

Early alcoholism
According to Jellinek, blackouts are a hallmark of this phase. These are short intervals of amnesia during or shortly after a drinking bout. But many alcoholics progress to advanced stages without ever experiencing blackouts.

More crucial to this phase is a tendency to drink surreptitiously. At cocktail parties the first few drinks are gulped rapidly. A few drinks at home before going out precede a social evening, which will involve heavy drinking. The drinker becomes preoccupied with alcohol and will go to great lengths to ensure that a bottle is available at home, hidden in a desk drawer at the office or in the car. He or she becomes concerned lest the supply be exhausted on a day when no liquor stores are open. Though preoccupied with alcohol, the drinker is extremely defensive and will go to great lengths to deny the existence of any problem.

Phase III

The crucial phase

At this stage, the alcoholic has become truly addicted. He or she has *lost control,* a phenomenon that led to the famous slogan of Alcoholics Anonymous, "The first drink is fatal." In fact, during the crucial phase, drinkers are usually not entirely out of control and a single drink does not invariably progress to drunkenness. In some studies, up to half of advanced alcoholics can avoid getting drunk on the first occasion of drinking after an interval of sobriety. They fight to maintain control and may set up a regimen for themselves—not drinking at home alone, drinking only when in a good mood, or drinking only beer or wine. But it is a losing battle.

This loss of control displays cultural variations. American and British drinkers, who are predominantly whiskey drinkers, often progress to a drunken state within hours after the first drink. French alcoholics, who prefer wine, behave quite differently. Instead of sober intervals alternating with drunken sprees, the French tend to drink continuously, yet may rarely if ever appear to be drunk. They are unable to abstain from drinking and will consume some wine almost every hour of the day, maintaining a fairly fixed blood alcohol level.

During the crucial phase, a drinker's life situation begins to disintegrate. In a frantic endeavor to solve personal problems, he or she may change many aspects of relationships, which are blamed for the drinking. Divorces and job changes are frequent in this phase. And for the first time, the drinker may begin to experience withdrawal symptoms, including delirium tremens after a spree.

Phase IV

The chronic phase

At this point, alcohol has triumphed. The victim often goes on benders, becoming inebriated day and night for periods of a week or more. Concerns about maintaining a façade of respectibility are lost. The alcoholic will drink anything that contains alcohol, even hair tonic. No further effort is made to forestall the disintegration of his or her personal life, including family and occupation. Physical damage to the liver and brain has usually occurred by this time.

These four phases of alcoholism were derived from a sample of Alcoholics Anonymous members at an end stage of social and physical disruption and do not apply to all problem drinkers (Pattison, 1966). Many heavy-drinking males in their twenties slack off and *stop drinking* excessively in their thirties without treatment. With the advent of polymorphous drug abuse, including amphetamines, psychedelic drugs, and heroin, a pattern of multiple addictions has become evident in many young people, who may also be alcoholics. Some spree drinkers go on benders resembling those of the worst skid-row alcoholics but can stop drinking abruptly and commence a month or more of total sobriety. Equally perplexing are individuals, like the leading lady of the movie *I'll Cry Tomorrow,* who plummet from their first Brandy Alexander to advanced alcoholism in weeks or months.

Alcohol withdrawal

Delirium tremens

The most dreaded feature of alcohol withdrawal is delirium tremens, the DT's. The physical symptoms of withdrawal that culminate in delirium tremens range from tremulousness and agitation to convulsions followed by motor disorganization. Delirium tremens proper, which follows the convulsions after an interval, consists of extreme agitation, hyperactivity, and frightening visual hallucinations. The work of Victor and Adams (1953) and Isbell et al. (1955) has firmly documented the relationship between these symptoms and an abrupt lowering of blood alcohol levels.

The first withdrawal symptoms are tremulousness and a feeling of uneasiness and nausea upon waking after a night of drinking. There may be some visual hallucinations, but the patient is fairly alert and lucid and can recognize the hallucinations as unreal at this stage, which usually peaks about twenty-four hours after drinking stops. Generalized convulsions resembling the grand mal form of epilepsy may occur soon after. The patient is unconscious, flails the arms and legs, and loses control over bladder and bowels.

The constellation of symptoms called delirium tremens appears two or more days after convulsions, about seventy-two to ninety-six hours after the individual has stopped drinking. The hallucinations are characteristically visual. The patient may behold all manner of small, strange, and terrifying animals, bugs, vegetation, or inanimate objects circling about. These inspire extreme fear which, in turn, spawns a pronounced agitation and hyperactivity. Victims will run about frantically in an effort to escape the frightening objects that pursue them. Auditory hallucinations are rare, so there is little difficulty in distinguishing delirium tremens from acute schizophrenic breakdown. Also in contrast to schizophrenia, individuals suffering delirium tremens are confused and disoriented. They do not know who or where they are, and they are truly delirious.

DT's occur only after heavy drinking for many weeks or months. This explains why many alcoholics who are forcibly deprived of their drug by being jailed may not develop DT's; they simply have not consumed enough alcohol over a long period. DT's can occur while an individual is still drinking, but this does not contradict the assertion that they are symptoms of withdrawal. Signs of abstinence occur in both animals and human beings after a decline in blood alcohol from previously higher levels; they do not require complete disappearance of alcohol from the blood (Ellis and Pick, 1970; Mello and Mendelson, 1978; Victor and Wolfe, 1973).

Recent research points toward the causes for specific symptoms of DT's. Magnesium is well known to diminish the excitability of neurons. Severe alcoholics have low blood magnesium levels. Victor and Wolfe (1973) showed that the tendency to develop convulsions, precipitated by shining a light at patients' faces, correlates inversely with serum magnesium levels. Alcoholics in whom photic stimulation elicits convulsions have lower blood magnesium levels than equally advanced alcoholics who do not react with convulsions. Moreover, those with a low magnesium level are more likely to go on to develop full-blown delirium tremens. Intravenous injections of magnesium sulfate can prevent the development of the light-induced seizures.

After they stop drinking, many alcoholics display withdrawal symptoms, including tremor, hallucinations, and even convulsions, but only about 5 percent of the alcoholics admitted to hospitals with obvious complications of alcoholism develop all the symptoms of delirium tremens. Of these, about 15 percent die, usually from the effects of overheating, heart failure, or by killing themselves in confusion and terror.

Alcohol and other central nervous system depressants, such as barbiturates and antianxiety drugs like diazepam (Valium) and chlordiazepoxide (Librium), are thought to act at similar sites in the brain. Withdrawal symptoms from barbiturates are essentially identical to alcoholic withdrawal symptoms. Moreover, there is cross-tolerance among all these drugs. If a person is tolerant to one of them he or she will also be tolerant to the others. Thus, one can suppress the withdrawal symptoms of a barbiturate addict with alcohol and those of an alcoholic with barbiturates or with antianxiety drugs such as Librium or Valium. Since these latter two drugs are safer than barbiturates, they have a major role in treating DT's. Intravenous fluids, replacing the vitamins and electrolytes such as magnesium that are lost or deranged in alcoholics, are an equally important part of the treatment.

Acute alcoholic hallucinosis

Like delirium tremens, acute hallucinosis appears after a heavy alcoholic binge and may represent a withdrawal reaction, though the evidence is not so clear as

with DT's. The major symptoms of acute hallucinosis are auditory hallucinations occurring in the presence of a clear sensorium. Patients hear voices which
are usually threatening, often accusing them of vile sexual acts. Unlike DT's,
the patients are not confused and remain fully aware of who and where they are.
Visual hallucinations are rare. Along with the auditory hallucinations, victims
develop delusions which seem designed to put the hallucinations into a conceptual framework that gives them some sort of meaning, such as an FBI or com-
munist plot against them. They are usually terrified of what is happening to
them, try to escape, and may even attempt suicide.

Hallucinosis can be easily mistaken for an acute schizophrenic breakdown.
Upon recovery from hallucinosis, however, patients usually display full insight
into what happened, which is uncommon in schizophrenia. Recovery takes
place over a period of about a week to a month. Individuals who continue to
experience auditory hallucinations and delusions may in fact have experienced
a schizophrenic breakdown.

Wernicke's and Korsakoff's psychosis

Because of their poor nutritional state, alcoholics suffer many debilities that are
primarily the result of vitamin deficiencies. Polyneuritis, an inflammation of the
peripheral nerves caused by vitamin B deficiency, is common in chronic alcoholics. Two psychoses are associated primarily with deficiency of thiamine (vitamin B_1): Wernicke's syndrome and Korsakoff's psychosis.

Wernicke's syndrome is technically referred to as "polioencephalitis hae-
morrhagica superior" because the brains of these patients at autopsy show evidence of hemorrhages into superior parts of the brain, including the thalamus
and mammillary bodies as well as the brain stem. Wernicke's syndrome begins
acutely with excitement, confusion, and frequently delirium. Over a period of
several days, patients typically develop double vision as hemorrhage and tissue
death begin to affect nuclei of the third and sixth cranial nerves in the brain
stem, which regulate eye movements. Memory is disturbed and sometimes patients become somnolent and stuporous before dying. About 16 percent of patients with Wernicke's syndrome die within a month of the appearance of
symptoms. Treatment with large doses of thiamine together with adequate general nutrition usually stabilizes patients, and often they recover their mental
functions (Victor and Adams, 1953).

Korsakoff's psychosis may be a less acute manifestation of brain changes
similar to those of Wernicke's syndrome. It also appears to result from vitamin
deficiency and can be at least partially reversed with thiamine. Sometimes patients recover from delirium tremens or acute hallucinosis and pass rapidly into

Korsakoff's psychosis, though the onset is usually more gradual. The major features are extreme memory defects. To compensate for memory loss, the patients confabulate to an extraordinary degree, fabricating farfetched, sometimes absurd stories in response to questions they are unable to answer factually. Patients display a great loss of introspection and judgment, tending to appear jovial despite a serious disability. They are very suggestible and incorporate events described by others into their own pseudo-reminiscences.

The extent to which a patient displays Wernicke's or Korsakoff's symptoms depends upon the areas of the brain involved. Korsakoff's symptoms tend to be associated with lesions in the cerebral cortex, while it is predominantly brain stem lesions that underlie Wernicke's symptoms.

Causes of alcoholism

Genetic factors

Drinking is certainly a learned behavior. Thus, whatever biological factors influence the development of alcoholism, environmental factors still must play a major and possibly an overriding role.

Adoption studies have provided impressive evidence for genetic determinants of the vulnerability to alcoholism. Adopted children with an alcoholic biological parent have twice the probability of developing alcoholism as adopted children whose biological parents are not alcoholic. Moreover, the likelihood of becoming an alcoholic is just as great for the biological child of an alcoholic adopted and raised by nonalcoholic parents as for children raised by their alcoholic biological parent (Goodwin, et al., 1973; Goodwin et al., 1974).

Twin studies have also provided evidence of genetic factors in alcoholism. If one of a pair of identical twins becomes alcoholic, the co-twin has a 50 percent chance of also becoming alcoholic. Fraternal twins, whose genetic makeup is no more similar than that of nontwin siblings, have a much lower concordance for alcoholism.

Though these studies indicate that genetics plays a role in making individuals vulnerable to alcoholism, the evidence is not as strong as for psychoses such as schizophrenia and manic-depressive illness.

Psychosocial factors

Drinking is thought by many to be a learned behavior reinforced by the ability of alcohol to reduce anxiety. Most people can attest to the lessening of anxiety and inhibitions associated with drinking. This effect of alcohol is readily demonstrated in animals. Like barbiturates and antianxiety drugs such as Valium, alcohol reduces an animal's fear of performing tasks which promise an electric shock along with food reward (Barry and Miller, 1962; Conger, 1951). In human beings, reduction of emotional tension by alcohol can be demonstrated by measuring the galvanic skin response (Wallgren and Barry, 1970). These studies have led to an anxiety-reduction model of alcoholism (Jellinek, 1960). According to this theory, alcoholics start out as "relief drinkers" using alcohol to ease tension, then drink more heavily as their situation in life grows more difficult and pressured, and finally are "hooked" when drinking becomes an end in itself.

Recent evidence that alcoholics become *more* anxious after they drink has cast doubt on this model (Mello and Mendelson, 1978). Nevertheless, it may be that before they become addicted, alcoholics-to-be derive pleasure and relief of tension from drinking. After becoming heavy drinkers, perhaps they lose control and continue to indulge even though it makes them feel worse.

Cross-cultural studies have also examined the tension-reduction hypothesis of drinking behavior. One would predict a greater incidence of alcoholism in societies with a high degree of conflict and tension. Surveys of different primitive societies tend to support this idea (Bacon, 1973). Hunting tribes have more alcoholism than agrarian communities. Because hunters must worry from day to day about where the next meal will come from and have many tense moments killing game, one could argue that theirs is an anxiety-laden culture compared with the more stable social structure of agricultural communities (Horton, 1943).

Among primitive societies studied by Bacon (1973), those with infrequent drunkenness and low consumption of alcohol generally:

1. Take care of the physical and emotional needs of their infants and children (indulge dependency needs).
2. Use, on the whole, permissive rather than punitive methods of socialization.
3. Exert relatively little socialization pressure toward achievement and independence.
4. Tolerate dependent behavior in adulthood.
5. Engage in communal eating.
6. Relate folk tales which tend to describe the world as essentially kind and friendly.

Thus, a stable social structure as well as tolerance of dependent behavior correlates with a low incidence of heavy drinking. These conclusions coincide with the work of McClelland and his colleagues (1972), who associate a need to drink with conflicts over assertiveness and dependency. Societies that are conducive to alcoholism "often put a man in a conflict situation in which he wants or is expected to be assertive and yet must be obedient. He responds by dreaming of solving the conflict by being powerful in a primitive, non-instrumental, impulsive way and finds in alcohol a means of promoting these dreams, of buying, at least temporarily, the strength he needs'' (McClelland et al., 1972).

This "need for power" hypothesis is supported by observations that alcoholics often behave in an expansive, pseudo-masculine way. Of course, such behavior might well be the consequence of alcohol addiction rather than its cause. Prospective studies in which individuals with particular personality characteristics are followed for several years before the onset of heavy drinking are more persuasive, and they suggest a different pattern. In one such study, men who became heavy drinkers were characterized in adolescence by impulsiveness, considerable sensitivity to criticism, and a lack of awareness as to how their behavior affects other people (Jones, 1968). Women who tend to become alcoholics differ somewhat. They don't display as much overbearing impulsiveness, tending instead to be shy, dependent, and irritable (Jones, 1968).

In summary, there is limited evidence that certain types of personalities are more vulnerable than others to alcoholism. Among men a possible indicator of future drinking problems is conflict between dependence and independence needs coupled with a tendency toward impulsivity. But because so many ill-defined sociocultural as well as biological factors apparently influence an individual's propensity toward heavy drinking, one cannot delineate an "alcoholic personality" that would be of any use in diagnosis.

Treatment

Conventional individual psychotherapy, especially of the insight-oriented, psychoanalytic type, has been notoriously unsuccessful in dealing with alcoholics. Many psychotherapists refuse to take on alcoholics as patients. The impulsive behavior of the alcoholic, like that of the sociopath, runs counter to the self-discipline required for success in intensive psychotherapy. Outcomes have been more favorable with directive approaches, either in a medical setting or in groups such as Alcoholics Anonymous.

Medical aspects

Treatment for alcohol withdrawal symptoms does not usually present major problems unless the patient is in an advanced stage, suffering from delirium tremens, Wernicke's, or Korsakoff's syndrome. Agitation and tremulousness can be relieved readily with the antianxiety drugs Librium and Valium. These agents have relatively little abuse potential, and even substantial doses carry no risk of excessive central nervous system depression. It is almost impossible to commit suicide with these drugs since massive doses only produce sleep for one or two days.

Disulfiram (Antabuse) is often useful in conditioning the patient to avoid alcohol. Disulfiram inhibits aldehyde hydrogenase, the enzyme that degrades acetaldehyde, which is the first breakdown product of ethyl alcohol. Thus, if an individual taking disulfiram also consumes alcohol, the blood levels of acetaldehyde rise rapidly. This produces marked nausea and lowers blood pressure, and symptoms can be violent symptoms. If enough alcohol is consumed, the lowered blood pressure may precipitate fatal shock, though this is unlikely to occur with the low daily doses currently used in treating alcoholics. Because the drug is excreted very slowly, a person is unable to tolerate alcohol for about four to five days after a dose.

The main difficulty with disulfiram treatment, as with all other methods of therapy for alcoholism, is that the patient must be motivated to continue to take the drug regularly. Few professionals experienced in the treatment of alcoholism recommend disulfiram as the sole method of treatment. Instead, patients taking the drug are urged to obtain additional psychosocial therapy, usually through Alcoholics Anonymous.

Alcoholics anonymous
There are many different approaches to individual and group psychotherapy with alcoholics. Because alcoholism affects such a large proportion of the working population, many large industrial concerns have developed specialized treatment programs. Most effective psychotherapeutic approaches incorporate principles developed by Alcoholics Anonymous.

Alcholics Anonymous was started by two alcoholics in Ohio in 1935 and spread rapidly through the nation and to many other countries; there are now about half a million members. The therapeutic program of AA depends largely on group sessions which are attended consistently two or more times a week. Meetings focus intensively on discussions of members' past or present problems with alcohol. They include frequent testimonials by recovered alcoholics describing the sharp contrast between life before and after joining AA.

A major tenet of AA philosophy is that even many years after terminating alcohol consumption, an individual is still an alcoholic, only now in remission. Members view alcoholism much like a congenital intolerance to a dietary constituent; for alcoholics it happens to be alcohol, while for other people it may be chocolate or seafood. It follows from this AA belief that recovered alcoholics should remain totally abstinent. Evidence from other quarters, however, indicates that a certain proportion, perhaps up to 30 percent of alcoholics, can return to social drinking without losing control again. The controversy over whether recovered alcoholics should ever drink socially is unresolved.

Several impartial evaluations of Alcoholics Anonymous attest to its efficacy in helping members recover from heavy drinking problems (Bacon, 1973; Leach, 1973; Leach et al., 1969). About 40 percent of those who join AA never drink again after their first attendance. About 25 percent drink sporadically but then become totally abstinent within a year, while another 20 percent have several relapses of heavy drinking but then are alcohol-free within two to five years after joining AA. No other form of therapy can match this record.

Nonetheless, these figures do not take into account the fact that many alcoholics attend only one or two meetings (hence are not technically members) and then drop out to return to heavy drinking. Despite the large membership of AA, it still represents less than 10 percent of the problem drinkers in the United States. Differences in personality between those who stay with AA and remain abstinent and those who drop out or do not enter have never been fully characterized. Some studies indicate that AA has the least success among alcoholics of low socioeconomic status and also among those who have major psychiatric disorders. In its first survey about five years after the organization was founded, an AA publication concluded, "Those who do not recover are people who cannot or will not completely give themselves to this simple program, usually men and women who are constitutionally incapable of being honest with themselves. There are such unfortunates. They are not at fault; they seem to have been born that way. They are naturally incapable of grasping and developing a manner of living which demands rigorous honesty" (Leach, 1973).

References

Bacon, M. K. Cross-cultural studies of drinking and alcoholism progress. In *Alcoholism: Progress in research and treatment,* eds. P. G. Bourne, and R. Fox, Academic Press, New York, 1973.

Barry, H., and Miller, N. E. Effects of drugs on approach-avoidance conflict tested repeatedly by means of a "telescope alley." *J. Comp. Physiol. Psych., 55:*201–210, 1962.

Calahan, D., and Cisin, I. H. American drinking practices: Summary of findings from the national probability sample. Extent of drinking by population subgroups. Q. J. Study of Alcohol, 29:130, 1968.

Calahan, D., and Cisin, I. H. Measurement of massed vs. spaced drinking. *Q. J. Study of Alcohol, 29:*642, 1968.

Chafetz, M. E. Alcoholism and alcoholic psychosis. In *Comprehensive textbook of psychiatry,* vol. 2 eds. A. M. Freedman, H. I. Kaplan, and B. J. Saddock. Williams and Wilkins, Baltimore, p. 1331, 1975.

Conger, J. J. The effects of alcohol on conflict behavior in the albino rat. *Q. J. Study of Alcohol, 12:*1–20, 1951.

Diagnostic and statistical manual of mental disorders, 2nd ed. American Psychiatric Association, Washington, D.C., p. 45, 1968.

Ellis, F. W., and Pick, J. R. Experimentally induced ethanol dependence on rhesus monkeys. *J. Pharmacol. Exp. Ther., 175:*88, 1970.

Glatt, M. M. Drinking habits of English (middle class) alcoholics. *Acta. Psychiat. Neurol. Scand., 37:*88, 1961.

Goodwin, D. W., Schulsinger, F., Hermansen, L., Guze, S. B., and Winokur, G. Alcohol problems in adoptees raised apart from alcoholic biological parents. *Arch. Gen. Psychiat., 28:*238–243, 1973.

Goodwin, D. W., Schulsinger, F., Moller, N., Hermansen, L., Winokur, G., and Guze, S. B. Drinking problems in adopted and nonadopted sons of alcoholics. *Arch. Gen. Psychiat., 31:*164–169, 1974.

Horton, D. The functions of alcohol in primitive societies: A cross-cultural study, *Q. J. Study of Alcohol, 4:*199, 1943.

Isbell, H., Fraser, H., Wikler, A., Belleville, R., and Eisenman, A. An experimental study of the etiology of rum fits and delirium tremens. *Q. J. Study of Alcohol. 16:*1, 1955.

Jellinek, E. M. The First (1943) Summer Session of the School of Alcohol Studies, Yale University, *Q. J. Study of Alcohol, 4:*187–194, 1943.

Jellinek, E. M. Phases of alcohol addiction. *Q. J. Study of Alcohol, 13:*673–678, 1952.

Jellinek, E. M. *The disease concept of alcoholism,* Hillhouse Press, New Haven, 1970.

Jones, N. C. Personality correlates and antecedents of drinking patterns in males. *J. Consult. and Clin. Psychol., 32:*2–12, 1968.

Leach, B., Norris, J. L., Dancy, T., and Bissel, L. Dimensions of Alcoholics Anonymous:1935–1965. *Int. J. Addictions, 4:*507–541, 1969.

Leach, L. Does Alcoholics Anonymous really work? In *Alcoholism: Progress in research and treatment,* eds. P. G. Bourne and R. Fox, Academic Press, New York, 1973, pp. 245–284.

McClelland, D. C. Davis, W., Kallin, R., and Warner. E. *The drinking man, alcohol and human motivation.* Free Press, New York, 1972.

Mello, N. K., and Mendelson, J. H. Alcohol and human behavior. In *Handbook of psychopharmacology,* vol. 12, eds. L. L. Iversen, S. D. Iversen and S. H. Snyder. Plenum Press, New York, 1978, pp. 235–317.

Pattison, E. A critique of alcoholism treatment concepts, with special reference to abstinence. *Q. J. Study of Alcohol, 27:*49–71, 1966.

Ray, O. S. *Drugs, society and human behavior.* C. V. Mosby Co., St. Louis, 1972, p. 90.

Victor, M. and Adams, R. D. The effect of alcohol on the nervous system. *Ass. Res. Nerv. and Ment. Disorder, 32:*526, 1953.

Victor, M. and Wolfe, S. M. Causation and treatment of the alcohol withdrawal syndrome. In *Alcoholism: Progress in research and treatment,* eds. P. G. Bourne and R. Fox. Academic Press, New York, 1974, pp. 137–169.

Wallgren, H., and Barry, H., III *Actions of alcohol, Vol. 1: Biochemical physiological and psychological aspects.* Elsevier, Amsterdam, 1970.

14. Organic brain disturbance: general features

The organic abnormalities of the brain are relevant to an understanding of psychopathology because emotional disturbances are often the most prominent symptoms in conditions as diverse as brain tumors, central nervous system syphilis, and degenerative disorders such as Huntington's Chorea. Professionals concerned with diagnosing emotional illness should be familiar with the various types of organic brain syndromes in order to avoid tragedies such as mistaking an individual with an early, operable brain tumor for a case of schizophrenia. Organic brain disease is also important from a theoretical perspective. Certain disturbances of feeling and thought occur consistently after damage to specific brain regions. Through an understanding of diverse forms of organic brain disturbance, one can gain insight into ways in which particular brain regions regulate diverse forms of emotional behavior.

The term *organic brain syndrome* is an imperfect one. It refers to mental disturbances that are presumed to stem from specific changes in the structure and function of the nervous system. This is in contrast to "functional" disorders such as schizophrenia and manic-depressive illness, in which no clearcut abnormality of the brain has yet been demonstrated. Of course, abundant genetic evidence indicates that many cases of schizophrenia and depression stem from specific biological vulnerabilities which may be just as definitely organic but are unknown. General paresis was thought to be functional, like schizophrenia, until specific changes in the brain were detected microscopically and the syphilis microorganism was demonstrated in patients' brains. Differentiating organic and functional behavioral disturbances is often difficult. Just as psychiatric symptoms occur in organic brain disease, individuals with functional psychosis often seem somewhat organic. For instance, individuals with acute mania, severe agitated depression, or acute schizophrenia may have clouded consciousness, which suggests brain damage (Langfeldt, 1960).

Organic brain syndromes may be acute or chronic. The acute type has a sudden onset, as the term implies; for example, delirium tremens of alcoholism is an acute brain syndrome. The principal sign of an acute brain syndrome is a clouding of consciousness, which is apparent either as reduced wakefulness, some confusion, or a combination of both. The former may be only drowsiness or it may progress to coma. In their confusion, patients misjudge things they perceive. Because of their mistaken perceptions, they readily form delusions, which sometimes resemble the delusions of schizophrenics. Visual illusions—mistaking one thing for another—and hallucinations—seeing things that aren't there—are prominent features of the acute brain syndrome. Because victims fail to integrate what they perceive in a meaningful way, they tend to forget whatever has happened while they were disturbed. Their sensory thresholds are lowered so that they become excitable and may be so startled by ordinary occurrences that they fall into a state of terror.

Whereas a mild organic disturbance may provoke only some clouding of consciousness, persons with more severe disturbances become delirious. The hallmark of delirium is a loss of orientation for time and place. Patients are sufficiently confused that they tend to deal mostly with imaginary experiences. They become restless, hyperactive, and frequently will run about the room in agitated terror.

With the more gradual onset of chronic brain syndrome, neither extreme delirium nor more profound clouding of consciousness develops. Whereas patients with acute brain syndrome have similar symptoms regardless of the site of the lesion, those with chronic disturbances have more clearly delineated clinical patterns that often indicate the specific part of the brain which has suffered injury.

A diagnosis of organic brain disturbance is established by the characteristic abnormalities in memory and intellectual functioning and, at later stages, by the loss of orientation for time, person, and place. However, these intellectual defects are often preceded by emotional changes that mimic functional disturbances.

Mild, moderate, and sometimes even severe depressive symptoms may be the harbingers of a progressive brain deterioration. They seem to arise from loss of the individual's mental capacity to seek new challenges and human relationships. The lack of aspiration often progresses to a state of apathy. On the other hand, many patients display a labile emotionality. Crying or laughing can be provoked by seemingly trivial events. The most minor frustration will trigger a reaction of rage. Individuals become impulsive and will sometimes commit antisocial acts.

The suspicion that an organic brain disturbance is involved should be aroused by such emotional changes in a person who has been stable and well adjusted for many years.

Adaptation to intellectual impairment

Kurt Goldstein (1948) described in careful detail how brain-damaged individuals attempt to compensate for their impairment. Lacking the ability to deal with their environment in abstract intellectual terms, patients operate in a "concrete" manner. For instance, they may be able to "Use scissors, open a door with a key or smoke a cigarette, but when asked to mimic the movements required for any of these tasks, they are completely at a loss" (Slater and Roth, 1969). Patients try to organize everything in their life in a stereotyped, meticulous way and become agitated by any interference with their "organic orderliness." The normally chaotic behavior of small children is particularly vexing to brain-damaged adults.

One manifestation of this concreteness is an inability to shift from one item to another. Patients seem bound to particular stimuli, but not in the way that normal people concentrate on what interests them. At the same time that they seem fixated on a stimulus, failing to divert their attention to something that is clearly more important, patients are nonetheless distracted by irrelevancies.

Brain-damaged persons are easily overwhelmed by intellectual stresses. When confronted with problems they cannot handle, sometimes as uncomplicated as simple arithmetic, individuals may have a castastrophic reaction, becoming agitated, violently angry, and bursting into tears. To defend themselves from such reactions, victims tend to organize their environments in ways that avoid complexity. They may become socially withdrawn or may set for themselves a schedule of diverting frantic activity, much of it meaningless.

Effects of damage to specific brain regions

For many years researchers have debated whether the symptoms of organic brain syndrome depend on the location of the lesion in the brain or the amount of tissue damaged. Probably both are important as well as the nature of the disease process itself, whether infection, tumor, or trauma. The extensive redundancy of neural circuits throughout the brain was highlighted years ago by the classic experiments of Karl Lashley (1929). Lashley showed that the extent of performance deficit in rodents was strictly dependent on the mass of tissue excised. The same deficit followed removal of a given weight of brain substance regardless of which cerebral region was lesioned. Chapman and Wolff (1959) evaluated intellectual deficiency in human beings after surgery for brain tumors. They found that losses of memory and orientation tended to depend upon the weight of brain tissue removed regardless of its location. When less than 120 grams of brain were removed, these intellectual functions remained intact, though patients still suffered the emotional disturbances associated with brain damage.

Frontal lobes

The frontal lobes are more extensively developed in humanity than in any other species. Of all parts of the brain which advance throughout evolution, the frontal lobes show the most significant changes in size and complexity as one ascends from lower mammals through monkeys and other primates to humanity.

The motor functions of the frontal lobes are straight-forward. The prominent corticospinal pathway originates in the large pyramidal neurons whose cells are in the motor area of the frontal lobes just anterior to the central sulcus (Figure 14.1). Damage to this pathway in patients suffering a stroke accounts for the typical paralysis of muscles of the face and limbs. Other portions of the frontal lobes located almost exclusively in the dominant hermisphere (left side in both right-handed and left-handed individuals) are concerned with speech formation. Lesions in this area result in impairment of speech, either its motor components (output), the ability to comprehend speech (input), or both.

The functions of the frontal lobes of greatest interest for psychopathology involve sites which are distinct from the motor and speech areas. The frontal lobes enable people to coordinate their feelings, perceptions, and thoughts in planning effective future action, essentially the most "human" of brain activities. Such functions are relatively subtle and difficult to pinpoint in conventional experiments on animals. Nor do studies of human beings who have suffered frontal lobe damage always provide a clear picture. Indeed, in some tests of psychological performance very little impairment can be detected in patients with frontal lobe injuries. Nonetheless, there is now a general consensus as to the kinds of behavior that are regulated by the frontal lobes, an area regarded as "that part of the brain which quickly and effectively orients and drives the individual, with all his percepts and concepts formed from past life experiences, toward action that is projected into the future" (Adams and Victor, 1977).

Early studies of the influence of frontal lobe removal in chimpanzees showed changes in apparent personality characteristics. The lesioned chimps seemed abnormally tame and socially indifferent, with some tendency to forget and a limited loss of problem-solving abilities. These types of alterations suggested that removal of the frontal lobes might lessen the abnormal behavior patterns of schizophrenics, severe depressives, and obsessive patients. Accordingly, in the 1940s and early 1950s thousands of psychiatric patients were subjected to frontal lobotomies. Whether symptomatic improvement was ever sufficient to justify this form of psychosurgery is dubious, though Egon Moniz received the Nobel prize in 1949 for its development. The large number of patients who underwent this operation provided abundant data to permit inferences about frontal lobe functions.

Typically, these patients and others with frontal lobe damage show a lessening of aggression and anxiety that goes along with a diminished concern over the consequences of their actions. Patients seem to lose control over their emotional expression and often behave with an inappropriate kind of jocularity. Previously reserved individuals may begin to tell bawdy stories. Patients may be boastful and grandiose or "incontinent" of their emotions, sometimes laughing and then crying in short succession after negligible provocation. Such emotional reactions seem unrelated to genuine feelings. Despite the display of emotionality, patients' sensibilities are shallow and blunted. This pattern of behavior occurs quite dramatically in patients with brain syphilis, a disease in which damage tends to be greatest in the frontal regions.

Frontal lobe patients show a slight impairment of intelligence, which is most apparent in tasks requiring concentration. Their attention wanders, and they appear unable to carry out planned activities or to shift from one task to another. Initiative is impaired and in general so are most mental processes. In extreme cases, patients are virtually mute.

Temporal lobes

The temporal lobes have long been known to mediate specific sensations, especially audition. The upper portion of the temporal lobe, buried within the Sylvian sulcus and referred to as the *transverse gyrus of Heschl,* is a crucial auditory receptive zone. Individuals with lesions here become deaf. Damage to other parts of the temporal lobe does not result in deafness but may impair the integration of auditory information, indicating that these areas are secondary processing centers for information about sound. Some lesions can produce "psychic deafness," in which auditory acuity is preserved but the patient can't recognize what is presented. Interestingly, the processing of information about words and other sounds differs. Some patients with temporal lobe lesions can't recognize music—*amusia*—while others do well with music but have difficulty recognizing words.

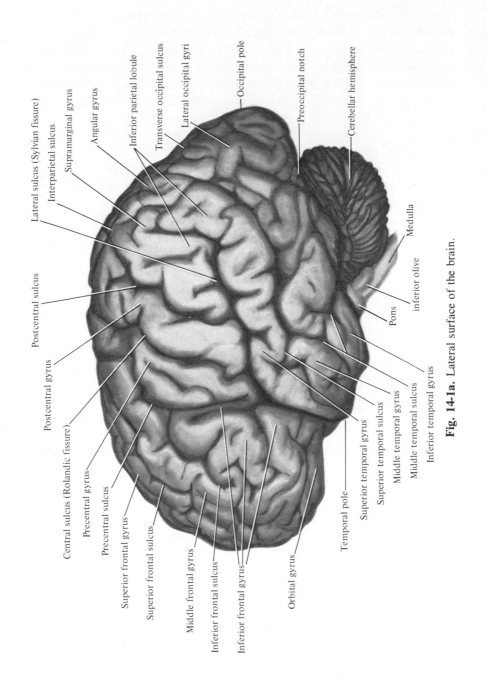

Fig. 14-1a. Lateral surface of the brain.

Lateral sulcus (Sylvian fissure)
Interparietal sulcus
Supramarginal gyrus
Angular gyrus
Inferior parietal lobule
Transverse occipital sulcus
Lateral occipital gyri
Occipital pole
Preoccipital notch
Cerebellar hemisphere

Postcentral sulcus
Postcentral gyrus
Central sulcus (Rolandic fissure)
Precentral gyrus
Precentral sulcus
Superior frontal gyrus
Superior frontal sulcus
Middle frontal gyrus
Inferior frontal sulcus
Inferior frontal gyrus
Orbital gyrus

Medulla
inferior olive
Pons

Temporal pole
Superior temporal gyrus
Superior temporal sulcus
Middle temporal gyrus
Middle temporal sulcus
Inferior temporal gyrus

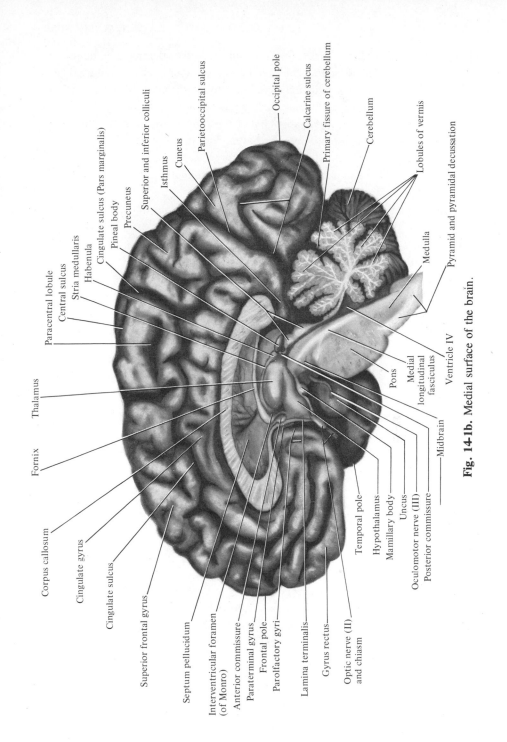

Corpus callosum

Fornix

Thalamus

Cingulate gyrus

Cingulate sulcus

Superior frontal gyrus

Septum pellucidum

Interventricular foramen
(of Monro)

Anterior commissure

Paraterminal gyrus

Frontal pole

Parolfactory gyri

Lamina terminalis

Gyrus rectus

Optic nerve (II)
and chiasm

Paracentral lobule

Central sulcus

Stria medullaris

Habenula

Cingulate sulcus (Pars marginalis)

Pineal body

Precuneus

Superior and inferior colliculi

Isthmus

Cuneus

Parietooccipital sulcus

Occipital pole

Calcarine sulcus

Primary fissure of cerebellum

Cerebellum

Lobules of vermis

Medulla

Pyramid and pyramidal decussation

Ventricle IV

Pons

Medial
longitudinal
fasciculus

Midbrain

Posterior commissure

Oculomotor nerve (III)

Uncus

Mamillary body

Hypothalamus

Temporal pole

Fig. 14-1b. Medial surface of the brain.

Distortions of auditory perception also accompany temporal lobe abnormalities. In some instances, sounds may be heard more loudly or less loudly than is normal. Some words or sounds may seem peculiarly disagreeable to the patient. Often words seem to repeat themselves. These auditory illusions may progress to hallucinations. Frequently elementary sounds are heard, such as pure tones, whistles, or clangs. Alternatively, the hallucinations are of musical themes or voices. In *temporal lobe epilepsy,* the auditory hallucinations may be indistinguishable from those of schizophrenics and the epileptic may be convinced of their reality.

The temporal lobes also play a role in visual perception, though they are less important in this regard than the occipital lobes. Some lesions of the temporal lobe produce a visual field defect in which the victim cannot see objects in the upper contralateral quadrant of the visual field.

The *hippocampus,* a portion of the temporal lobe, is one of the most crucial parts of the brain in regulating memory, especially the consolidation of immediate events into long-term memory. Patients with bilateral hippocampal lesions can remember a grocery list only if they keep repeating it to themselves. If they are distracted for a minute, all is forgotten.

Parietal and occipital lobes

The parietal lobes are usually regarded as higher-order integrators of sensory information, crossing the boundaries between the modalities of vision, touch, and hearing, but with special emphasis on tactile and visual information processing.

Lesions of the parietal lobes don't cause direct sensory loss. Thus, the sense of touch as well as sensitivity to heat, pain, and vibration are preserved. However, the patient cannot put this information together when making efforts to recognize the shape of presented objects. The resulting defect is called *astereognosis.*

Since our awareness of our own body image and our relationship to other objects in space requires an appreciation of spatial relations, it is not surprising that patients with temporal lobe defects experience abnormalities of body image perception. Many patients with cerebral strokes that cause paralysis and also affect the parietal lobes seem indifferent to or unaware of their paralysis. Some patients will admit only to a slight weakness, despite total paralysis. Others will deny that the affected limb belongs to themselves. Patients with a lesion of one temporal lobe will neglect totally one side of their body, failing to dress or groom the affected side.

Some neurologists have speculated that more global disturbances of self-awareness may reflect parietal lobe dysfunction (Adams and Victor, 1977). The depersonalizatin that occurs in drug-induced or psychotic states might conceivably involve an inability of the patient to place the self in space. When schizophrenics or severe depressives deny that they exist, their behavior is reminiscent of patients with disturbed parietal lobe function who refuse to recognize part of their body.

The occipital lobes are primarily, if not exclusively, concerned with visual perception. In this sense they are "purer" in their role than other areas of the cerebral cortex which subserve multiple activities. When the occipital area is damaged on one side, the patient experiences a loss of vision in a specific visual field. Destruction of both occipital lobes results in total blindness. This blindness can be as complete as that which occurs when both eyes are removed. In this sense, the occipital cortex is more directly involved in immediate sensory perception than any other part of the cerebral cortex. Incomplete occipital lesions produce a partial loss of sight that is often associated with other visual abnormalities. Illusions and hallucinations are common. The hallucinations may be elementary ones of dots of light, colors, stars, or geometric patterns. The hallucinated objects may be stationary or may zigzag, pulsate, or oscillate. Complex hallucinations involve all manner of objects, people, or landscapes with intricate scenery. As with the auditory hallucinations associated with temporal lobe abnormalities, visual hallucinations following occipital lobe injury may be recognized by the patient as false perceptions or they may be taken for real.

References

Adams, R. D., and Victor, M. *Principles of neurology*. McGraw-Hill, New York, 1977, p. 288.

Chapman, L. F., and Wolff, H. G. the cerebral hemispheres and the highest integrative functions of man. *Arch. Neurol., 1:*357, 1959.

Goldstein, K. *Aftereffects of brain injuries in war: Their evaluation and treatment*. Grune and Stratton, New York, 1948.

Langfeldt, G. Diagnosis and prognosis of schizophrenia. *Proc. Royal Soc. Med., 53:*1047, 1960.

Lashley, K. *Brain mechanisms and intelligence*. University of Chicago Press, Chicago, 1929.

Slater, E., and Roth, M. *Clinical psychiatry*. Williams and Wilkins, Baltimore, 1969, p. 490.

15. Age-related mental deterioration

All people undergo some intellectual deterioration with age. The psychopathologist's task is to discriminate between the normal aging process and clinically serious alterations, sometimes a subtle distinction. The most obvious change in mental functioning of elderly people is their loss of memory. Generally they lose the capacity to recall recent events, while memories of childhood or emotionally significant events in young adulthood remain intact. The elderly tend to become somewhat rigid and dogmatic, because it is difficult for them to assimilate novel ideas. Numerous studies of intellectual functioning in the aged have emphasized the difficulties they experience in developing innovative concepts despite the fact that their judgment and good sense may be superior to that of younger and mentally more facile persons. As they age, some people become emotionally constricted in their outlook on life and lose all sexual interest. Others maintain an active sex life and use their retirement years to explore new interests or to revive old hobbies.

In certain ways the senile dementias and psychoses are merely accentuations of the normal aging process, but there are some notable differences. Emotional and intellectual disturbances severe enough to warrant hospitalization are surprisingly frequent in the aged. About 0.6 to 0.8 percent of the general population suffers from *senile psychosis,* a frequency approaching the incidence of schizophrenia. As the proportion of elderly individuals in the population continues to increase, this incidence will probably also rise.

Age-related mental deterioration is one of our major public health problems. About 4 to 5 percent of the 25 million Americans over sixty-five qualify for a diagnosis of senile dementia (Butler, 1978). It is well established that age-related dementias are associated with a markedly shortened life expectancy, reduced from an average of sixteen years in most men and women aged sixty-five to only about five years. From these statistics, it appears that 100,000 to 200,000 deaths each year in the United States result from senile dementia.

At least two distinct types of brain alterations are associated with mental deterioration among the aged. One is the death of brain tissue following a loss of blood supply associated with cerebral arteriosclerosis that usually results from a stroke. The other consists of degenerative changes in brain tissue that frequently correlate with the aging process but for which there is no known cause. Such changes are referred to simply as "senile" pathology, and the corresponding clinical picture is called *senile dementia*. A similar clinical entity occurs in middle-aged persons and is called *presenile dementia*.

Senile dementia

The major features of senile dementia include an overall decline in intellectual performance and specific disturbances of memory. Personal habits deteriorate and emotions become either labile or blunted. Since these clinical features seem like an accentuation of normal aging processes, many investigators have questioned whether a genuine entity of senile dementia exists or whether it is merely one pole of the normal distribution curve of elderly people.

The evidence for genetic factors in senile dementia is consistent with the view that it is a genuine disease entity. In the classic twin studies of Kallman (1951), there was only an 8 percent concordance rate for senile dementia in fraternal (dizygotic) twins, while the concordance rate for identical (monozygotic) twins was 43 percent. Family studies also indicate a genetic component in determining the vulnerability to senile dementia. The risk of developing senile dementia among children, siblings, spouses, and parents of afflicted individuals is about four times greater than the risk in the general population. By contrast, there is no enhanced risk for any other form of psychosis in these families (Kallman, 1951; Larsson et al., 1963).

One question that can be addressed by genetic studies is whether senile and presenile dementia represent distinct disease entities rather than the same condition which varies in age of onset. Several workers have examined the incidence of senile and presenile dementia in relatives of patients with presenile dementia (Akesson, 1969; Larsson et al., 1963; Slater and Cowie, 1971). The incidence of presenile dementia is greatly elevated in these relatives, but there also is some increase in the frequency of senile dementia. Thus, there may be a genetic association between the two conditions, though this question is still not fully resolved.

Several workers have attempted to discern the mode of inheritance of the dementias (Heston, 1977). Though all have obtained similar findings indicating a strong genetic component, interpretations vary. One view is that both senile and presenile dementias are inherited as autosomal dominant traits (Larsson et al., 1963); another is that multiple genes determine the dementias in the same way that they regulate the inheritance of intelligence and diabetes.

If senile dementia is a polygenic disorder, then the disposition to develop dementia is present to varying degrees in a major portion of the population and may account for the commonplace observation that while some people preserve all their mental faculties unimpaired to the age of ninety, others who are not clinically demented still seem notably slowed by the time they are sixty. To investigate what might account for such variability, Kallman and collaborators initiated an extensive longitudinal study of 134 normal twins (Jarvik, 1978; Jarvik et al., 1972; Kallman and Sander, 1949). Their fate suggests that genetic factors are responsible, at least in part, for intellectual changes with age even in normal subjects. For instance, identical twins tended to remain more similar in intellectual functioning than fraternal twins even after having been out of school for at least forty years.

The well-known reduction of life expectancy for individuals with dementia has its counterpart in the normal population. Those who were still alive thirty years after initiation of the Kallman study had performed better than the nonsurvivors on cognitive tests given when the study commenced. At that earlier time, survivors and nonsurvivors did not differ in physical health.

The researchers also obtained evidence for a role of emotional factors in determining physical survival. They found that "critical loss" of a loved one, a home, or financial stability was related to a shortened lifespan. Among eleven twin pairs, all the twin partners who died first had suffered such a critical loss, whereas none of their co-twins who survived longer had undergone this kind of loss.

Brains of individuals with senile dementia show clear-cut abnormalities, though their source is unknown. There is degeneration in parts of the cerebral cortex; a loss of nerve cells is apparent, and the remaining cells are shrunken. Most characteristic are the "senile plaques," circular or star-shaped structures that seem like cerebral "scars" incorporating fragments of dead nerve and glial cells. Analysis of the number of these plaques in brain tissue has provided a means of assessing the relationship between brain damage and psychological impairment as well as the relationship of senile dementia to the normal aging process (Blessed et al., 1968; Roth et al., 1967). In one study, a large number of patients admitted to hospitals with either psychiatric or physical disorders were given psychometric tests of intelligence. The brains of those who subsequently died were analyzed for the frequency of senile plaques. There was a highly significant correlation between decrements of intellectual performance and the incidence of plaques both in patients with senile dementia and in those who had no psychiatric diagnosis. These findings suggest that the pathology of senile dementia lies on a continuum with normal aging of the brain.

Most cases of senile dementia begin after the age of seventy. Defects of memory are the first symptoms, usually involving a marked loss of recall for recent events even though childhood memories seem intact. At about the same time or soon thereafter, patients become less enthusiastic about their activities and their emotional responses seem blunted. Once the first symptoms make their appearance, the disease usually progresses fairly rapidly. At first, individuals will attempt to compensate for their disturbance by adopting rigid, inflexible regimens of routine behavior and by speaking in clichés. After a period of time these defensive maneuvers fail, and the person's conversation becomes inappropriate and ultimately incoherent. Patients experience delusions, which represent their endeavors to give some meaningful framework to their confusion and disorientation. Often they lose control of their bladder and bowels.

For reasons which are unclear, there is a preponderance of women among senile dementia patients.

Presenile dementia

Symptoms like those of senile dementia afflict individuals as young as forty, who are, therefore, diagnosed as having *presenile dementia.* In the most common form of presenile dementia, *Alzheimer's disease,* pathological changes in the brain are essentially the same as those of sentile dementia, though somewhat more severe. Alzheimer's disease affects about 0.1% of the population, which means that its incidence is about one-tenth that of senile dementia. Like senile dementia, Alzheimer's disease has a genetic component. There seem to be at least two genetic forms of the condition. A substantial number of cases occur in families in which every affected person has an affected parent and in which 50 percent of children are affected, with the same frequency in males and females. For these patients the disease appears to be inherited according to an autosomal dominant pattern. In most cases, however, families fail to display an extremely high incidence of dementia and the disorder appears to be determined by multiple genes.

Though the symptoms of Alzheimer's disease are similar to those of senile dementia, they are more severe and there are some definite differences. At an early stage patients will confabulate—that is, fabricate elaborate false stories in an effort to conceal their disturbance. Major involvement of the temporal and parietal lobes of the brain impairs the ability to perform complex motions and to understand the significance of statements by others or of objects perceived in the environment. Frequently, patients have symptoms resembling those of Parkinson's disease, exhibiting marked muscular rigidity and peculiar puppetlike movements. At later stages, victims decline into a vegetative state and either cannot talk at all or utter only meaningless words and phrases.

Pick's disease is a much less common form of presenile dementia than Alzheimer's disease. It too has a genetic basis and apparently is related to a dominant autosomal gene. The brain damage is somewhat selective, being most prominent in the frontal and to a lesser extent the temporal lobes. Microscopically, there is wide destruction of nerve cells and an overgrowth of glial cells to replace them. The senile plaques of Alzheimer's disease are not apparent.

The symptoms of Pick's disease differ from those of Alzheimer's disease in the same way that the regional pathology in the brain differs. Whereas the parietal lobe abnormalities in Alzheimer's disease give rise to difficulties in comprehending speech and spatial relationships, the frontal lobe damage of Pick's disease causes deficits in emotional regulation resembling those of brain syphilis. Patients with Pick's disease lose insight and self-restraint. Among the first symptoms may be the telling of bawdy tales in polite company. Even at a stage when memory and general intellect are intact, patients display an empty facial expression and a foolish smile.

Cerebral arteriosclerosis

To a certain extent, the factors underlying mental symptoms in patients with cerebral arteriosclerosis are fairly straightforward. About half of the patients have definite high blood pressure, which should predispose to arteriosclerosis. However, one cannot readily predict the extent of cerebral arteriosclerosis from the condition of peripheral blood vessels. Even the degree of involvement of retinal arteries does not correlate with that of cerebral vessels. However, pathologists have found a surprisingly close parallel relationship between the status of blood vessels in the kidney and brain.

Psychosis and dementia due to arteriosclerosis usually appear only after a series of strokes, which are technically referred to as *cerebrovascular accidents* (*CVA*). The two major types of CVA's are thrombosis and hemorrhage. A cerebral thrombosis is very much like a coronary thrombosis. A blood clot lodges in one of the medium-sized or small cerebral arteries; areas of brain tissue supplied by the vessel die and do not regenerate. Hemorrhage is due to the bursting of a small cerebral artery, usually secondary to hypertension.

The nature of a patient's symptoms depends, to some extent, on the location of the CVA. However, there are certain common characteristics. Among the first symptoms are headaches, very brief blackouts, and some dizziness. Patients' personality traits are exaggerated, and they tend to be hyperemotional. Only later does memory begin to deteriorate. Patients will then have difficulty concentrating and grasping new situations.

In contrast to senile dementia, patients with arteriosclerosis generally retain their personality structure and sound judgment until advanced stages of the disease. They often possess excellent insight into the nature of their condition, and as a result they are somewhat more depressed than patients with senile dementia.

After nerve cells die in one area of the brain, those in another will usually take over the lost function. Following a CVA, therefore, a person's intellectual and motor functions can return. And for the same reason the symptoms of cerebral arteriosclerosis fluctuate considerably. Patients who have reached a state of confusion may undergo striking remissions and subsequently perform well in their jobs for fairly long periods of time. On the other hand, at a very early stage with negligible overall impairment, individuals sometimes have attacks of acute delirium and lose contact with their surroundings almost completely. These symptoms of delirium usually clear in a few days or weeks.

Despite such vicissitudes, the overall course in cerebral arteriosclerosis is downhill, as it is in presenile and senile dementia. Still, concerted efforts to rehabilitate these patients socially, intellectually, and physically can result in several additional years of meaningful, rewarding life.

Differentiating arteriosclerotic changes and senile dementia

Before the 1950s it was generally assumed that everyone developed cerebral arteriosclerosis, with aging to a greater or lesser extent, and that this accounted for the intellectual deterioration commonly observed in elderly people. It is now clear that cerebral arteriosclerosis and senile dementia are distinct entities. Contrary to earlier assumptions, arteriosclerosis is much less common than senile dementia, which accounts for 80 percent of all hospitalized demented patients. Since the prognosis for senile dementia and cerebral arteriosclerosis may differ, it is important to distinguish the two conditions.

As already discussed, the neuropathology of the two diseases differs considerably (Tomlinson et al., 1970). There are also clinical differences. Senile dementia is substantially more common in women than men, while the reverse is true for arteriosclerosis. Since arteriosclerotic brain changes follow vascular strokes, they are usually heralded by the fairly sudden appearance of isolated

psychological deficits such as difficulty in recognizing objects or in comprehending speech. By contrast, senile dementia develops gradually without local-
izing signs.

As vascular clots or hemorrhages subside, the symptoms of cerebral arteriosclerosis may improve, at least for a while. This waxing and waning with
occasional episodes of abrupt clouding of consciousness is not usually seen in
senile dementia. Additionally, emotional changes are more frequent with cerebral arteriosclerosis than dementia. On the other hand, except for some lability
and a tendency to depression, patients with cerebral arteriosclerosis have a better preserved personality structure than senile demented individuals. The personal habits and demeanor of arteriosclerotics are generally more socially appropriate so that they can function within the community and avoid
institutionalization for a reasonably long period of time (Roth, 1978).

Relationship of dementias and affective disorders

One of the hallmarks of functional mental illness, such as schizophrenia and the
affective disorders, is that the patients display no signs of organic brain disorder. Nevertheless, researchers have noted in recent years that some severely
depressed patients display symptoms which are almost indistinguishable from
those of dementia (McHugh and Folstein, 1979). About 15 to 20 percent of elderly depressed patients suffer cognitive impairment resembling that of dementia. Most frequently these individuals become confused as to exactly where
they are, what time it is, and who is in their environment. Their memory for
recent events is impaired, and they give inappropriate answers to questions.
Their scores on standard intelligence tests are low (Steinberg and Jarvik, 1976;
Stromgrem, 1977).

Some psychiatrists have labeled this disorder a *pseudo-dementia* and have attributed it to the emotional distractedness of depressed individuals. If emotional
distress and distraction were the sole causes, young depressed patients should
appear just as demented as older individuals. But this "dementia" of the
depressed is apparent only in elderly patients. Moreover, the symptoms mimic
true dementia so faithfully that experienced clinicians cannot distinguish the
two conditions by the nature of the intellectual impairment alone. However, it
is clear that brain changes responsible for the depression also account for the
associated intellectual deterioration. The dementia of depressed patients clears
promptly when depressive symptoms are relieved by traditional antidepressant
medication, whereas these drugs are ineffective in conventional senile dementia.

Clinically, one can usually differentiate the dementia associated with depression from irreversible senile dementia by observing the patient's affective symptoms. Though patients with senile dementia are somewhat dejected, they usually do not manifest the extreme apathy, self-denigration, insomnia, and hopelessness of the truly depressed. Sometimes, however, the dementia symptoms of the depressed individual may be sufficiently extreme that they obscure the affective components of the disorder. If the patient has a history of earlier manic or depressive episodes, the primary disturbance is more likely affective. And if the dementia has had a fairly rapid onset coincident with affective symptoms, this increases the likelihood that depression is the correct diagnosis.

A mixed condition of serious depression and dementia due to cerebral arteriosclerosis or senile dementia often presents life-threatening clinical problems. This occurs in about 20 percent of patients with arteriosclerotic dementia and less often in those with senile dementia. The depressive symptoms then cause the dementia itself to worsen. Of greatest concern is the high suicidal risk for these individuals. It is well established that suicidal propensities increase markedly when severe depression develops in the presence of organic brain disturbance, whether caused by dementia, epilepsy, or chronic alcoholism.

References

Akesson, H. O. A population study of senile and arteriosclerotic psychoses. *Human Hered., 19:*546–566, 1969.

Blessed, G., Tomlinson, B. E., and Roth, M. The association between quantitative measures of dementia and of degenerative changes in the cerebral gray matter of elderly subjects. *Br. J. Psychiat., 114:*797, 1968.

Butler, R. N. Alzheimer's disease—senile dementia and related disorders: The role of NIA. In *Alzheimer's disease: Senile dementia and related disorders,* eds. R. Katz- man, R. D. Terry, and K. L. Bick, Raven Press, New York, 1978, pp. 5–9.

Heston, L. L. Alzheimer's disease, Trisomy 21 and myeloproliferative disorders: Associations suggesting a genetic diathesis. *Science, 196:*322–323, 1977.

Jarvik, K. F., Blum J. E., and Varma, A. O. Genetic components and intellectual functioning during senescence; 20 year study of aging twins. *Behav. Genet., 2:*159–171, 1972.

Jarvik, L. Genetic factors and chromosomal aberrations in Alzheimer's disease, senile dementia and related disorders. In *Alzheimer's disease: Senile dementia and related disorders,* eds. R. Katzman, R. D. Terry, and K. L. Bick, Raven Press, New York, 1978, pp. 272–277.

Kallman, F. J. Comparative adaptation, social and psychometric data on life histories of senescent twin pairs. *Am. J. Human Genet., 3:*65, 1951.

Kallman, F. J., and Sander, G. Twin studies on senescence. *Am. J. Psychiat. 106:*29–36, 1949.

Larsson, T., Sjogren, T., and Jacobson, G. Senile dementia. *Acta Psychiat. Scand. 39,* suppl. 167, 1963.

McHugh, P. R., and Folstein, M. F. Psychopathology of dementia: Implications for neuropathology. In *Cogenital and acquired cognitive disorders,* ed. R. Katzman. Raven Press, New York, 1979, pp. 17–30.

Roth, M. Diagnosis of senile and related forms of dementia. In *Alzheimer's disease: Senile dementia and related disorders,* eds. R. Katzman, R. D. Terry, and K. L. Bick. Raven Press, New York, 1978, pp. 71–86.

Roth, M., Tomlinson, B. E., and Blessed, G. The relationship between quantitative measures of dementia and of degenerative changes in the cerebral gray matter of elderly subjects. *Proc. Royal Soc. Med. 60:*254, 1967.

Slater, E., and Cowie, V. *The genetics of mental disorders.* Oxford University Press, London, 1971.

Steinberg, D. E., and Jarvik, M. E. Memory functions in depression. *Arch. Gen. Psychiat., 33:*219–244, 1976.

Stromgrem, L. S. Memory and depression. *Acta Psychiat. Scand., 56:*109–128, 1977.

Tomlinson, B. E., Blessed, G., and Roth, M. Observations on the brains of demented old people. *J. Neurol. Sci., 2:*205–274, 1970.

16. Brain syphilis

Syphilis can affect every organ of the body; and so, before the advent of penicillin for its treatment, medical students were taught that "If you understand all the manifestations of syphilis, then you know all of medicine." Even now, syphilis provides a model of how some forms of emotional disorder may derive from specific biological disturbances. Until the early twentieth century, general paralysis of the insane, the end product of syphilitic invasion of the central nervous system, was classified as a mental or emotional affliction; it was the province of psychiatrists, not bacteriologists.

Though syphilitic infection itself was well recognized 500 years ago, only in the early 1900s was the infection found to be the cause of general paralysis, also called general paresis. Up to a third of all patients in mental hospitals suffered from this condition, so the discovery of the responsible microorganism and its treatment with penicillin may be regarded as one of the great therapeutic advances in psychiatry.

Symptoms and mechanisms of syphilitic infection

Even though syphilis can be readily treated, each year in the United States about one million new cases go without treatment. In several of its stages, syphilis can be asymptomatic for long periods of time, only to emerge later, producing serious, irreversible damage throughout the body.

The syphilis microorganism is much larger than most bacteria; it is referred to as a spirochete, specifically *Treponema pallidum*. Because *Treponema palli-*

dum is readily killed by soap, drying, and heat, syphilis is not spread by coughing, sneezing, or by contact with objects handled by an infected person. The organism is most commonly transmitted by direct contact with moist body surfaces of infected individuals, usually mucus membrances of their sexual organs. The spirochete can penetrate wet skin through a scratch and can also penetrate an intact mucus membrane. Sexual intercourse, kissing, and biting are the most common means of spread.

After a spirochete has entered the body, it passes through the lymphatic channels to lymph nodes, from which it enters the blood stream and then moves rapidly through the body. Once lodged in body tissues, the spirochete may lie dormant for long periods, sometimes up to forty years. The first manifestation of the disease is a hard ulcer or pimple at the site where the organism entered the body. This diagnostic *chancre* makes its appearance about three to five weeks after infection and, even in the absence of treatment, it disappears within a month so that the patient may assume he or she is cured.

The chancre stage is referred to as *primary syphilis*. Six weeks after the appearance of the chancre, *secondary syphilis* arrives in the form of a reddish rash covering the entire body. Depending on its severity, the rash may be associated with headache, loss of appetite, and fever.

The rash regresses spontaneously so that the patient is again lulled into a false sense of security for a latent phase of several years before the sometimes fatal manifestations of *tertiary syphilis* make their appearance. These include inflammatory lesions of all organs of the body, most frequently the cardiovascular system and the brain.

History of general paresis

What seems to have been a virulent form of syphilis was noted in Europe about 500 years ago. It has been speculated that the infection was brought from the West Indies by members of Christopher Columbus' expedition. Indeed, accounts of Columbus' last years suggest that he suffered from syphilitic infection and succumbed to general paresis. Another major epidemic occurred during the Napoleonic wars, when the infection was spread by French soldiers traveling through the Mideast and Europe. The French physician Bayle first described *general paralysis of the insane,* without using that phrase, as a specific syndrome with characteristic changes in behavior and brain tissue. About that time the psychiatrist Calmeil referred to the disease as general paralysis of the insane or *general paresis,* a flagrant misnomer which has been maintained to the present day. Calmeil did not mean true paralysis of the limbs, as occurs after a stroke, but a general debility and weakness, which is actually manifested by only a third of patients (Bruetsch, 1959).

Several nineteenth century physicians noted the relationship between general paresis and an earlier history of syphilis, but the prolonged interval between infection and emotional symptoms made most authorities skeptical. As late as 1877 Krafft-Ebing, well known for his sexual studies, believed that general paresis was due to any or all of the following: "Heredity, dissipation (Bacchus and Venus), smoking of 10–20 Virginia cigars, excessive heat and cold, trauma to the head, exhaustive efforts to make a living, weak nerves and fright" (Krafft-Ebing, 1877). He made no mention of syphilis. Soon after the identification of *Treponema pallidum* in 1913, Hideyo Noguchi and Joseph Moore visualized spirochetes in the brains of general paretics, establishing unequivocally the cause of the disease (Noguchi and Moore, 1913).

Symptoms of general paresis

The behavioral disturbances of general paresis result from infection of the brain tissue, the *parenchyma,* distinct from the blood vessels or meningeal coverings of the central nervous system. This form of brain syphilis is also referred to as *encephalitis.* The spirochete moves out of capillaries directly into brain tissue, breaking through the "blood-brain barrier" more readily than most bacteria. General paresis occurs more often in whites than blacks, even though the latter have a higher frequency of syphilitic infection. These observations, together with the fact that only about 5 percent of untreated people afflicted with syphilis develop general paresis, suggest that certain individuals are vulnerable to brain infection.

General paresis usually commences ten to fifteen years after the primary infection, though the interval can range from three to forty years. The first symptoms are vague ones such as insomnia, headache, restlessness, and giddiness. The most dramatic and characteristic changes are alterations in mood and judgment, which accompany a gradually worsening dementia. Patients appear expansive and superficially euphoric. They will boast about their remarkable accomplishments in life and vast wealth, and often squander their personal funds in profligate gifts to friends and strangers. Though paretics in this way resemble manics, there are some fairly clear-cut differences. The paretic lacks the clever playfulness and infectious mood of the manic, seeming instead naive and childish. A typical patient, after being taken to the hospital, told the office attendant, "I am going to the wardens of the prisons in the state and all the other states and I am going to buy the prisoners. I'll have an agreement with the warden to take their prisoners and put them to work on farms, and I'll charge each prisoner $300 for doing it and for getting him out of jail. I made $105,000 with prisoners just last week'' (Kolb, 1973).

This quotation illustrates a characteristic loss of judgment which reflects the progressive deterioration of the ability to conceptualize clearly. As memory and thought processes fail, the patient fabricates fantastic stories to cover up his or her impairment. At first the gaps in judgment may be subtle. More than in most other organic brain disturbances they involve moral and social functions. Slater and Roth (1969) described patients whose first symptoms seemed like the indiscretions of someone mildly drunk: ''A well-known lawyer, asked to propose a toast at a dinner, regaled the assembled company with a recital of bawdy songs. . . . A politician, seated on the platform at the annual congress of his party was observed to pick his nose assiduously throughout the proceedings.'' The disabilities develop gradually and go unnoticed by the person's family for some time unless brought out by a sudden change in environment: ''A school teacher who had been observed to grow anxious, depressed and a little forgetful (but otherwise seemed normal) was sent for a three-week holiday in France which he was visiting for the first time in his life. There he contracted a bigamous marriage, ordered three motor cars and was finally arrested after a particularly brutal assault on a man in a nightclub'' (Slater and Roth, 1969).

Some patients are more often depressed than expansive. Others show few clearly emotional disturbances. Instead, there is a gradual loss of mental alertness and ambition, a progressive forgetfulness, and finally profound confusion and inability to comprehend conversation.

Most distressing are congenital cases of general paresis. Since the circulating spirochete readily passes through the mother's placenta, infants are born infected with syphilis. Though syphilis was once the leading cause of stillbirth, babies may be totally asymptomatic. After the ten- to fifteen-year incubation period for general paresis, however, its symptoms become apparent in adolescence. These patients are less responsive to penicillin than adults and progress over four to five years to complete deterioration of higher brain functions, culminating in a vegetative state and death.

The frontal lobes of the brain are the area which is most severely affected by the spirochete. One of the early indications of this is the deterioration of the patient's social judgment. A large number of soldiers in World War I who suffered gunshot wounds to the frontal lobes showed similar behavior. These clinical observations were extremely valuable in determining the behavioral functions of the frontal lobes.

The dementia of brain syphilis is first apparent in difficulty with abstract thinking, which becomes impoverished and concrete. Ultimately, the degeneration reaches a point where patients don't even recognize friends and family.

Meningovascular syphilis

In some patients the spirochetes do not reach the brain parenchyma, causing instead inflammation in the blood vessels of the meningeal linings of the brain. As the inflammation progresses, blood flow is retarded or halted so that some areas of brain tissue die.

Because the occlusion of blood vessels is a direct way of damaging brain tissue, the symptoms of meningovascular syphilis develop more rapidly than those of general paresis. Since the regional pattern of damaged brain tissue is unlike that of general paresis, the mental abnormalities are somewhat different.

Patients first feel vaguely ill, experiencing fatigue, headache, and difficulty sleeping. They may be slow and forgetful, somewhat careless of detail. In contrast to general paresis, patients retain considerable insight into their problems, which may provoke anxiety. The disorder is most frequently mistaken for a severe anxiety neurosis. As the disease progresses, however, the patient's consciousness becomes clouded, sometimes to the point of delirium. An organic disturbance of brain function can be diagnosed by observing that the pupils of the eyes are unequal in size and fail to constrict in response to light. These changes may subside for a while only to return later.

Brain abnormalities in syphilis

Brain syphilis is described above as having two distinct forms—meningovascular syphilis, which affects primarily the meninges or linings of the brain with associated blood vessel involvement, and encephalitic syphilis, in which the inflammation involves the brain substance or parenchyma itself. In fact, all brain disorders in syphilis start at the meninges. In some patients the inflammation does not reach the brain substance so that only meningovascular symptoms are present, while in other cases neuronal cells throughout the brain are involved.

The syphilitic organism *Treponema pallidum* generally enters the central nervous system between three and eighteen months after the initial infection. Thus, if a patient has no central nervous symptoms by twenty-four months following first exposure, there is only a 1 in 20 chance that he or she will develop neurosyphilis. If the central nervous system is still unaffected five years after infection, the likelihood of subsequent involvement is only about 1 percent.

Since the meningeal lining, where all brain syphilis begins, is immediately adjacent to the cerebrospinal fluid, the best way to diagnose neurosyphilis is by spinal fluid examination. Antibodies to *Treponema* can be detected in infected individuals by conventional and convenient tests. This meningeal inflammation occurs in about 25 percent of all individuals who are infected with syphilis. However, in most instances the inflammation fails to produce any central nervous symptoms and can be diagnosed only by spinal fluid examination. Treatment with penicillin at this stage completely aborts the infection and prevents the development of advanced neurosyphilis.

Once the infection progresses from the meninges to the brain parenchyma, a series of destructive events combine to produce the clinical picture of general paresis. The meninges are thickened and infiltrated with white blood cells, which are also present in the small blood vessels that line the meninges. Neuronal cells of the cerebral cortex degenerate and are replaced by glial cells, which proliferate considerably. By far the greatest damage occurs in the frontal and temporal regions. These entire lobes shrink markedly and the adjacent ventricular space expands, which is readily detected by x-ray studies. The major damage to the frontal lobes accounts for the similarity of general paretic symptoms to those of some patients with frontal lobe damage from other causes.

Treatment

The first effective therapy for brain syphilis was the somewhat improbable induction of high fever by superimposing a malarial infection. For years physicians had noticed that some mental patients improved after suffering a febrile illness such as malaria, tuberculosis, or typhoid fever. Wagner-Jauregg decided to induce fever intentionally for therapeutic purposes. After some poor results with streptococcus infections and typhoid vaccines, a World War I soldier who had contracted malaria on the Balkan front was mistakenly admitted to the psychiatric hospital at the University of Vienna. Taking serendipitous advantage of this bureaucratic mixup, Wagner-Jauregg innoculated three general paretics with the soldier's blood and was astonished by the improvement in mental symptoms when the patients recovered from their 105° fever. In the therapy program he evolved, paretics received eight to twelve malaria infections with fevers up to 105°, which were then terminated with quinine. For this discovery Wagner-Jauregg received the Nobel prize in 1927, the first and only psychiatrist ever to have been so honored (Wagner-Jauregg and Bruetsch, 1946).

Untreated, both general paresis and meningovascular syphilis invariably end in death. Malaria therapy produced complete recovery in about a third of all patients, including many *whose brain deterioration was already advanced.* Massive doses of penicillin can now eliminate symptoms in 80 percent of patients. Even advanced cases improve sufficiently to permit a return to fairly normal life in the community.

In controlling syphilis, public health measures are at least as important as drug treatment. Because patients may have symptoms for only brief periods during the primary and secondary phases of the disease, they are often unaware of their condition until may years later when several organs of the body have been ravaged. Educating the public to detect early signs such as the chancre and the rash of secondary syphilis is imporant. Locating exposed individuals, after detecting an infected patient, is equally crucial. In the United States all physicians are required to report cases of syphilis to health authorites, who then trace and alert all the individual's sexual contacts. The Wasserman serum test for syphilis is an efficient means of diagnosing early infection. When applied to cerebrospinal fluid, the Wasserman test establishes syphilitic invasion of the central nervous system. All individuals with positive Wasserman tests should be treated with large doses of penicillin.

References

Bruetsch, W. L. Neurosyphilitic conditions. In *American handbook of psychiatry,* ed. S. Arieti. Basic Books, New York, 1959, pp. 1003–1020.

Kolb, L. C. *Modern clinical psychiatry.* W. B. Saunders, Philadelphia, 1973, p. 229.

Krafft-Ebing, Von R. Zur Kenntnis des paralytischen Irreseins beim weiblichen Geschlect. *Arch. Psych., 7:*182, 1877.

Noguchi, H., and Moore, J. W. A demonstration of Treponema pallidum in the brain in cases of general paralysis. *J. Exp. Med., 17:*232, 1913.

Slater, E., and Roth, M. *Clinical psychiatry.* Williams and Wilkins, Baltimore, 1969, p. 522.

Wagner-Jauregg, J., and Bruetsch, W. H. The history of the malaria treatment of general paralysis. *Am. J. Psychiat., 102:*577, 1946.

17. Epilepsy

Most people think of epilepsy in terms of attacks in which victims lose consciousness totally and fall to the ground, foaming at the mouth, with their arms and legs flailing violently for a substantial period of time. Such indeed is the typical picture of a grand mal seizure, which was historically the principal type of epilepsy of concern to physicians who, in Greek, Roman, and medieval European cultures, called it the "falling sickness" or "falling evil." However, there are many kinds of epilepsy. In some, the level of consciousness is disturbed minimally if at all. In others, few if any body movements are apparent. The epilepsies are best defined in terms of the electrical activity of the brain as conditions in which a hyperexcitable group of nerve cells periodically undergoes repetitive discharge. The eminent nineteenth century neurologist Hughlings Jackson referred to epilepsy as "an occasional, an excessive and a disorderly discharge of nerve tissues." The nature of a typical seizure is highlighted by the derivation of the term *epilepsy,* which comes from Greek words meaning "to be seized by forces from without." Though epileptics are treated primarily by neurologists, the brain abnormalities underlying epilepsy are often associated with changes in emotional behavior that have important theoretical as well as practical ramifications.

Epilepsy is also a major disease in social terms. In the United States the number of epileptics is probably over 2 million. Most of these individuals are fully competent members of society, yet many suffer economic and social penalties because of the longstanding but quite erroneous stereotype of epileptics as "weird," irresponsible, and dangerous individuals.

Causes

There are two major classes of epilepsy—those for which a cause is obvious, and hence are referred to as *symptomatic,* and those for which physicians have failed to detect a specific brain lesion, and hence are referred to as *idiopathic.* Symptomatic epilepsy is usually associated with a brain tumor, trauma to the head, encephalitis, and metabolic or endocrine disease.

In children the most common symptomatic source of epilepsy is high fever. In the absence of fever, recurrent seizures in a child or adolescent are usually associated with idiopathic, primary epilepsy with no demonstrable physical abnormality in the brain. However, if recurrent seizures first appear in adult life, structural brain damage is the most common source. During young adult life brain tumors are the most frequent cause, while in later years vascular strokes predominate. The four principal structural abnormalities giving rise to seizures are head trauma, brain tumor, brain abscess, and vascular strokes.

The risk of epilepsy following head injury is closely related to whether or not the missile penetrates the skull and the *dura mater,* the external lining of the brain. When the dura has been pierced, more than 50 percent of victims develop seizures, while the likelihood is only about 5 percent if no penetration has taken place. Even if a seizure occurs following head injury, the patient may not develop recurrent epilepsy. When the seizure appears within the first week of injury the risk of epilepsy is only about 25 percent, while the incidence rises to 70 percent if the first seizure occurs later (Jennett et al., 1973).

Brain tumors are the major fear of most people who experience a first seizure in adult life. However, tumors are responsible for adult onset epilepsy in only about 10 percent of cases (Currie et al., 1971). Of course, the overriding fear with tumors is that they might be malignant. Surprisingly, the tumors most likely to cause seizures are benign ones such as meningiomas; malignant tumors produce seizures only half as frequently as meningiomas.

Brain infections with abscesses frequently cause epilepsy. About 70 percent of patients recovering from abscesses develop epilepsy, most often of the generalized grand mal types (Legg et al., 1973). In the elderly, vascular strokes are far and away the most frequent source of epilepsy. After the age of fifty, at least half of all seizures are attributable to strokes. Usually the first seizure appears within one week following the stroke.

Idiopathic seizures, for which there is no obvious structural cause, are the most common. About 1 percent of the world population suffers from idiopathic epilepsy, a proportion similar to the incidence of schizophrenia or diabetes. As with these two conditions, there is substantial evidence that the vulnerability to develop epilepsy is genetically determined. There is a fairly high incidence of seizures in first-degree relatives of epileptics. When one examines the EEG patterns of relatives of epileptics, a very high proportion have abnormalities. About 50 percent of the siblings of epileptics with petit mal, focal, and temporal lobe disorders have clear-cut abnormalities (Bray and Wiser, 1964; Metrakos and Metrakos, 1961). This rate is consistent with a dominant mode of inheritance. Only one-fourth of the relatives with aberrant EGG's ever experience seizures, so that if one were to rely on evidence of clinical epilepsy, the strong genetic trend indicating a dominant inheritance pattern would not be apparent.

Studies comparing identical (monozygotic) and fraternal (dizygotic) twins have provided equally strong evidence of a genetic component in epilepsy. If one of a pair of identical twins is epileptic, the likelihood is 77 to 85 percent that the co-twin will have experienced seizures or will have an abnormal EEG. For fraternal twins this concordance rate is only between 7 and 27 percent (Inoue, 1960; Lennox, 1951).

Some types of seizures have a low genetic loading. Among small children who experience considerable brain damage at birth and subsequently develop seizures, only 5 percent have a family history of seizures. One severe form of epilepsy that is associated with various brain abnormalities—infantile spasms—has only a small genetic component. This condition is discussed below (see page 176).

Febrile convulsions are frequent in children up to the age of three to five. While the great majority of these individuals never develop epilepsy, their likelihood of subsequent epilepsy is higher than in the general population. Interestingly, the susceptibility to seizure accompanying high fever appears to be genetically determined. The likelihood of some form of seizures, frequently related only to high fever, is about 50 percent in relatives of children experiencing febrile convulsions (Livingston, 1972; Wallace, 1972).

Varieties

Grand mal

These seizures are best known to the general public. The patient loses consciousness completely just before body movements commence. First, there is a *tonic* phase in which most of the body's muscles become tense and the individual stops breathing. Within a few seconds to a minute the *clonic* phase begins, with rhythmic trembling and flailing of the arms, legs, and trunk. This pattern continues for a few minutes and then stops or the entire tonic-clonic sequence may repeat itself. After the seizure has ended, the patient gradually regains consciousness but suffers from a *post-ictal* period of confusion, drowsiness, somnolence, and headache which can last anywhere from several minutes to seventy-two hours.

A dramatic and clinically important part of the seizure is the *aura,* which is reported by about half of grand mal epileptics. The aura is usually a vague sensation of discomfort lasting for a few seconds. Sometimes the aura may be sharply localized, such as a tingling in one finger. In severe cases of epilepsy which require brain surgery, a localized aura enables the surgeon to pinpoint the site of the lesion in the brain.

Often the aura is experienced as a remarkably altered state of consciousness suggestive of transcendental states of mystics or of the effects of psychedelic drugs. Understanding central mechanisms responsible for these auras may shed light on the central nervous system correlates of altered states of consciousness. Dostoyevsky, an epileptic, described the aura preceding his seizures as an awesome, almost spiritual state. In fiction he characterized this experience most vividly in *The Idiot:*

There was a moment or two in his epileptic condition, almost before the fit itself, when . . . his brain seemed to catch fire at brief moments. . . . His sensation of being alive and his awareness increased tenfold at those moments which flashed by like lightning. His mind and heart were flooded by a dazzling light. All his agitation, all his doubts and worries seemed composed in a twinkling, culminating in a great calm, full of serene and harmonious joy and hope, full of understanding and the knowledge of the final cause. . . . It was not abnormal and fantastic visions he saw at that moment, as under the influence of hashish, opium or spirits . . . these moments were merely an intense heightening of awareness.

Petit mal

These seizures are also referred to as "absence" seizures since the individual remains awake but the face appears vacant as he or she loses awareness for a period of five to ten seconds. Except for rolling of the eyes or blinking of the eyelids, there are no motor expressions of petit mal epilepsy. The patient's stream of consciousness seems to be interrupted for a few seconds, after which he or she returns to the previous activity with no post-ictal confusion.

Petit mal seizures occur almost invariably in children and tend to disappear by adolescence. The majority of these children never suffer from any other type of seizure. Clinically, petit mal epilepsy is one of the most innocuous forms, yet it is characterized by grossly abnormal EEG's with large waves and spikes occurring at a frequency of three per second on both sides of the brain.

Focal seizures

As the name suggests, these disturbances involve discrete areas of the brain without spread to other regions. If they are sensory areas, the seizure is characterized by a strange feeling in one part of the body which lasts for less than a minute. If motor areas of the brain are affected, physical movements such as trembling of a single limb will occur. Sometimes both motor and sensory components are involved. Patients do not usually lose consciousness.

Minor motor seizures

Some minor motor seizures are not serious, while others are associated with severe brain damage. *Myoclonic jerks* are literally jerks of the arms or legs. Many normal individuals experience myoclonic jerks just as they are falling asleep. *Akinetic seizures* are related to myoclonic jerks and petit mal epilepsy. They are called akinetic because children so afflicted seem to fall to the ground suddenly and passively. However, the seizures are not due to relaxation but to contraction of muscles. The muscles of the neck and hip flex so that the children tend to fall forward and often injure their face. While petit mal epilepsy and myoclonic jerks are not usually associated with brain damage, akinetic seizures generally occur in children with considerable brain damage and marked mental retardation. Akinetic epilepsy occurs mainly in children younger then eight years.

Infantile spasms

Children with this disorder have the worst outlook of all epileptics. The condition becomes apparent in children before their first birthday. It is probably caused by brain malfunctions similar to those responsible for akinetic seizures but manifested in a younger age group. The whole body flexes and extends as the child cries and loses consciousness. Fully 90 percent of children with infantile spasms become severely retarded. The EEG patterns of these children show disturbances spread more widely through the brain than in almost any other type of brain disease. Infantile spasms are more resistant to control by anticonvulsant drugs than any other form of epilepsy.

Febrile convulsions

These are the most common form of seizure in children. About 5 percent of children suffer at least one febrile convulsion (Lennox-Buchtal, 1973). The convulsion is clearly due to the higher body temperature rather than other features of the infection which is the usual precipitant, since seizures can be induced experimentally in animals by elevating body temperature through any of a variety of techniques. The form of the seizure is usually grand mal. Of greatest concern is the possibility that the seizures may become repetitive, a condition referred to as *status epilepticus,* with attendant danger of severe brain damage and even death.

Follow-up studies indicate that most children experiencing a single febrile convulsion are not likely to suffer permanent sequels as measured by academic performance and neurological examination (Ellenberg and Nelson, 1977; Hauser et al, 1977). However, the possibility of subsequent impairment even in the absence of clear-cut organic brain disturbance has been demonstrated in well-controlled studies. In a series of fourteen identical twins in which only one of each pair had experienced febrile convulsions, definite intellectual deficit was apparent in the twin who had experienced convulsions (Schiottz-Christensen and Bruhn, 1973). The twins who had had seizures showed statistically significant reductions in academic performance and in the performance scale of IQ tests compared to the normal twins. However, no evidence of organic brain damage was present upon neurological examination or EEG recording, emphasizing that subtle brain damage can readily escape detection in conventional neurological evaluations.

Psychomotor or temporal lobe epilepsy

The two names for this disorder convey its main characteristics. Patients display abnormalities of both psychological and motor behavior, and electrical disturbance invariably involves the temporal lobes. Of all the seizure disorders, this type is most closely associated with specific forms of psychopathology. Though grand mal epilepsy is the most common type in children, psychomotor seizures predominate in adults. Many children who experience grand mal seizures develop into psychomotor epileptics as they pass through adolescence.

The symptoms of psychomotor seizures are more variable than those of other types of epilepsy. Some seizures are characterized only by abnormal thoughts and feelings. Feelings of anxiety and peculiar sensations of having been in the same situation before (*deja vu*) are common. Individuals may feel depersonalized, like strangers in their bodies. Some experience dreamlike episodes. The seizures may involve perceptual changes, such as expansion or constriction of visual images, or strange distortions of objects seen, heard, smelled, or tasted.

Motor activities involving fairly complicated yet automatic series of movements often constitute the major manifestation of the psychomotor seizure. The simplest automatisms are chewing, swallowing, retching, or lip smacking. Some individuals perform complicated acts of dressing and undressing. Often these behaviors appear to be influenced by the environment. For instance, a patient may display violent behavior toward an individual who earlier frustrated him or her. There have been a few reports of psychomotor epileptics who have murdered others while undergoing a seizure.

Temporal lobe epileptics have different characteristic personality patterns. Some are irritable, paranoid, and prone to violence upon slight provocation.

Others are obsessive, fussy, extremely cautious in their behavior, and overly concerned with details. Many, however, are normal between seizures.

The most consistent behavioral abnormality of psychomotor epileptics is a decrease in sexual activity (Blumer and Walker, 1967). The pattern is one of a global hyposexuality affecting both men and women. Patients have very little interest in sexual activity, and they have difficulties in performance. Many men are entirely unable to attain erections or to ejaculate. Female psychomotor epileptics are not readily aroused, usually do not have vaginal secretions during erotic stimulation, and almost always fail to attain orgasm. These changes indicate the importance of the temporal lobes in mediating sexual activity. The decreased sexuality associated with hyperexcitation in the area of the temporal lobes, which include the limbic system underlying the temporal cerebral cortex, finds a reverse counterpart in animal studies involving destruction of the temporal lobes. Ablation of these structures in monkeys results in pronounced hypersexuality.

Temporal lobe epilepsy and violence
Some researchers believe that many violent crimes, serious automobile accidents, and suicides may derive from temporal lobe abnormalities which are not detectable by currently available techniques. Mark and Ervin (1970) are major proponents of this point of view. They have studied numerous persons who manifested episodic violence but whose brain function appeared to be completely normal when examined exhaustively by conventional neurological procedures. Only by directly implanting electrodes into the temporal lobes of the brain could they identify specific abnormalities. A typical case they studied was that of Jennie W., a double murderess at the age of fourteen:

While she was babysitting with her stepsisters, she was very disturbed by one youngster's constant crying, so she put a plastic bag over the child's head and suffocated her. . . . While she was being questioned by a psychiatrist, she confessed that she had killed another younger stepsister who was thought to have died of pneumonia. . . . The physicians at the state hospital did a thorough medical and psychiatric examination without finding any abnormality; the opinion of the psychiatric staff . . . was that Jeannie in *no way differed* from hundreds of other prisoners accused of a serious crime. [At the Massachusetts General Hospital] the results of the neurological examination, the brain wave examination, the brain scan and the final x-ray films of her brain were all normal. . . . The brain waves recorded from the surface of the temporal lobe itself . . . were quite normal; recordings from the amygdala were also normal. But the recordings from an electrode directly in the hippocampus were strikingly abnormal (Mark and Ervin, 1970).

Mark and Ervin argue that large numbers of incarcerated criminals may suffer from similarly undetected brain disorders. The violent behavior of many of their patients was alleviated by treatment with anticonvulsant drugs or, in some cases, by bilateral surgical destruction of the amygdala within the temporal lobe. Might not many violent prisoners be rehabilitated if adequately evaluated and treated? Mark and Ervin themselves evaluated 400 prisoners in a large penitentiary and detected EEG abnormalities in half of them. They found the incidence of epilepsy to be ten times higher among prisoners than in the general population. Moreover, in their series of 400 violent prisoners, about half reported symptoms resembling those of temporal lobe epilepsy, such as altered states of consciousness or an aura preceding violent behavior.

The work of Mark and Ervin and other researchers reporting similar findings has stirred up a great deal of controversy. Some researchers maintain that abnormal EEG's do not prove the existence of brain pathology because many perfectly normal people have aberrant EEG's. Similarly, "altered state of consciousness" is a broad enough description to apply, on occasion to everyone.

At a more subjective level, many find it difficult to accept the notion that criminal behavior could derive from anything other than an abnormal environment. Moreover, the concept of psychosurgery is repugnant to many, even if the surgeons can demonstrate relief of severe symptoms. Because no one understands human brain functioning fully, opponents of psychosurgery believe that possible deleterious effects of the operations can never be adequately predicted. They point to the harm done to large numbers of psychiatric patients who underwent prefrontal lobotomies with subsequent behavioral deterioration and no demonstrable improvement in their psychiatric symptoms.

Relationship to schizophrenia of psychomotor epilepsy

Psychomotor epilepsy may also serve as an experiment of nature to shed light upon the central nervous system abnormalities underlying schizophrenia. Psychotic disturbance that is clinically indistinguishable from schizophrenialike psychosis occurs in temporal lobe epilepsy much more commonly than in other forms of seizures. In one study (Guerrant et al., 1962) 20 percent of psychomotor epileptics displayed psychotic behavior compared to only 4 percent of patients with grand mal epilepsy. In the same study 47 percent of psychomotor epileptics showed some evidence of organic brain abnormalities with impaired memory, attention, concentration lability of affect, and slowed speech. Only 27 percent of grand mal epileptics and 4 percent of a matched group of general medical patients displayed such changes.

In another study (Slater et al., 1963) 80 percent of a group of psychotic epileptics displayed temporal lobe abnormalities. These patients manifested all the cardinal symptoms of schizophrenia. However, the overall pattern of psychosis tended to differ somewhat from classic schizophrenia. For most of the epileptic psychotics, affective response to the environment was not as bizarre and inappropriate as in classic schizophrenia. Moreover, even after many years of psychotic disturbance, some patients failed to undergo personality deterioration. Still, the close mimicry of true schizophrenia was highlighted by the fact that two-thirds of the patients who had previously been evaluated by psychiatrists who were ignorant of their history of epilepsy had received a diagnosis of schizophrenia. Support for the clinical impression that temporal lobe epileptics have more personality quirks than other epileptics or normal individuals comes from standardized psychological testing (Rodin et al., 1976). Patients with temporal lobe disease showed more anxiety during interview, a higher paranoia score on Minnesota Multiphasic Scale testing, and more personality disturbance in other psychological tests than other epileptics or control subjects.

The frequency of this schizophreniform condition in psychomotor epileptics is much higher than could be accounted for by a random association of schizophrenia and epilepsy. Unlike schizophrenics, these patients have no family history of psychosis. Interestingly, the extent of psychotic symptoms varies inversely with the frequency of epileptic seizures (Flor-Henry, 1969). Temporal lobe seizures themselves may somehow alleviate whatever disturbance accounts for the schizophreniclike symptoms.

The exact source of this epileptic psychosis is unclear. It is not likely to be due to anticonvulsant medication, since it occurs in untreated epileptics and since patients who have other forms of epilepsy treated with the same drugs that temporal lobe epileptics receive fail to develop the psychosis. The symptoms cannot be a direct effect of the epileptic discharge because anticonvulsants suppress the discharge but fail to influence the emotional symptoms. The psychotic symptoms respond best to drugs used in treating schizophrenia, suggesting again that the brain abnormalities in this disorder are similar to those of classic schizophrenia.

Treatment and outcome

The advent of effective anticonvulsant drugs has greatly improved the outlook for epileptics. The two most valuable drugs in the treatment of epilepsy are phenobarbital, a long-acting barbiturate, and diphenylhydantoin (Dilantin). These two agents, along with a large number of less commonly used drugs, are administered either alone or in various combinations. They are able to control almost all cases of epilepsy.

The mechanism of action of the anticonvulsant drugs is unknown. They were discovered, for the most part, on the basis of their ability to antagonize electrically induced convulsions in animals. Since virtually all drugs that affect brain function do so by interacting with one or another neurotransmitter, one might speculate that anticonvulsants should either mimic the effects of major inhibitory neurotransmitters or block actions of excitatory transmitters. Interestingly, the most recent sophisticated neurophysiological studies indicate that diphenylhydantoin and phenobarbital possess both properties (MacDonald and Barker, 1979). The excitatory neurotransmitter acting at the largest proportion of brain synapses appears to be the amino acid glutamic acid. The major inhibitory amino acid in the brain quantitatively is also an amino acid, γ-aminobutyric acid (GABA). Diphenylhydantoin and phenobarbital facilitate the electrical effects of GABA and block those of glutamic acid.

For those who do not respond to drug treatment, surgical removal of the epileptic focus may be considered. In this case, it is important to establish the exact location of a specific lesion that can account for all the patient's symptoms. If the patient suffers from diffuse abnormalities, removal of a single area is not likely to prove helpful.

It had once been thought that a deterioration of intellect was one of the manifestations of epilepsy. Clear-cut organic brain damage associated with dementia does take place after many years of controlled seizures. However, patients whose seizures are suppressed by medication generally have unimpaired intelligence (Chaudry and Pond, 1961; Rodin, 1968). The only epileptics with consistent and severe mental retardation are those with minor seizures.

Historically, there appears to be a greater association of genius than of mental retardation with epilepsy. After reviewing the literature, Livingston (1954) made the following list: "Among the great men of history who are reported to have had epileptic seizures are: Apostle Paul, Buddha, Socrates, Alexander the Great, Julius Caesar, Mohammed, Blaise Pascal, Peter the Great, Handel, Gustave Flaubert, Paganini, Lord Byron, Feodor Dostoyevsky, Algernon Charles Swinburne, Sir William Pitt, Napoleon Bonaparte, Alfred the Great, Louis XIII of France, Swedenborg and Vincent van Gogh."

References

Blumer, D., and Walker, A. E. Sexual behavior in temporal lobe epilepsy. *Arch. Neurol. 16:*31–43, 1967.

Bray, P. F., and Wiser, W. C. Evidence for a genetic etiology of temporal–central abnormalities in focal epilepsy. *N. Eng. J. Med., 271:*926, 1964.

Chaudry, M. R., and Pond, D. A. Mental deterioration in epileptic children. *J. Neurol. and Psychiat., 24:*213, 1961.

Currie, S., Heathfield, K. W. G., Henson, R. A., and Scott, D. F. Clinical course and prognosis of temporal lobe epilepsy. A survey of 666 patients. *Brain, 94:*173, 1971.

Ellenberg, J. H., and Nelson, K. B. Febrile seizures, tested intelligence and learning disorder. *Neurology, 27:*342, 1977.

Flor-Henry, P. Psychosis and temporal lobe epilepsy. *Epilepsia, 10:*363, 1969.

Guerrant, J., Anderson, W. W., Fischer, A., Weinstein, M. R., Jaros, R. M., and Deskins, A. *Personality in epilepsy.* C. C. Thomas, Springfield, Ill., 1962.

Hauser, W. A., Annegers, J. F., and Kurland, T. Febrile convulsions: Prognosis for subsequent seizures. *Neurology, 27:*341, 1977.

Inoue, E. Observations on 40 twin index cases with chronic epilepsy and their co-twins. *J. Nerv. and Ment. Diseases, 130:*401, 1960.

Jennett, B., Teather, D., and Bennie, S. Epilepsy after head injury. Residual risk after varying fit-free intervals since injury. *Lancet, 2:*652, 1973.

Legg, N. J., Gupta, P. C., and Scott, D. F. Epilepsy following cerebral abscess. A clinical and EEG study of 70 patients. *Brain, 96:*259, 1973.

Lennox, W. G. The heredity of epilepsy as told by relatives and twins. *J. Am. Med. Assoc., 146:*529, 1951.

Lennox-Buchtal, M. A. Febrile convulsions—a reappraisal. *Electroen. Clin. Neurophysiol.,* suppl. *32,* 1973.

Livingston, S. *The diagnosis and treatment of convulsive disorders in children.* C. C. Thomas, Springfield, Ill., 1954, p. 183.

Livingston, S. *Comprehensive management of epilepsy in infancy, childhood and adolescence.* C. C. Thomas, Springfield, Ill., 1972.

MacDonald, R. L., and Barker, J. L. Enhancement of GABA mediated postsynaptic inhibition in cultured mammalian spinal cord neurons: A common mode of anticonvulsant action. *Brain Res., 167:*323–336, 1979.

Mark, V. H., and Ervin, F. R. *Violence and the brain.* Harper & Row, New York, 1970.

Metrakos, K., and Metrakos, J. D. Genetics of convulsive disorders, II: Genetic and encephalographic studies in centrencephalic epilepsy. *Neurology, 11:*474, 1961.

Pond, D. A. Psychiatric aspects of epileptic and brain damaged children. *Br. Med. J., 2:*1377, 1961.

Rodin, E. A. *The prognosis of patients with epilepsy.* C. C. Thomas, Springfield, Ill., 1968.

Rodin, E. A., Katz, M., and Lennox, K. Differences between patients with temporal lobe seizures and those with other forms of epileptic attacks. *Epilepsia, 17:*313, 1976.

Schiottz-Christensen, E., and Bruhn, P. Intelligence, behavior and scholastic achievement subsequent to febrile convulsions: An analysis of discordant twin pairs. *Develop. Med. Child. Neurol., 15:*565, 1973.

Slater, E. A., Beard, W., and Glithero, E. Periods of schizophrenia-like psychosis in epilepsy. *Br. J. Psychiat., 109:*95, 1963.

Wallace, S. J. Etiological aspects of febrile convulsions. *Arch. Dis. Childhood, 47:*171, 1972.

18. Psychosomatic disorders

ROBERT L. SACK, M.D.,
University of Oregon Health Sciences Center

Psychosomatic illness has been a controversial topic in medical science. Although many physicians, dating back to the ancient Greeks, have noted the relationship between emotions and illness, scientific evidence has not always been easy to generate. Particularly challenging has been the attempt to understand the chain of events starting with mental processes and leading eventually to organ damage. This chain has many links, including the relationships among mind, brain, endocrine functions, and organ vulnerability. In large part, these relationships remain dimly understood. Nevertheless, an impressive amount of evidence has now been accumulated to support the notion that psyche (mind) and soma (body) are linked in the induction of some diseases.

Before going on, it is necessary to define some terms. *Psychosomatic illness* refers to those diseases in which psychological factors lead to structural or functional damage to an organ. Certain illnesses, such as peptic ulcer disease, high blood pressure (hypertension), neurodermatitis, ulcerative colitis, migraine headaches, hyperthyroidism, and asthma are often mentioned as having psychosomatic determinants, but many other diseases have been considered as well.

Psychosomatic illness must be distinguished from several other categories of illness which also involve psychological factors. For example, some patients suffer symptoms of physical illness but no organic damage can be demonstrated. These patients may have undue concern over bodily functions and may be highly sensitive to any deviation from their usual bodily sensations. These patients suffer from somatic anxiety and are termed *hypochondriacal*. Occasionally such patients have intense and dramatic symptoms in many parts of the body; they may even seek surgery in an attempt to find the cause or to obtain relief. Such patients are now recognized as a distinct category termed *somatization disorder* (DSM-III, 1979) and require careful medical management lest they suffer harm from needless surgery or diagnostic tests.

Conversion reactions represent another category of psychologically related illness. Patients with conversion reactions develop symptoms that usually resemble those of neurological disease, such as blindness, paralysis, numbness, or amnesia. They have no conscious control of their symptoms. These reactions are often related to some specific overwhelming psychological trauma or conflict. For example, a soldier may develop blindness after witnessing a horrible battle. Conversion reactions can be quite disabling; however, careful examination of the nervous system reveals no organic dysfunction. These reactions may subside gradually or may be actively treated by hypnosis, suggestion, or the alleviation of the precipitating stress.

Occasionally, individuals will consciously feign a physical illness in order to be excused from some responsibility or to gain some privilege. This is called *malingering*. By mimicking illness, for example, a prisoner may try to get transferred from jail to a hospital in order to secure greater comforts. Such patients have to be detected through careful examination.

The distinctions between malingering, conversion symptoms, and hypochondriacal complaints are not always easy to make. They may depend on some knowledge of the patient's motivation, which is not always easy to obtain. These illnesses all involve psychological determinants but are not psychosomatic since no structural damage to an organ is involved.

One additional way in which psychological factors may play a role in producing illness is through habits that are deleterious to good health. For example, obesity is a predisposing factor in the development of high blood pressure. Smoking and lack of exercise pose an increased risk for heart attacks. Overeating, smoking, and lack of exercise are all habits, that is, learned behaviors. Behavioral psychologists have become very interested in devising techniques to help people change these habits using the principles of learning theory (Williams and Gentry, 1977).

Thus, there are many intersections between psychological phenomena and disease. This chapter, however, will focus on one major theme: the proposition that psychological stress and conflict can lead to organ damage.

The psychosomatic hypothesis: an overview of the issues

In order to qualify as psychosomatic, an illness must be caused, at least in part, by some psychological state or process. Most often the noxious psychological process is called *stress*. In other words, we may hypothesize that an individual "under stress" is more likely to develop ulcers. Plausible as it sounds, this hypothesis is quite nonspecific since the word "stress" can mean so many things. It can refer either to an external environmental event, such as the occurrence of an economic depression, or to a consequent internal state, such as that which may result from worry about money lost in a depression. It would help if we referrred to external events which most people find disagreeable as *stressors* and to the internal state of disequilibrium as *stress*. In practice, however, the word "stress" is used in both ways.

Further issues emerge. There are a wide variety of problems with which people have to cope; thus, there are many potential stressors. Do all stressors produce similar physiological perturbations—that is, similar states of stress? Or do some stressors affect one organ while other kinds affect a different organ? In other words, is peptic ulcer disease the outcome of accumulated stress or is it specific to a certain kind of conflict—for example, having to contain anger felt toward a boss or other authority?

Furthermore, if peptic ulcer disease is the result of psychological conflict, what are the pathways which could link the mind, brain, and stomach? How does the brain generate emotional states, and how are these emotional states manifested in nervous or hormonal influences on the stomach?

Why do some people get ulcers under stress while others do not? What protects an individual from psychosomatic illness? Are the differences related to the way people perceive stressful events? Are the differences related to *organ vulnerability*—that is, an inherent tendency to develop ulcers, determined by genetic heritage?

These are the kinds of questions that surround the psychosomatic hypothesis. Clearly, there are many issues that warrant examination. In the remainder of the chapter, examples of research at several levels of inquiry will be discussed. Only examples can be provided since to review the evidence for the basis of each suspected psychosomatic illness would be a monumental task.

Stress and the social environment

In 1938, the British physician C. P. Donnison wrote a book entitled *Civilization and Disease* (Donnison, 1938). For many years, Donnison had served as a physician to a tribal reservation on the shores of Lake Victoria in Kenya. His curiosity was aroused by the observation that, out of 1,800 patients admitted to his hospital, he could find no case of high blood pressure. He hypothesized that traditional African societies produced less stress for their citizens because the cultures were very stable and well adapted to their natural habitat. He thought that these cultural factors were the main reason for the low incidence of hypertension.

Ten years later in Glasgow, Scotland, an epidemiologist, J. Halliday, supported Donnison's work by reporting a higher incidence of peptic ulcers, diabetes, coronary artery disease, and high blood pressure in urban versus rural, nonindustrialized communities (Halliday, 1949).

Since Donnison and Halliday, there has been wide speculation and research on the question of the noxious effects of advanced Western civilization on health. In general, commentators and researchers have asserted that modern societies tend to be highly unstable, requiring an inordinate amount of adaptation from their citizens. This instability leads to states of chronic tension and uncertainty which eventually undermine health through the development of psychosomatic illness.

An interesting study on this question was conducted by Stewart Wolf and his associates (Stout et al., 1964). They compared the annual death rate in two Pennyslvania towns, Roseto and Bangor. Roseto was, at the time of their study, composed almost entirely of Italian-Americans who maintained much of their native culture, giving them a sense of security, stability, and self-appreciation. Not far away in Bangor, the population was ethnically mixed, rather contentious, and definitely Americanized. Wolf and his co-workers found that the death rate from heart attack was much lower in traditional Roseto than in modern Bangor. This difference could not be explained by diet; indeed, the Italian-Americans of Roseto were fond of olive oil and lard and were twenty pounds overweight compared to the U.S. average.

Marmot and associates (1975, 1976) addressed the question of social disruption and illness by studying Japanese-Americans in the process of cultural transition. They observed that the gradient for coronary heart disease increased from 1.8 per thousand in native Japanese to 3.2 in Hawaiian-Japanese, compared to 9.8 in American Caucasians. Furthermore, a study of the prevalence of coronary artery disease in 3,800 Japanese-Americans living in the San Francisco area revealed that the incidence of coronary heart disease was 2.5 times greater in the acculturated than in the traditional Japanese. The most traditional population had a rate approximately that of native Japanese, while the least traditional group approximated the Caucasian-Americans. This finding was unaffected when the comparison was controlled to rule out the influence of

Westernization of diet, smoking, blood triglycerides (a form of fat), blood cholesterol, blood pressure, relative weight, and blood sugar.

Although Japan is a modern industrialized society, Matsumoto (1970) argued that, in contrast to other Western industrialized cultures, Japanese culture remains tightly integrated and tensions are kept within limits by intense social support. For example, in Japan children are encouraged to be dependent on their parents. Industries are paternalistic and seldom fire an employee once he or she is hired. Japanese have ritualized means of relaxation, including the tea shop and the communal bath. The fabric of the society is tightly woven by the attitude that personal obligation and duty are more important than individual fulfillment. Marmot's studies suggest that, as a Japanese individual relinquishes these cultural buffers to stress in favor of American customs, he or she becomes vulnerable to stress-related heart disease.

High blood pressure (hypertension) is another illness which has been studied from the psychosocial viewpoint. Chronically elevated blood pressure can lead to strokes and heart failure. In most societies the incidence of high blood pressure rises with age. However, there are some societies in which blood pressure remains quite constant with age. Such societies tend to be found in remote, isolated locations. For example, the small group living on the South Sea island of Puka Puka has normal blood pressure which persists for life (Cassel, 1975). By contrast, their more heavily Westernized cousins who live several hundred miles down the Cook Island chain in the administrative capital of Rarotonga have consistently higher blood pressure that shows the typical rise with age (Cassel, 1975).

Societies free of hypertension are found among all racial groups, in all parts of the world, making it unlikely that such differences could be explained by genetic factors alone. Henry and Cassel (1969) surveyed many of these cross-cultural studies of blood pressure and found that within a particular racial stock, blood pressure tends to rise with age more rapidly in urban, nontraditional groups. The rise is particularly rapid among societies in which the population is under collective stress, as when they have been geographically dislocated or are the objects of scapegoating and persecution.

Although these observations are compelling arguments for a social stress factor in the development of hypertension, there is one simple but confounding variable that has been most difficult to control—namely, the dietary intake of salt (Page, 1976). People who have remarkably low blood pressures throughout life often live in areas of the world where salt has been relatively inaccessible and where salt intake is very low by U.S. standards. The introduction of Western civilization invariably increases the amount of salt in the diet. Thus, the intriguing link between high blood pressure and the psychosocial stresses of civilization must await further knowledge of the relationship between salt intake and high blood pressure.

Stressful events

Up to now, we have focused on broad social and cultural differences in the environment as determinants of psychosomatic illness, utilizing comparisons between traditional and modern societies. The next question is whether psychosomatic illness in Western society is more likely to occur at times of personal stress. Some of the most notable work on this issue has been done by Holmes and Rahe. These investigators constructed a questionnaire to quantify the degree of major change in a person's life over a year's time (see Table 18.1). In developing this scale, marriage was given an arbitrary value of 50 (Holmes and Rahe, 1967). The initial subjects were asked to rate certain events in their lives as more or less demanding of readjustment than marriage. In this way, a series of numerical values was assigned to typical life-change events such as divorce, pregnancy, changing residence, changing jobs, and securing a mortgage (see Table 18.1). Of interest was the finding that subjects rated certain pleasant events, including marriage and promotions, as equally demanding as some unpleasant events.

After developing this scale, Holmes and Rahe then correlated the individual life change scores with medical histories (Rahe, 1972). They found that as the life-change score increased, the probability of the occurrence of disease increased. Furthermore, they found that the types of illness that correlated with life change were not necessarily classic psychosomatic illnesses; all types of major illness seemed to bear a relationship to life turmoil.

The death of a spouse is the most stressful event on the Holmes-Rahe scale. In 1969, Parkes and his associates followed up 4,486 widowers, fifty-five years or older, for nine years after the death of their wives. During the first six months, 213 widowers died; this was 40 percent above the statistically predicted rate. After the first year, the widowers did not differ from the general male population in their mortality rate. Thus, the period of bereavement must be considered a time of greater risk for physical illness.

In summary, there is evidence that major life changes, bereavement, and social disruption play a part in the occurrence of coronary artery disease, hypertension, and perhaps other diseases as well. Nevertheless, given a certain degree of conflict or change, some people develop illness and others do not. What can be said about individual susceptibility to psychosomatic illness?

Table 18-1 The Holmes-Rahe life change scale

Family

Death of spouse	100
Divorce	73
Marital separation	65
Death of close family member	63
Marriage	50
Marital reconciliation	45
Major change in health of family	44
Pregnancy	40
Addition of new family member	39
Major change in arguments with wife	35
Son or daughter leaving home	29
In-law troubles	29
Wife starting or ending work	26
Major change in family get-togethers	15

Personal

Detention in jail	63
Major personal injury or illness	53
Sexual difficulties	39
Death of a close friend	37
Outstanding personal achievement	28
Start or end of formal schooling	26
Major change in living conditions	25
Major revision of personal habits	24
Changing to a new school	20
Change in residence	20
Major change in recreation	19
Major change in church activities	19
Major change in sleeping habits	16
Major change in eating habits	15
Vacation	13
Christmas	12
Minor violations of the law	11

Work

Being fired from work	47
Retirement from work	45
Major business adjustment	39
Changing to different line of work	36
Major change in work responsibilities	29
Trouble with boss	23
Major change in working conditions	20

Financial

Major change in financial state	38
Mortgage or loan over $10,000	31
Mortgage foreclosure	30
Mortgage or loan less than $10,000	17

Stress and the individual

The individual psychology of patients with psychosmatic illness was the major interest of two eminent psychiatrists of the 1940s and 1950s, Franz Alexander and Flanders Dunbar. They engaged patients with psychosomatic illness in extensive interviews which included explorations of fantasies, childhood memories, and underlying motivations. Dunbar (1954) described the "ulcer personality," the "coronary personality," the "arthritic personality," and many more. She produced evidence from clinical studies that these personality profiles were quite consistent for each category of illness.

Alexander (1950), a psychoanalyst, developed the theory that each psychosomatic illness was the manifestation of a state of chronic tension in a particular part of the autonomic nervous system which was, in turn, activated by a specific unresolved, unconscious conflict. For example, peptic ulcer disease was explained as the product of chronic activation of stomach secretory activity by unresolved "oral-dependent" yearnings.

When the ideas of Dunbar and Alexander were first introduced, they generated considerable excitement since they linked dynamic psychology and personality theory with the rest of medicine. Eventually these approaches proved rather disappointing, however. Other observers were skeptical that illness could be so specifically linked to one personality type or to one basic conflict. Furthermore, therapy based on these principles was not particularly effective for psychosomatic illness. Thus, for a time, the very concept of psychosomatic illness lost credibility in medical circles.

However, some personality theories of psychosomatic illness have enjoyed a revival in the last decade. The most notable example (clearly in the tradition of Dunbar) is the popular theory which relates coronary artery disease to a "Type A" personality pattern. According to the originators, Friedman and Rosenman (1974), Type A individuals are driven by the urgency of time pressure, are excessively competitive, and are prone to undue hostility when frustrated; in other words, they are the picture of the "hard-driving executive." Persons who are just the opposite, that is, easygoing, are labeled "Type B." In an eight-year follow-up of 3,000 men, the rate of coronary artery disease was found to be twice as high for the Type A's as for the Type B's.

Another example of current investigation into personality patterns of patients with psychosomatic illness is provided by the studies of Sifneos (1972). He has extensively studied patients with psychosomatic illnesses such as asthma, hypertension, and ulcerative colitis and has compared them to neurotic psychiatric patients. According to his findings, the psychosomatic patients have an impoverished fantasy life and very poor dream recall. They have a difficult time finding words to express feelings but are fluent in describing physical symptoms and sensations.

The physiology of the stress response

In order for acute or chronic psychological stress to induce disease in an organ, the stress would have to be transmitted from the brain to that organ by the autonomic nervous system or by some neuroendocrine pathway. The autonomic nervous system and the neuroendocrine pathways are the only routes by which the brain can directly affect the activity of the internal organs. Both the autonomic nervous system and the neuroendocrine system are relatively autonomous, taking care of the routine business of keeping the internal environment constant. However, this ordinary reflex activity can be overridden by higher centers of the brain when they sense some change in the environment and prepare the body to meet it.

Perhaps these relationships can be best illustrated by an example. Suppose we encounter a bear while hiking in the woods. The sequence of physiological responses, starting with the brain, might be analyzed as follows. The cerebral cortex would be involved in perceiving the bear, remembering that bears can be dangerous, reasoning that the best plan of action would be to leave the area, and initiating the motor activity which would carry us back down the trail. In other words, the cerebral cortex is essential for the cognitive functions of perceiving stress and coping with it.

Of course, the missing ingredient in this sequence is the element of fear. Because we feel afraid upon encountering a bear, the cognitive sequence of perceiving, planning, and acting is carried out with great urgency. Furthermore, fear activates physiological responses which are necessary for a successful escape.

Fear is mediated in that part of the brain underlying the cortex called the *limbic system*. The limbic system is older on the evolutionary scale than the cerebral cortex. Many studies have shown that the structures of the limbic system are involved with basic drive states such as fear, hunger, sexual excitement, and aggression. For example, electrical stimulation of the cat hippocampus, a limbic structure, results in apparent bewilderment and anxiety, together with intense attention to something the animal seems to sense in the environment. On the other hand, stimulation of the amygdala, another limbic structure, results in intense rage reactions. Similar kinds of emotions have been generated in conscious humans by stimulation of these regions during brain surgery.

The limbic structures are shaped like a "C," forming a ring around an even older, more basic structure called the *brain stem*. The brain stem contains centers which are involved in regulating basic vegetative functions. For example, the centers for temperature control, blood pressure regulation, and sleep-wake activation are located in the brain stem. The brain stem passes information to the internal organs by way of the autonomic nervous system. Thus, the emotion of fear, generated in the limbic system, influences the nearby brain stem structures to alter the activity of the internal organs. Upon meeting a bear, our blood pressure rises, we begin to breath rapidly, our heart starts to pound, and our muscles fill with blood.

The autonomic nervous system has two major divisions, the sympathetic and the parasympathetic. In general, the *sympathetic system* mediates the response to challenges presented by the environment. The adrenal medulla is a specialized and enlarged sympathetic ganglion. When stimulated, the adrenal gland releases epinephrine, which is also called adrenaline. The *parasympathetic system* is involved during periods of physiological restoration—for example, when digesting a meal. Table 18.2 lists the effects of sympathetic and parasympathetic stimulation on various internal organs. Both divisions of the autonomic nervous system have been implicated in psychosomatic illness, as we will see below.

Besides the autonomic nervous system, the other major route by which psychological stress is transmitted to the internal organs is the *hypothalamic-pituitary neuroendocrine system*. The *hypothalamus* lies at the base of the brain and receives input from most other parts of the brain. Electrical messages from other brain areas are translated to chemical messages in special hypothalamic cells. These cells are stimulated by the usual synaptic mechanisms, but instead of passing along an electrical message, they secrete polypeptide hormones. These polypeptides from the hypothalamus, also known as *releasing factors,* travel down into the pituitary gland via a special blood vessel network.

The *pituitary,* sometimes called the *master gland,* secretes hormones into the general circulation when activated by hypothalamic polypeptide hormones. The

Table 18-2 Typical responses of organs to autonomic nerve impulses

Organ	Sympathetic	Parasympathetic
Eye (pupil)	Constriction	Dilation
Heart	Increased rate and contractility	Decreased rate and contractility
Arteries	Constriction	Dilation
Lungs (bronchial muscles)	Relaxation	Constriction
Stomach and intestines		
Motility	Decrease	Increase
Secretion	Inhibit	Stimulate
Gall bladder	Relaxation	Contraction

pituitary hormones may act directly on other organ systems, or they may stimulate other endocrine glands such as the thyroid and adrenal cortex to release hormones.

Thus, in addition to autonomic arousal, psychological stress can activate a chain of hormonal responses which eventually alters the activity of the internal organs. Although these hormonal responses may be activated when we encounter a bear, they may become even more critical if he catches us and causes some bodily injury. The effects of hormonal activation on survival in the face of extreme stress were first studied by Hans Selye beginning in the 1930s. He demonstrated that a wide variety of stressors, including heat, cold, trauma, and psychological threats, produce a coordinated physiological response which includes a major increase in the secretion of the adrenocortical hormone cortisol. He called the overall response to stress the *general adaptation syndrome,* or *GAS.* The characteristic pattern includes an initial phase of generally lowered resistance immediately following a stress, a stage of resistance when counteractive mechanisms are called into play, and a state of exhaustion marked by the collapse of adaptive responses. For example, if the bear were to catch us and we lost a significant amount of blood, our blood pressure would drop, we would become weak, and we would be in a state of "shock." However, the pituitary-adrenal system, anticipating this kind of disaster, begins to release cortisol into the bloodstream even before we begin to lose blood. Cortisol helps to restore blood pressure and physical strength. If blood continues to be lost or is not replaced, these compensatory mechanisms are exhausted, blood pressure again drops, and we expire. Selye believed that chronic psychological stress would stimulate the GAS to some degree and that the continued activation of compensatory mechanisms could be damaging to the organs of the body.

It is intriguing that the autonomic response to stress can sometimes be activated without involving the pituitary-adrenal system. For example, Mason and associates (1976) showed that men who were fully briefed to understand and cooperate in an experiment showed no change in cortisol metabolite excretion during three hours of exhausting exercise even though they nearly doubled their urinary catecholamine excretion (a reflection of adrenomedullary response).

Henry (1976) has constructed an interesting theory which integrates much of what we know about the adrenomedullary and pituitary-adrenocortical systems. He suggests that the sympathetic, adrenomedullary systems are activated when the organism is challenged in its control of the environment. It prepares the organism for "fight or flight." For example, in lower animals this would occur when a predator or rival is encountered. In human beings, the response may be activated not only by physical threats but by related symbolic threats posed, for instance, by arguments and traffic jams. If control over the environment is lost or injury occurs, the most adaptive response is to withdraw and conserve energy. Henry hypothesizes that the experience of loss of control is a major stimulus for the activation of the pituitary-adrenal response. He suggests that the syndromes of grief and depression represent a loss of control in psychological terms; indeed, very high levels of cortisol have been measured in depressed patients (Sachar, 1976).

Organ damage in psychosomatic illness

The final step in the chain from psyche to soma is the connection between emotional disturbance and the induction of pathological changes in the body's structure or function—in other words, disease. Since the major links between the brain and the internal organs are the autonomic nervous system and the pituitary-endocrine system, the question to be examined is whether intense or prolonged activation of these systems, particularly by psychological stimuli, can lead to disease.

Acute, overwhelming fright or despair has been reported to result in sudden death. For example, voodoo deaths are supposedly caused by the victim's belief that an evil spell has been cast over him. Such cases have not been sufficiently medically verified or studied to show for certain the mechanism of death. Of interest, however, is the phenomenon, described by Richter, of sudden death in the wild Norway rat. These animals commonly die from cardiac arrest when they are transferred from one cage to another. Richter (1957) found that he could prevent these deaths occasionally by the injection of the drug atropine, which blocks the activity of the vagal nerve, the major outflow nerve of the parasympathetic nervous system. He concluded that the cardiac arrest was due to intense vagal stimulation of the heart, activated by the rat's fear response.

A common example of parasympathetic overactivity in human beings is the *vaso-vagal reflex*. When activated, this reflex produces a sudden momentary decrease in heart rate. This reflex is responsible for fainting—for example, during the drawing of a blood sample. Apparently it was common among Victorian women under conditions of acute emotional stress. Athletes who have slow heart rates because of their physical conditioning are more prone to this reflex, giving rise to the somewhat amusing occurrence of a football player fainting after a blood test.

Ordinarily, the vaso-vagal reflex is quite benign; however, it may be significant under certain circumstances. For example, it has been suggested as the mechanism for sudden death in some people who die after diving into a cold swimming pool, a known stimulus to vagal activity. In addition, it may be significant for people who already have poor coronary circulation (Engle, 1978).

With most psychosomatic illnesses, sudden stress resulting in acute damage to an organ is not usually the hypothesized mechanism. Rather, it is assumed that a chronic or recurrent stress response gradually causes some destructive change in the anatomy or physiology of an organ.

For example, a number of investigators have shown that operant conditioning schedules which require a high level of vigilance in order to avoid an electric shock will induce significant hypertension in monkeys (Herd et al., 1969). Furthermore, experimental conflict situations, such as associating food reward with an electric shock, can induce significant hypertension, especially in animals predisposed to developing high blood pressure (Harris et al., 1973). When animals are removed from such stressors, blood pressure typically returns to normal. However, if hypertension is sustained for long periods of time by these methods, anatomical changes in the walls of arteries take place. As increased stretching pressure persists, the muscle cells in the artery walls begin to produce fibrous material for increased structural support. This has the effect of thickening the artery walls, making them less elastic. When the blood pressure is reduced, the walls stay thickened. These thickened artery walls may themselves contribute to elevated blood pressure. A vicious cycle is thus established (Wolinsky, 1972).

Sympathetic nervous system activation is known to release fatty acids and glycerol from the fat tissues. It has been hypothesized that sympathetic adrenal medullary stimulation could repeatedly raise blood fatty acid levels and thus, by way of several biochemical steps, leave fat deposits on the walls of arteries, contributing to the disease known as *atherosclerosis* (Carruthers, 1969). Thus, repeated stress could predispose an individual both to high blood pressure and to arteries partially occluded with fatty deposits. Neither of these effects has been conclusively proven in human beings.

It would take too much time and space to describe analagous mechanisms in other diseases, such as peptic ulcer, asthma, and ulcerative colitis. In order to analyze each disease, one would have to ask: What is the normal physiology of the organ? What are the major mechanisms controlling the physiology? What is the usual response to stimulation by the autonomic nervous system? What influence do pituitary or adrenal hormones have on the organ? Are the effects of autonomic stimulation or hormonal interaction induced by stressors sufficient to cause organ damage eventually? These are the difficult but crucial questions in the field of psychosomatic medicine research today (Weiner, 1977).

Interventions

What can be done to prevent, control, or reverse the adverse effects on health of psychological stress? Looking back at the many possible levels of causation, it is no surprise that many kinds of remedies have been proposed.

Beginning with the most general level, it has been suggested that we should pay more attention to the stimulus factors in our physical environment. For example, it may be important to control the level of noise in the environment in order to reduce excess psychological stimulation (Anticaglia and Cohen, 1970). Perhaps the organization of space in cities needs to take into account the effects of crowding on the physiological stress response. An easily accessible park where one may unwind would be an important psychological resource.

Secure, sustaining interpersonal relationships are unquestionably a major buffer in times of crisis. For example, Nuckolls and associates (1972) studied the outcome of pregnancy as it related to the Holmes-Rahe Life Change Scale. The degree to which a woman was surrounded by a network of husband, family, and friends was assessed. Women with a high number of life changes and poor social support were much more likely to experience complicated pregnancies than women who had undergone a similar number of changes but who had supportive relationships.

To the extent that personality traits are involved in the response to stress, they may perhaps be modified through psychotherapy. Although psychoanalytic approaches to psychosomatic patients as advocated by Alexander (1950) proved to be expensive and inconsistently effective, more recent studies of psychotherapy have shown psychosomatic patients to be among those most benefited (Hill, 1977). The focus of psychotherapy with such patients is often to encourage the expression of emotions directly and thus to relieve the tension which produces destructive effects on affected organs. As noted by Sifneos (1972), psychosomatic patients may have great difficulty expressing their feelings directly and may need to be taught ways of verbalizing their emotions and discharging their feelings appropriately.

The Type A personality described by Friedman and Rosenman is as much a life style as a personality type. Type A individuals may be helped by being taught to organize their lives so that they are not under the constant strain of time pressure (Suinn, 1977). The motivation for their competitive drives may be examined, and they may be helped to find ways to base their self-esteem on other aspects of their lives than just striving to "get ahead."

Modifying the activity of the autonomic nervous system and hormonal responses to stress has been a major technique for dealing with psychosomatic illness. Thus, an array of drugs has been discovered which block the effects of the sympathetic nervous system in elevating blood pressure. Other drugs which are effective in the treatment of high blood pressure may act on the blood pressure regulation centers in the brain. One of the time-honored ways of treating peptic ulcer disease is to administer anticholinergic drugs which block the parasympathetic stimulation of the stomach and thus diminish acid production. This stimulation may also be blocked by surgically cutting the parasympathetic vagal nerves to the stomach.

These examples of the treatment of high blood pressure and peptic ulcer disease involve drugs which act on the autonomic nervous system. Another approach to psychosomatic illness involves the use of antianxiety agents and sometimes antidepressent drugs, which presumably modify the individual's central nervous system response to stress. These drugs are extremely popular in medical practice, although research on their efficacy in psychosomatic illness has not been extensive.

Another promising technique for the modification of bodily response to stress involves the use of *biofeedback* (Shapiro and Sunvit, 1979). This technique utilizes electronic instruments which amplify various physiological events and display them so that the individual can become aware of their fluctuations. For example, tension in the neck muscles is usually only dimly perceived. However, if electrodes are placed in these muscles, an individual can readily obtain feedback about the degree of tension. With practice, he or she can learn to relax these muscles more effectively, thus leading to a state of generalized relaxation.

Many physiological functions can be modified through biofeedback. These include blood pressure, skin temperature, gastric and intestinal motility, and EEG activity. Biofeedback has been demonstrated to have lasting therapeutic benefits in the control of high blood pressure. In addition, it has been quite effective for the treatment of tension headaches. It may be useful in treating migraine headaches and some kinds of peripheral vascular diseases.

Biofeedback is expensive and time-consuming. Other researchers have found that a variety of relaxation techniques, including progressive relaxation training and transcendental meditation, can produce therapeutic benefits for patients with psychosomatic illnesses. These techniques are relatively easy to learn and can be practiced at home without elaborate equipment.

References

Alexander, F. *Psychosomatic medicine; Its principles and applications.* Norton, New York, 1950.

Anticaglia, J. R., and Cohen, A. Extra-auditory effects of noise as a health hazard. *Am. Indust. Hygiene Assoc. J.,* May–June, 1970, pp. 277–281.

Carruthers, M. E. Aggression and atheroma. *Lancet, 2:*1170–1171, 1969.

Cassel, J. Studies of hypertension in migrants. In *Epidemiology and control of hypertension,* ed. P. Oglesby. Stratton Intercontinental Medical Book Corp., New York, 1975, pp. 41–58.

Diagnostic and Statistical Manual of Mental Disorders (DSM-III). Prepared by the Task Force on Nomenclature and Statistics of the American Psychiatric Association, 1979.

Donnison, C. P. *Civilization and disease.* Wood, New York, 1938.

Dunbar, F. *Emotions and bodily changes.* Columbia University Press, New York, 1954.

Engle, G. L. Psychologic stress, vasodepressor (vasovagal) syncope and sudden death. *Ann. Int. Med., 89:*403–412, 1978.

Friedman, M., and Rosenman, R. H. *Type A behavior and your heart.* Alfred A. Knopf, New York, 1974.

Halliday, J. L. *Psychosocial medicine: A study of the sick society.* Heinemann, London, 1949.

Harris, A. H., Gilliam, W. J., Findley, J. D., and Brady, J. V. Instrumental conditioning of large magnitude, daily 12-hour blood pressure elevations in the baboon. *Science, 182:*175–177, 1973.

Henry, J. P. Mechanisms of psychosomatic disease in animals. *Adv. Vet. Sci. Comp. Med., 20:*115–145, 1976.

Henry, J. P., and Cassel, J. C. Psychosocial factors in essential hypertension: Recent epidemiologic and animal experimental evidence. *Am. J. Epidemiol., 90:*171–200, 1969.

Herd, J. A., Morse, W. H., Kelleher, R. T., and Jones, L. G. Arterial hypertension in the squirrel monkey during behavioral experiments. *Am. J. Physiol., 217:*24–29, 1969.

Hill, O. The psychological management of psychosomatic diseases. *Br. J. Psychiat., 131:*113–126, 1977.

Holmes, T. H., and Rahe, R. H. The social readjustment rating scale. *J. Psychosom. Res., 11:*213–218, 1967.

Marmot, M. G., and Syme, S. L. Acculturation and coronary heart disease in Japanese-Americans. *Am. J. Epidemiol, 104:*225–247, 1976.

Marmot, M. G., Syme, S. L., Kagan, A., Kato, H., Cohen, J. B., and Belsky, J. Epidemiologic studies of coronary heart disease and stroke in Japanese men living in Japan, Hawaii and California: Prevalence of coronary and hypertensive heart disease and associated risk factors. *Am. J. Epidemiol, 102:*514–525, 1975.

Mason, J. W., Maher, J. T., Hartley, L. H., Mougey, E. H., Perlow, M. J., and Jones, L. G. Selectivity of corticosteroid and catecholamine responses to various natural stimuli. In *Psychopathology of human adaptation,* ed. G. Serban. Plenum Press, New York, 1976, pp. 147–171.

Matsumoto, Y. S. Social stress and coronary heart disease in Japan. A hypothesis. *Milbank Mem. Fund Q., 48:*9–36, 1970.

Nuckolls, K. B., Cassel, J., and Kaplan, B. H. Psychosocial assets, life crisis and the prognosis of pregnancy. *Am. J. Epidemiol., 95:*431–441, 1972.

Page, L. B. Epidemiologic evidence on the etiology of human hypertension and its possible prevention. *Am. Heart J., 91:*527–534, 1976.

Parkes, C. M., Benjamin, B., and Fitzgerald, R. G. Broken heart: A statistical study of increased mortality among widowers. *Br. Med. J., 1:*740–743, 1969.

Rahe, R. H. Subjects' recent life changes and their near-future illness reports. *Ann. Clin. Res., 4:*250–265, 1972.

Richter, C. P. On the phenomenon of sudden death in animals and man. *Psychosom. Med., 19:*191–198, 1957.

Sachar, E. J. Neuroendocrine abnormalities in depressive illness. In *Topics in psychoendocrinology,* ed. E. J. Sachar. Grune and Stratton, New York, 1976.

Shapiro, D., and Sunvit, R. S. Biofeedback. In *Behavioral medicine: Theory and practice,* eds. O. F. Pomerleau and J. P. Brady. Williams and Wilkins, Baltimore, 1979, pp. 45–73.

Sifneos, P. E. The prevalence of "alexithymic" characteristics in psychosomatic patients. In *Topics in psychosomatic research,* ed. H. Freyberger. Karger, Basle, 1972.

Stout, C., Morrow, J., Brandt, E. N., Jr., and Wolf, S. Unusually low incidence of death from myocardial infarction: Study of an Italian American community in Pennsylvania. *J. Am. Med. Assoc., 188:*845–849, 1964.

Suinn, R. M. Type A behavior pattern. In *Behavioral approaches to medical treatment,* eds. R. B. Williams, Jr., and W. B. Gentry. Ballinger, Cambridge, Mass., 1977, pp. 55–65.

Weiner, H. *Psychobiology and human disease.* Elsevier, New York, 1977.

Williams, R. B., Jr., and Gentry, W. D., eds. *Behavioral approaches to medical treatment.* Ballinger, Cambridge, Mass., 1977.

Wolinsky, H. Long-term effects of hypertension on the rat aortic wall and their relation to concurrent aging changes. *Circ. Res., 30:*301–309, 1972.

19. Sexual organs: structure and function

The physiology of human sexual organs has been examined in detail only in recent years and largely through the pioneering work of Masters and Johnson (1966). Knowledge of the basic anatomy and physiology can be very helpful in understanding why individuals suffer from one or another form of human sexual inadequacy.

Male sex organs

One of the most striking aspects of male sexual function is the process of erection during which the penis can double in size in five to ten seconds. Erection is produced by an influx of blood into uniquely structured tissues within the penis. The penis is composed of three cylinders. The two largest ones run side by side on the upper part and are called the *corpora cavernosae;* the smaller one, which encases the urethra, a channel for both semen and urine, is called the *corpus spongiosum.* As their names imply, these structures are both cavernous and spongy. How they function is best understood by analogy with a sponge, which is shriveled and small when dry, yet swells up when filled with liquid. The corpora cavernosae contain a network of compartments or sinuses connected indirectly with blood vessels. Erection of the penis is determined almost entirely by its blood flow. During sexual excitement, small arteries or *arterioles* to the penis become dilated. Blood then flows rapidly into the penis, filling up the sinuses, enlarging the spongy tissue and making the penis erect. The increased blood flow does not leave the penis as rapidly as it enters because

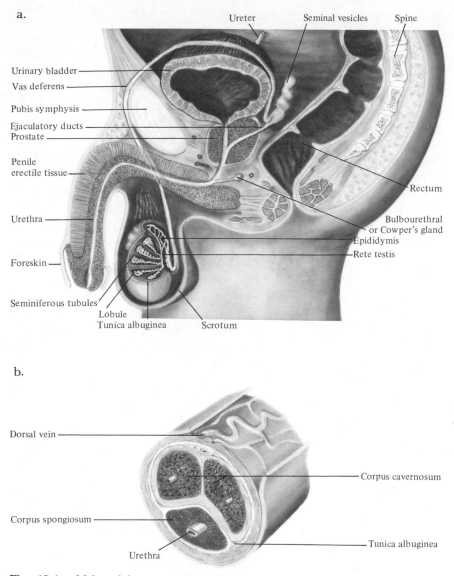

Fig. 19-1a. Male pelvic organs shown in cross section. **b.** Cross section through the penis.

unique valves located in the veins of the penis slow the return of blood to the rest of the body.

What triggers erection and what causes detumescence, the loss of erection? Sexual arousal and inhibition, which regulate penile erection, originate in the brain and then pass down neuronal pathways through the spinal cord to the sexual organs by way of the sympathetic and parasympathetic nerves. These two major classes of nerves to the penis are part of the *involuntary nervous system,* which explains why one cannot consciously control penile erection. Parasympathetic nerves generally enhance functions of the body associated with a quiet, relaxed state such as slowing the heart rate and increasing digestive movements of the intestine. By contrast, sympathetic nerves prepare the body for emergency by speeding the heart rate, increasing blood pressure, dilating bronchi to facilitate rapid breathing, and halting digestive processes. Penile erection is brought about by a firing of parasympathetic nerves, which cause the arterioles of the penis to dilate so that blood can rush in, fill the sinuses, and cause the penis to swell. The organ becomes stiff and erect because the corpora cavernosae are surrounded by a tough fibrous coat which restrains the swelling.

After ejaculation the penis undergoes *involution,* shrinking to its usual flaccid size. This appears to occur because firing of the sympathetic nerves, which takes place with orgasm, constricts the arterioles, and the accumulated blood then departs via the veins. When men lose erection as a result of some distracting event, it is probably because anxiety or a shift of attention has caused sympathetic nervous discharge.

The most sensitive part of the penis is the rounded head or *glans,* which possesses many more sensory nerves than does the rest of the organ. The most sensitive portion of the glans itself is the rim or *corona* and a small, thin piece of skin on the underside of the glans called the *frenulum.*

Many men are concerned about the size of their penis. Do short men have small penises? In their extensive studies, Masters and Johnson evaluated this question and found no correlation between the size of the penis and the rest of the body. Moreover, there was no correlation between the length of the penis in its flaccid and erect phases.

Myths abound as to the relationship of penile anatomical dimensions and sexual functioning. The size of the erect penis does not determine its ability to fill a vagina. The vagina is only a potential space which is distended by the penis. Its walls literally stretch apart to accommodate the penis regardless of its size.

Another myth holds that circumcision, by removing the skin overlying the penile glans, makes men more susceptible to sexual excitation and to premature ejaculation. However, during the thrusting of intercourse the prepucial skin of uncircumcised men retracts so that the glans is exposed to as much excitement in an uncircumcised as in a circumsised individual.

The "accessory" sex organs of the man include the prostate gland, the seminal vesicle, and Cowper's glands. Despite vast amounts of research on the prostate gland, scientists still do not know just what the prostatic secretions contribute to the biological function of semen. Of all the male sex organs, the prostate gland is the most susceptible to a variety of disorders. By middle age a large percentage of adult males suffer from *benign prostatic hypertrophy.* With age the muscle cells of the prostate enlarge in size and number. Since the prostate surrounds part of the urethra, this makes for painful, difficult urination. The enlarged prostate can be cut back by a fairly simple operation in which a drill encased within a tube is inserted and then literally chops away the enlarged prostate.

After this *transurethral prostatectomy,* urethral valves are damaged so that ejaculation takes place into the bladder and no semen is expressed during ejaculation. However, the capacity to maintain an erection and to ejaculate is usually unaffected by the operation. Thus, this type of operation should not interfere with sexual activity. With cancer of the prostate a more radical operation is employed which frequently cuts the nerves to the penis and results in impotence.

The *seminal vesicles* are two small, saclike organs whose function is also unclear. Their secretions may contain chemicals which maintain the vigor of sperm. The duct of the seminal vesicles joins together with the duct of the vas deferens, which carries sperm from the testes, to form the *ejaculatory duct.* The ejaculatory duct empties into the prostatic urethra near the opening through which the prostatic secretions themselves emerge.

Cowper's glands, also called the *bulbourethral glands,* are substantially smaller than the prostate and seminal vesicles and are located in a small area just between the prostate gland and the body wall. Their secretions empty into a narrow area called the membraneous urethra, just where the urethra emerges from the prostate gland and leaves the body to enter the penis. As with the other accessory glands, no one knows with certainty the function of Cowper's secretions. Chemically, these secretions are alkaline and may serve to neutralize the acidic environment of the urethra, which would otherwise be lethal for sperm. Cowper's secretions emerge just before ejaculation. They appear as a small drop of clear, sticky fluid at the tip of the penis when a man is highly excited. At the time of this discharge, it is still possible to delay ejaculation.

The ancients must have been aware of the biologic importance of the testes, since the word derives from the same roots as "testament," "testify," and "testimony." In early times, men would take oaths by holding their hands on their testes. The testes not only produce sperm but also elaborate the male sex hormones, or *androgens,* the most prominent of which is *testosterone.* Separate populations of cells are devoted to elaborating sperm and testosterone, respectively. Once produced, the sperm undergo a long and tortuous journey through the seminiferous tubules, which give rise to a single coiled tube, or *epididymis.*

The epididymis merges into the *vas deferens,* a straight tube that ascends out of
the scrotum and into the abdomen through the inguinal ring. Because of its superficial location, the vas deferens is an ideal target for sterilizing operations.
Vasectomy requires only a small cut in the scrotum, performed under local anesthesia, after which the surgeon need only tie off the vas.

Changes during arousal and orgasm

Masters and Johnson divided the sexual cycle of both men and women into four
phases. First is the phase of *excitement* or arousal. The *plateau* phase is a
vaguely defined period after sexual arousal has begun during which "sexual
tensions are intensified and subsequently reach the extreme form from which
the individual ultimately may move to orgasm" (Masters and Johnson, 1966).
After orgasm takes place the *resolution* phase restores the sexual apparatus to
baseline. The one major difference between the sexual cycle of men and
women is that, during resolution, a woman can be aroused to a second, third,
or fourth orgasm. For most men, there is a *refractory period* of thirty to ninety
minutes during which arousal is not feasible.

Most of the changes during the sexual cycle in both men and women are
caused by two principal alterations in the sex organs: vasocongestion and muscle contraction. Erection begins in the excitation phase. During the plateau
phase, it becomes more "permanent" and is less likely to subside in the presence of distracting stimuli. This stability may be related to a further engorgement of blood which "locks" the venous valves in place, preventing blood
from leaving the penis.

Just as the penis swells with blood so do the testes, which enlarge by 50 percent. Because of the tightness of the capsule of the testes, most men can sense
the feeling of tenseness associated with this swelling. When men and women
pet but the man does not ejaculate, the swollen testes may become painful.
Contraction of the muscles surrounding the vas deferens literally pulls the testes
up during excitement until they press against the body wall.

There are two stages to the male orgasm, both of which involve contractions
of muscles associated with the sex organs. In the first stage, the tubular system
leading out from the testes and culminating in the vas deferens contracts, along
with the seminal vesicles and prostate gland. The fluid from these three organs
collects in the prostatic portion of the urethra, where it is accommodated by a
simultaneous expansion of this portion of the urethra.

At about this time, the tight sphincter muscle at the outlet of the bladder
seals shut. This keeps urine out of the semen so that the ejaculate is free of
urine. The same mechanism also prevents semen from flowing backward into
the bladder.

This first stage of ejaculation takes about two to three seconds and does not involve the expelling of semen from the penis. Yet the male feels a sensation of "ejaculatory inevitability." At this point ejaculation is indeed inevitable, and attempts to "hold back" by intense concentration cannot succeed but will only diminish enjoyment of the ongoing orgasm.

In the second stage of ejaculation, the muscles that surround the penis contract four or five times at intervals of about one second. This timing is essentially identical to the time frame for contractions of the woman's sexual organs during orgasm.

Contrary to myth, the distance that semen is propelled forward is not related to the likelihood of impregnating the woman. Semen is never deposited in proximity to the ovum. Instead, the sperm swim uphill into the uterus to meet the egg. It is the motility of individual sperm which correlates best with fertility.

Female sex organs

The medical terminology for the female external genitals suggests a history of male chauvinism. *Vulva,* the most frequently used term, derives from a Latin word meaning "covering." The more technical designation for vulva is *pudendum* from the Latin *pudere,* meaning "to be ashamed," so that "pudendum" translates literally as "a thing of shame."

The major external genitals are the mons pubis, the major and minor lips, the clitoris, and the vaginal opening itself. The *mons pubis* is essentially a small mass of fatty tissue which is covered by pubic hair.

The major lips, or *labia majora,* are the outermost folds of skin which cover the external genitals. They merge with the general body skin in the back portion near the anus, while in the front they come together a small distance above the clitoris. The major lips are analogues of the skin of the scrotum, the scrotal sac.

The minor lips of *labia minora* are the second, inner covering of the vagina. The *labia minora* are thinner layers of skin than the major lips and are devoid of hair. They enclose the vestibule, which includes the openings for both the vagina and the urethra as well as the ducts of the greater vestibular or Bartholin's glands. In front, the major and minor lips come together and divide into two small folds of skin called the *prepuce* of the clitoris. Anatomically this is analogous to the prepuce of the penis, which is removed during circumcision.

Because the minor lips closely surround the vagina, they are stretched back and forth as the penis thrusts in and out during intercourse. The minor lips, in turn, tug upon the prepuce, causing friction upon the clitoris and providing the major stimulation which elicits orgasm.

Except for some engorgement with blood, the outer lips are fairly quiescent

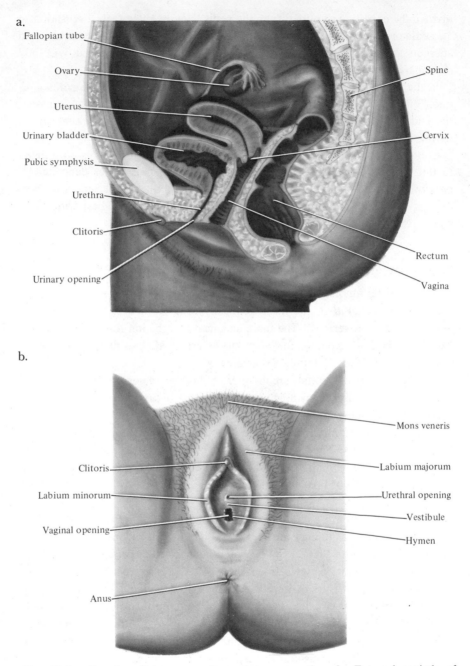

Fig. 19-2a. Female pelvic organs shown in cross section. **b.** External genitals of the female.

throughout the sex cycle. By contrast, the minor lips undergo pronounced changes. In the excitement phase the minor lips become swollen with blood to two to three times their normal size. As the plateau phase approaches, the size changes are succeeded by color alterations with their initial pinkness developing into a bright and sometimes dark red, which signifies that orgasm is close at hand.

Despite much concern throughout history over the hymen, no specific function is yet known for this structure. In the young girl, the hymen is not completely closed; small holes allow for the passage of menstrual fluid. It is traditionally held that an intact hymen signifies that a girl is a virgin. Though this is generally the case, occasionally flexible hymens remain intact even after several episodes of intercourse. A torn hymen certainly does not prove that a girl has been having intercourse, as the hymen is readily torn during exercise or through the use of tampons.

The *clitoris* is the most crucial sex organ for orgasm. Like the penis, the clitoris contains two corpora cavernosa, but it lacks a corpus spongiosum. Also like the penis, the clitoris possesses a swelling at its end referred to as the glans.

During the sex cycle the clitoris undergoes a number of changes. Unlike the penis, it does not respond immediately to stimulation by becoming erect. Instead, the initial event during sexual arousal in a woman is lubrication of the vagina. During excitement the clitoris does become congested with blood. It increases in diameter and remains enlarged throughout the rest of the sexual cycle. One of the most striking features of the plateau phase in women is that the prominent, erect clitoris retracts beneath its prepuce so that it is not observable until orgasm is complete. Though the clitoris cannot be stimulated directly at this stage, it is still affected by hand manipulations in the general area of the vulva or by penile thrusting, both of which stimulate the clitoris indirectly by pulling down on the overlying prepuce. Direct stimulation of the clitoris is probably a less effective means of bringing a woman to orgasm. The clitoris, especially its glans, is exquisitely sensitive and becomes rapidly "satiated" to stimulation, which can even be painful.

The vagina is slanted downward and forward. Thus, during intercourse the penis must tilt upward. Ignorance of this simple anatomical fact can render intercourse difficult. The outside opening of the vagina is surrounded by the bulbocavernosus muscles. Women possess some voluntary control over these muscles and so can cause pleasurable sensations in the male by alternately contracting and relaxing them. In some anxious women these muscles become tense. If this condition of *vaginismus* is severe enough, intercourse is impossible. Along with a lack of lubrication, tenseness of these muscles probably accounts for the majority of discomfort during a newly mated couple's first attempts at intercourse.

Changes during arousal and orgasm

Lubrication of the vagina is the hallmark of sexual arousal and often occurs within a few seconds of erotic stimulation.

During the excitement phase the inner two-thirds of the vagina lengthens and widens to provide a cavity where the ejaculate can fall. In the plateau phase the outer third constricts and its walls, engorged with blood, swell up to form a narrow tube which Masters and Johnson call the orgasmic platform. During orgasm all the female genitals except the ovaries contract. However, the dramatic contractions of the orgasmic platform exceed those of other parts of the female sexual system. Most women experience orgasm subjectively through the movements of the orgasmic platform.

Though many aspects of the sex cycle are similar in men and women, one major difference involves the timing of the various phases. The length of the resolution period is fairly constant among men. Most men are unable to have a new erection for thirty minutes to several hours after ejaculation. The length of this refractory period varies with age and is shortest in young men, some of whom can initiate active intercourse within ten minutes after ejaculating. By contrast, most women have little if any refractory period and can return to orgasm any time in the course of resolution.

Women vary more than men in the duration of the excitement and plateau phases. Many women require considerably more stimulation than men in preparation for orgasm. If their mates fail to delay their ejaculation for a long enough period, these women are unable to attain orgasm. They should not be regarded as suffering from orgasmic dysfunction. Instead the man and woman must learn to accommodate to each other's cycles.

Reference

Masters, W. H., and Johnson, V. E. *Human sexual response*. Little, Brown, Boston, 1966.

20. Human sexual inadequacy

William Masters and Virginia Johnson, pioneers in the study of sexual dysfunction, have often said that at least 50 percent of marriages are affected by some form of sexual inadequacy. If abnormalities in sexual functioning occur in half of all marriages, then one must seriously question what is meant by "normal" sexual behavior. There is certainly a wide range in the spectrum of normality. What is acceptable to a couple is probably just as important a criterion as any general standard. Women who were taught by their mothers that it is sinful to enjoy sex may never feel a need to have an orgasm. Are they to be judged frigid? The husband of such a woman might ejaculate within seconds of intromission. If this causes no distress to himself or his mate, one would be hard pressed to label him as suffering the dynsfunction of premature ejaculation.

Often it is difficult to judge one member of a pair as inadequate, as the fault in his or her performance may lie with the other partner. For instance, a woman may not reach orgasm if her mate is physically repulsive, emotionally distant, or ejaculates too soon. A man who dislikes his wife might well have difficulty attaining an erection in bed.

Despite such caveats, certain patterns of sexual activity do reflect dysfunction either when compared to the performance of most of the population or when judged against the needs and desires of the individual or his or her partner.

Among men the most common problems are *impotence,* which is usually defined as inability to maintain an erection, and *premature ejaculation,* difficulty in delaying ejaculation. The most common dysfunctions for women are failure to attain orgasm and painful intercourse.

Until recently most Western societies have failed to discuss these sexual inadequacies openly. Little attention was devoted to them in textbooks of psychopathology. Hardly any research into the causes and treatments of these problems was conducted. Yet, regardless of one's definitions, human sexual dysfunctions are probably at least as common as any other behavioral disorder. Moreover, with the advent of sex therapy by counseling techniques many of these disorders can be treated with considerable success.

Male sexual inadequacies

Premature ejaculation

The simplest definition of *premature ejaculation* is ejaculating too soon. There have been numerous approaches to defining an adequate duration for normal intercourse prior to ejaculation. Some authorities rely on arbitrary intervals, so that a man is a premature ejaculator if ejaculation occurs within thirty seconds, two minutes, or ten thrusts following intromission. Here the question of normality is relevant again, since the Kinsey researchers reported that about 75 percent of the men they interviewed ejaculated within two minutes of vaginal penetration (Kinsey et al., 1948). Masters and Johnson emphasize that a given symptom has meaning only in the context of interpersonal relationships. Accordingly they define a premature ejaculator as a man who "cannot control his ejaculatory process for a sufficient length of time during intravaginal containment to satisfy his partner in at least 50 percent of their coital connections" (Masters and Johnson, 1970).

Frequently premature ejaculators ejaculate immediately upon penetrating the vagina or even earlier, sometimes while observing their partner undressing. Such men worry constantly about their own sexual organs, and this worsens the situation since optimal sexual functioning requires a relaxed attitude. After many repeated episodes of premature ejaculation some men become so anxious about their performance that they develop difficulty in attaining erections, hence impotence.

Wives of premature ejaculators become frustrated because they rarely attain orgasm. Besides their psychological distress, these women often develop chronic pelvic and low back pain from the congestion with blood that occurs following many episodes of sexual arousal without orgasm. Thus the relatively discrete symptom of premature ejaculation can lead to a chronically escalating situation of marital discord.

Causes

In some instances, premature ejaculation can be due to physical causes. Prostatitis often gives rise to premature ejaculation. Because up to 20 to 30 percent of males suffer from chronic or acute prostatitis, and because chronic prostatitis often displays few other symptoms, patients suffering from early ejaculation should first have a urologic evaluation.

Most cases of premature ejaculation are probably determined by psychological mechanisms (Lief, 1975; Meyer, 1975). Psychoanalysts have suggested that premature ejaculation represents an aggressive act of the man against the woman, reflecting an unconscious wish to deprive the woman of sexual gratification. However, psychological profiles of individuals suffering from premature ejaculation have failed to disclose any unique pattern of psychopathology. The majority probably would not warrant any psychiatric diagnosis (Cooper, 1969, Lazarus, 1969, 1972).

Masters and Johnson believe that premature ejaculation stems from faulty learning as a result of early sexual experiences. For many of their patients, first sexual encounters occurred in unpleasant and even frightening circumstances which precipitated premature ejaculation and set in motion a pattern of behavior which was difficult to erase. For instance, some patients had their first experience with prostitutes who would urge them to "get it over with quickly."

Treatment

Reasoning that the penis of patients with premature ejaculation is hypersensitive to erotic stimulation, some physicians have recommended anesthetic creams or condoms to lessen the sensitivity. Others have advocated the use of alcohol, sedatives, or tranquilizers prior to intercourse. Greater success has been attained with conditioning procedures, which have been most extensively worked out by Masters and Johnson.

In initial sessions the program advocated by Masters and Johnson emphasizes that the couple learn to relax and enjoy each other's bodies without any attempt to perform sexually. After a few days they can engage in foreplay, but intercourse is still proscribed. Then systematic exercises specifically directed at the problem of prematurity commence. The wife stimulates her husband's penis until it is both firmly erect and highly excited; she stops just before ejaculation becomes inevitable. The aim of this procedure, developed by the urologist Semans (1959), is to train the male to recognize the sensation of extreme excitement and to control it. After repeating this procedure several times over a period of fifteen minutes, the wife carries it forward to her mate's ejaculation. Following several days of these exercises, intercourse is initiated with the male not attempting any thrusting. Gradually, the amount of male and female movement is increased until the male is able to maintain an erection long enough to satisfy his partner.

Before the new sex therapy counseling procedures were developed, psychotherapists had experienced very little success in treating this condition. By contrast, out of their 186 initial cases, Masters and Johnson reported only 4 failures and each of these involved complicating factors. They have concluded that unless the marital relationship has completely deteriorated, "there is negligible chance of therapeutic failure to reverse the male's rapid ejaculatory tendency" (Masters and Johnson, 1972). Other therapists have reported similar high rates of success (Kaplan, 1974; Meyer et al., 1975; O'Connor and Stern, 1972).

Impotence

Of the most common sexual inadequacies, impotence probably has the most devastating psychological effects. A woman who does not have orgasms can still partake in sexual intercourse. The same is true for most men with premature ejaculation. However, without an erection, a man cannot engage in intercourse. The true incidence of impotence is difficult to gauge, because many, perhaps most, victims feel too humiliated to report their problem to a physician or other therapist. It is well established that the ability to attain an erection decreases with age so that above the age of sixty about 20 percent or more of men have difficulty in attaining erection (Kinsey et al., 1948). However, a loss of erectile capacity or erotic feelings is by no means universal. In one study involving relatively healthy married men between the ages of seventy and seventy-nine, 43 percent reported full erectile functioning, and of those between the ages of sixty and sixty-nine, 62 percent had essentially normal sexual activity; the corresponding figure for individuals between fifty and sixty was 82 percent (Martin, 1977).

The term *impotence* is often used to describe any male sexual dysfunction. A more accurate label is *erectile dysfunction*. Most normal men at one time or another, especially in anxiety-provoking situations, fail to attain an erection suitable for sexual intercourse. Clinically significant impotence refers only to individuals who consistently fail to attain erections even with a suitable partner. The definition offered by Masters and Johnson holds that "when an individual male's rate of failure at successful coital connection approaches 25 percent of his opportunities, the clinical diagnosis of . . . impotence must be accepted" (Masters and Johnson, 1970). A distinction is often made between individuals with *primary impotence,* who have never attained an erection which permitted sexual intercourse, and *secondary impotence,* which refers to individuals who have had at least one instance of successful intromission.

Causes

Impotence can be determined by psychological factors, or it may arise as a consequence of specific organic abnormalities. One of the best-known medical causes of impotence is diabetes. About half of all male diabetics experience some erectile difficulties, largely a result of diabetic involvement of the nerves to the penis. Atherosclerosis can affect blood vessels to the penis and also produce impotence. Impotence has been associated with both abnormally low and high levels of secretion of thyroid hormone. Individuals with alcoholic cirrhosis or other liver disorders may be impotent because the liver fails to destroy circulating female sex hormones, especially estrogens. In these individuals, as well as in those in whom disorders of the testes reduce secretion of androgens, treatment with the male hormone such as testosterone can often relieve the symptoms.

Numerous drugs can cause impotence. Since penile erection is initiated by a firing of parasympathetic nerves, drugs which block their actions precipitate impotence in some individuals. The parent parasympathetic blocking drug is called *atropine*. Many drugs have atropinelike anticholinergic activity. Drugs used for the treatment of stomach ulcers, spastic colon, and other gastrointestinal distress are primarily anticholinergics. Most antihistamines have atropinelike properties. The major antidepressant drugs are potent anticholinergics. All too frequently a psychiatrist may treat a patient for depression with one of these drugs and, when impotence appears, may assume that it is just another symptom of depression.

Drugs used in treating high blood pressure interfere with both sympathetic and parasympathetic nervous activity and often inhibit both erection and ejaculation. Of all drugs, the agent most often linked to impotence is alcohol. Shakespeare knew well that drink "provokes the desire but takes away the performance." Often men will drink heavily prior to a sexual liaison with a new woman in order to feel relaxed enough to perform, only then to fail miserably.

It had been assumed that the great majority, about 90 percent of cases of impotence, were psychogenic in origin. However, recent evidence suggests that a much higher proportion than 10 percent have an organic basis, at least in part. In one study of sixty-two impotent men who presented themselves to a sex clinic with no other complaint, more than 50 percent had significant physical abnormalities which could account for their impotence. In contrast, control groups of men accompanying wives with sexual problems or groups of male premature ejaculators had a very low incidence of physical abnormalities (Lloyd and Schumacher, 1977). In a British study eleven of thirty-four impotent men showed organic abnormalities other than diabetes. Disorders included liver dysfunction, thyroid disease, and hypersecretion of prolactin. Treatment of the physical illness resulted in a recovery of normal erectile function (Mountjoy and Davies, 1969).

Among psychological causes, depression may be more closely associated with impotence than any other psychiatric condition. Indeed, severely depressed patients often first complain of impotence without ever mentioning that they feel depressed.

Among men with primary impotence, Masters and Johnson reported several typical backgrounds. Some of these men were raised by extremely seductive mothers. Others were brought up in households of extreme religious orthodoxy with a rigid suppression of sexual discussions. Many homosexuals never attain erections with women.

Some psychiatrists have speculated that the women's liberation movement has been associated with an increase in the incidence of sexual impotence. They propose that the increasing sexual assertiveness of women is perceived by young men as a threat (Ginsberg, 1972). On the other hand, the incidence of impotence may not have changed at all. Instead, in earlier times certain young men would not have discovered their impotence because the sexual reticence of young women would have saved them from exposure (Kaplan, 1977). In fact, sex therapy to relieve impotence usually involves making the woman more assertive, which actually helps the man.

Emotionally troubled childhoods occur less frequently in men with secondary impotence, especially those who have had normal functioning for many years only to experience difficulty in their mid-forties or fifties. Premature ejaculation is a frequent predecessor of secondary impotence. Often to forestall ejaculation, men will attempt to think nonsexual thoughts. This conscious suppression of sexual arousal, along with a frustrated wife's increasing tension and irritability, can frequently give rise to secondary impotence in premature ejaculators.

Heavy alcohol intake interferes with normal erection in all men. In some individuals, failure to perform while under the influence of alcohol triggers a fear that there is something wrong. Thus, in subsequent encounters, even while sober, the man is overcome with anxiety and fear of failure, which itself breeds further failure.

Treatment

True organic impotence can be treated by effective penile prostheses which have been available only in recent years. These devices should not be used in most cases of psychogenic impotence. Thus, differentiating psychogenic from organic causes of impotence is an important consideration. Recent studies of spontaneous penile erections during sleep afford a means for making such distinctions. Rapid eye movement (REM) sleep, the phase during which dreaming occurs, takes place in 20- to 30-minute periods at intervals of about 90 minutes throughout the night. In healthy men and boys, penile erections coincide with each REM period and thus total 90 to 120 minutes each night. Penile erections can be measured by simple strain gauges. During sleep, penile erection is normal in men with psychological impotence but greatly reduced in those with organic disorders (Schiavi, 1976).

Treatment of impotence according to the Masters-Johnson procedure involves the same basic principles already described for premature ejaculation. Initially, man and woman are instructed not to attempt intercourse but instead to "pleasure" each other's bodies. They begin by just gazing at one another and then caressing face, arms, and body. Gradually, they may begin to caress the genitals and then engage in oral stimulation. With this type of sexual stimulation slowly escalated over a period of weeks in a nonthreatening atmosphere, the male usually attains spontaneous erections. After several days the couple may now attempt intercourse, generally with the female in the superior position.

In their initial studies, Masters and Johnson reported a cure rate of about 75 percent for secondary impotence and 60 percent for primary impotence (Masters and Johnson, 1970). Subsequent researchers have not obtained such positive results. Some investigators feel that patients who elect to travel long distances to the Masters-Johnson clinic in St. Louis, spend two weeks "in residence," and pay a large fee are highly motivated individuals with the best prognosis. Other studies emphasize the existence of different subtypes of individuals with impotence. In one investigation, men whose impotence had a specific psychological or physical cause did well with sex therapy and equally well with no therapy or with a tranquilizer. By contrast, individuals whose impotence had developed slowly, steadily, and with no discernible cause failed to respond to any treatment, apparently because of longstanding, severe psychological disturbances (Ansaci, 1976).

While Masters and Johnson emphasize the fact that sexual dysfunction often occurs in individuals who do not qualify for any psychiatric diagnosis, numerous researchers have been impressed with the coexistence of sexual and psychiatric difficulties and with the poorer prognosis for sexual problems accompanied by severe emotional disturbance (Kaplan and Cole, 1972; Maurice and Guze, 1967; Meyer et al., 1975; O'Connor and Stern, 1972).

Female sexual inadequacies

Orgasmic dysfunction

The most frequent sexual complaint of married couples is difficulty of the wife in attaining orgasm. In his classic studies, Kinsey found that about a third of married women experience orgasm during intercourse rarely or not at all, confirming earlier extensive studies of Terman (1938). About a third of married women interviewed by Kinsey's group had orgasm during the majority of their marital intercourse, another third had orgasms about half the time, and the final third were virtually anorgasmic. Because of the great increase in sexual openness since Kinsey's studies of the 1940s, some researchers suggest that women today have less difficulty in attaining orgasm. No recent surveys have been conducted with the same rigor as the Kinsey studies, so that comparisons are difficult. In Kinsey's sample about 45 percent of women who had been married fifteen years reported that they always or nearly always reached orgasm in coitus, where a more recent study indicated a figure of 53 percent (Hunt, 1974). The proportion of women who never reached orgasm was 28 percent in the Kinsey sample and 15 percent in Hunt's work. Though these data might suggest a lessening of orgasmic dysfunction in the years since the Kinsey survey of the 1940s, the difference might be due only to variations in data acquisition and analysis.

The term *frigidity* may be applied to any female difficulty in sexual functioning. Some workers feel that "frigidity" should refer only to women who never attain sexual arousal and whose sexual organs do not lubricate during intercourse. Less severe than this *general sexual dysfunction* is orgastic dysfunction, in which a woman can be aroused but does not experience orgasm. The latter condition is much more frequent than the former (Kaplan, 1974).

Causes

There have been many theories to explain why some women are more apt to have orgasms than others. Kinsey believed that women varied in their intrinsic biological capacity to experience orgasm. In interviews with thousands of women he was impressed with the marked variability in orgasmic capacity. Some women reached orgasm within a matter of seconds and described five, six, or seven orgasms within minutes. The striking contrast between these women and others who never had orgasms seemed to him too dramatic to have been acquired through training or parental influences (Kinsey et al., 1953).

Psychoanalytic theory holds that orgasmic dysfunction derives from an inability to resolve the Oepidus complex. A simplistic, direct corollary of such a view is that increasing difficulty in sexual performance in women should closely parallel increasing levels of psychopathology. If this were the case, one would expect the greatest degree of orgasmic dysfunction in schizophrenic women. However, though the overall sexual activity of schizophrenic women is impeded by their disturbance, their frequency of orgasm is not much different from that of psychologically normal women (Landis et al., 1940; Winokur et al., 1958).

Some clinicians feel that orgasmic dysfunction is correlated with a fear that a woman's mate will abandon her or with a childhood in which sexuality was strongly suppressed (Fisher, 1973; Kaplan, 1974). A striking example in which an overly religious, rigid upbringing impeded female sexual functioning is reported by Goshen-Gottstein (1966). He surveyed an ultra-orthodox Jewish group living in Israel and found that hardly any women in the entire sect had ever attained orgasm. In one extensive study, detailed personality questionnaires revealed marked differences between women who were "orgastically adequate" and "orgastically inadequate" in that "the [orgastically] inadequate women tends to be less happy, less self-confident, less secure, less persistent and less well-integrated, more sensitive, and more moody, more exclusive in her friendships and more apt to conform to authority and conventions" (Terman, 1951).

Therapy

The most successful approach to the treatment of orgasmic dysfunction derives from the Masters-Johnson techniques. The initial phases of treatment are similar to those described for premature ejaculation and impotence. Kaplan (1974) has introduced an interesting innovation which differs somewhat from the standard Masters-Johnson routines. Masters and Johnson universally advocate that the man and woman carry out all their "exercises" together, always attempting to "pleasure" each other. For severely frigid women, Kaplan advocates that the woman initially endeavor to attain orgasm by solitary masturbation. Many of these women have developed such a negative reaction to male bodies that the presence of a man will preclude attaining orgasm at all. If masturbation is unsuccessful, Kaplan recommends the use of an electric vibrator, which provides extremely intense clitoral stimulation. Once the woman can attain an orgasm and thus recognize the attendant sensations, she begins practice with her mate. In the initial sessions, intercourse is not attempted. The man caresses his mate gently over her body and finally in her clitoral region. After gradual, nondemanding stimulation has facilitated her attaining orgasm at his hands, the couple may proceed to intercourse.

The overall success rate recorded by Masters and Johnson (1970) in treating orgasmic dysfunction is about 80 percent. As with male disabilities, other workers have not had such a high success rate in treating female orgastic dysfunction. Meyer et al. (1975) emphasizes that Masters and Johnson report their results in terms of "failures." Thus, instead of speaking of an 80 percent cure rate, they speak of a 20 percent failure rate. Among the inferred "successes" are a substantial number of equivocal instances of "improvement." In the short two-week intensive therapy program of Masters and Johnson, a couple will be judged as not having failed if they have begun to improve. Other workers have found that couples who only begin to improve during intensive treatment sub-sequently relapse. Thus, that may seem to be an initial 80 percent partial or complete success rate often eventuates in only a 40 to 50 percent long-term remission rate.

References

Ansaci, J. M. A. Impotence: Prognosis (a controlled study), *Br. J. Psychiat.,* *128:*194–198, 1976.

Cooper, A. J. Factors in male sexual inadequacy: A review. *J. Nerv. and Ment. Disor-ders, 149:*337, 1969.

Derogatis, L. R. Psychological assessment of sexual disorders. In *Clinical management of sexual disorders,* ed. J. K. Meyer. Williams and Wilkins, Baltimore, 1976.

Fisher, S. *The female orgasm: Psychology, physiology, fantasy.* Basic Books, New York, 1973.

Ginsberg, G. L. Personal communication, 1972.

Goshen-Gottstein, E. R. Courtship, marriage and pregnancy in "geulan," a study of an ultra-orthodox Jerusalem group. *Israel Ann. Psychol. and Related Dis., 4:*43–66, 1966.

Hunt, M. *Sexual behavior in the 1970's.* Playboy Press, Chicago, 1974.

Kaplan, H. S. *The new sex therapy.* Brunner/Mazel, New York, 1974, p. 374.

Kaplan, H. S. *The myth of the new impotence.* Presented at the American Academy of Psychoanalysis, May 1977.

Kaplan, H. S., AND Cole, R. Adverse reactions to the rapid treatment of sexual problems. *Psychosomatics, 13:*185–190, 1972.

Kinsey, A. C., Pomeroy, W. B., and Martin, C. E. *Sexual behavior in the human male.* W. B. Saunders, Philadelphia, 1948, pp. 236–238.

Kinsey, A. C., Pomeroy, W. B., Martin, C. E., and Gebbard, P. H. *Sexual behavior in the human female.* W. B. Saunders, New York, 1953.

Landis, C., Landis, A. T., AND Bolles, M. M. *Sex in development.* Harper & Row, New York, 1940.

Lazarus, A. A. Modes of treatment for sexual inadequacies. *Med. Aspects Human Sex. 3:*53, 1969.

Lazarus, A. A. Psychological causes of impotence. *Sexual Behavior, 2:*39, 1972.

Lief, H. I. *Medical aspects of human sexuality.* Hospital Publications, New York, 1975.

Lloyd, W. W., and Schumacher, S. Personal communication, 1977.

Martin, C. E. Personal communication, 1977.

Masters, W. H., and Johnson, V. E., *Human sexual response.* Little, Brown, Boston, 1966.

Masters, W. H., and Johnson, V. E. *Human sexual inadequacy.* Little, Brown, Boston, 1970, p. 157.

Maurice, W., and Guze, S. Sexual dysfunction and associated psychiatric disorders. *Psychiatry, 11:*534–539, 1967.

Meyer, J. Individual treatment of sexual disorders. In *Comprehensive textbook of psy-chiatry,* 2nd ed., eds. A. Freedman, H. Kaplan, and B. Sadock. Williams and Wilkins, Baltimore, 1975.

Meyer, J. K., Schmidt, C. W., Lucas, M. J., and Smith, E. Short term treatment of sexual problems: Interim report. *Am. J. Psychiat., 132:*170–176, 1975.

Mountjoy, C. Q., and Davies, T. F. Erectile impotence. *Br. Med. J.,* July 17, 1969, pp. 176–177.

O'Connor, J., and Stern, L. Developmental factors in functional sexual disorders. *N. Y. State J. Med., 72:*1838–1843, 1972a.

O'Connor, J., and Stern, L. Results of treatment in functional sexual disorders. *N. Y. State J. Med., 72:*1927, 1972b.

Schiavi, R. C. Sex therapy and psychophysiological research. *Am. J. Psychiat., 133:*562, 1976.

Semans, J. H. Premature ejaculation (ejaculatio praecox): A new method of therapy. *A. Urology, 52:*381–389, 1959.

Terman, L. M. *Psychological factors in marital happiness.* McGraw-Hill, New York, 1938.

Terman, L. M. Correlates of orgasmic adequacy in a group of 556 wives. *J. Psychol., 32:*115–172, 1951.

Winokur, G., Guze, S. B., and Pfeiffer, E. Developmental and sexual factors in women: A comparison between control, neurotic and psychotic groups. *Am. J. Psychiat., 115:*1097–1100, 1958.

21. Gender identity and role disorders

Men who dress themselves as women and women who dress themselves as men are known as *transvestites*. Eastern and Western, preliterate and modern cultures all contain a number of transvestites. Less common is *transsexualism,* in which the individual not only dresses as a member of the opposite sex but perceives himself or herself as having been "born into the wrong body" and nowadays strongly desires sex reassignment by surgery. The development of "sex change" operations during the past twenty years amid much publicity has focused attention upon this relatively rare condition. A common misconception is that transvestites and transsexuals are simply particularly effeminate homosexuals. In fact, individuals with gender identity disturbances have quite different psychosexual characters from homosexuals. Homosexuals view themselves as members of the sex to which they were born. They merely prefer sexual relationships with individuals of their own sex. Transvestites are often not homosexuals at all. Many of them are married and have normal sexual relationships with their spouses. Male transsexuals, on the other hand, do desire sexual relationships with other men. However, they view these as heterosexual relationships.

Many instances of transvestism and transsexualism have been described in Western history. King Henry III of France dressed in public as a woman with jeweled necklaces and low-cut dresses. Indeed, he introduced the term "Sa majesté" to be used in reference to the sovereign, a term which literally means "Her Majesty." The first colonial governor of New York, Lord Cornbury, dressed in women's clothes publicly while in office both in America and in England.

A technical name for transsexualism, *eonism,* derives from the Chevalier d'Eon. This biological male so effectively masqueraded as a woman that he became the closest rival to Madame de Pompadour as mistress for King Louis XV of France. After learning the chevalier's secret, the king regarded him as a trusted friend and even made use of his ability to assume a dual identity in secret missions to Russia, where d'Eon alternated dress as woman and man.

Determinants of sexual identity

An individual's gender identity is determined by both psychological and biological factors. It should come as no great surprise that if a boy is raised by his parents as a girl from the day of birth, he will experience sexual identity crises as an adult and will probably be effeminate. Biological factors, such as the influence of sex hormones on the brain, also affect later sexual behavior. The normal female has forty-four autosomal chromosomes and two sex chromosomes, both X. The biological male has the same forty-four autosomal chromosomes plus one X and one Y sex chromosome. Disorders of the sex chromosomes give rise to distinct clinical conditions.

At an early stage, the human fetus is both male and female. The precursors of the female gonads are called the *Mullerian ducts,* while the *Wolffian ducts* are progenitors of the male structures. In the fetal male, an unknown inhibiting substance causes a degeneration of the Mullerian ducts. At the same time, the male sex hormones or androgens promote the development of the Wolffian duct systems and subsequently of the male external genitals. In the absence of androgens or of the substance which inhibits the Mullerian system, an organism develops gonadally as a female. Thus, in the absence of hormone secretion, embryos become female; a special hormonal secretion is required to produce males.

Whereas there exist distinct analogues of separate male and female internal genitals, the external genitals derive from the same precursors. Thus, the tissue folds which give rise to the penis in a male are transformed into the clitoris in the female. The labia minora and clitoral hood are homologous to the skin of the penis. The scrotum of the man is equivalent to the woman's labia majora. As with the internal gonads, development of the external genitals is determined solely by androgens. If androgens are secreted by the fetus, the male genitals appear; if they are not, female genitals are formed.

Administration of minute amounts of androgens or estrogens directly into the brains of fetal or newborn rats dramatically alters subsequent sexual behavior (Gorski, 1966; Hamburg and Lunde, 1966; Phoenix et al., 1967). Sexual behavior patterns of monkeys can be influenced in a relatively subtle fashion by perinatal administration of different sex hormones. One can readily see how disturbances in the amount or timing of hormonal secretion could have considerable influence upon subsequent sexual differentiation. Several human sexual abnormalities can be definitely attributed to early hormonal malfunctions, and one can speculate that as yet undiscovered abnormalities might account for disorders which have been thought to be exclusively psychogenic in origin. Whether or not this is the case, the nature of the behavioral disorders in patients with identified chromosomal or hormonal defects can tell us a great deal about the way in which these early developmental processes influence adult gender identity.

Chromosomal errors

Turner's syndrome

Individuals with this condition lack one of the female X chromosomes. They possess a single X chromosome but no Y chromosome. Since male characteristics develop only when a Y chromosome exists, these individuals are female. However, they lack ovaries; hence the technical name for this disorder of *gonadal agenesis*. Upon operation, surgeons find only primitive streaks of tissue where the ovaries should have been. Such women are sterile, and lacking the ovarian hormones, or estrogens, they are sexually infantile in that their breasts and other secondary sex characteristics fail to develop until they are medically treated with estrogens. Additionally, some suffer from various abnormalities. Most are short, averaging about 4 feet 10 inches. Some have a small, almost absent neck, receding chin, folds about their eyelids resembling Oriental eyes, and hearing loss.

Girls with Turner's syndrome display few psychological problems. If anything, they seem somewhat more emotionally stable than physiologically normal girls, which is surprising in light of their short stature, the knowledge that they are sterile, and their failure to undergo puberty. The only consistently noted psychological dysfunction is a tendency to clumsiness in handling various objects and difficulty in perceiving subtle three-dimensional objects and directions accurately (Money, 1963).

Almost all of these girls have a strong female identity and display maternal interests from early childhood. Most of them marry and adopt children, for whom they appear to be excellent parents.

Klinefelter's Syndrome (XXY)

Individuals with this condition have an extra X chromosome. While most patients with Klinefelter's syndrome have only one extra X chromosome, some have two or three too many. In one sense, these individuals are chromosomally both male and female. Anatomically, however, they are not hermaphrodites, that is, individuals possessing both male and female gonads. Instead, they develop as males. They are characteristically slender and tall. Though they have testes, these fail to produce sperm, and in time the testes degenerate into connective tissue. The penis is small and at adolescence breasts develop, a condition called *gynecomastia*.

Men with Klinefelter's syndrome show a much broader range of intelligence than normal persons. Some are superior in IQ, yet the incidence of mental retardation is greater than in the general population. Emotional problems of all sorts are common, but there is no specific pattern. Some individuals are obsessional, others predominantly anxious, and there are also cases of depression and schizophrenia.

The apparently greater liability of Klinefelter patients to psychological disorders is accompanied by a similar tendency to sexual problems. Men with Klinefelter's syndrome have very little sexual drive. Androgen treatment increases sexual vigor in some patients, while others tend to be unresponsive (Jost, 1972; Money and Ehrhardt, 1972; Money and Pollitt, 1964; Money and Wang, 1966).

Of particular interest with regard to gender identity is the fact that among men with Klinefelter's syndrome there are numerous transvestites and transsexuals. Since both Klinefelter's syndrome and transsexualism are rare conditions, their coexistence even in a limited number of individuals is statistically improbable. Because the majority of Klinefelter's patients are not transsexuals, the chromosomal abnormality is probably not the sole explanation for subsequent transsexualism or transvestitism. Rather, the biological abnormalities of these patients may make them particularly vulnerable to environmental influences which precipitate psychosexual gender dysfunctions. Perhaps a similar interplay of biological factors and the environment is relevant to other psychosexual disorders.

The XYY syndrome

This disorder, which one might expect to produce "supermales," was discovered in a chromosomal screening of male prisoners. Several studies have since suggested that individuals with the extra Y chromosome were impulsive in a criminal fashion and tended to be sex offenders. Richard Speck, who sexually assaulted and murdered several nursing students in Chicago in a highly publicized case, was shown to have an XYY chromosome pattern.

Gonadal errors due to hormonal disorders

Testicular feminization

Individuals with this condition are genetically males. Sexual differentiation in the fetus takes place normally and the gonads develop as testes, while the Mullerian ducts regress so that the internal sex organs are exclusively male. The testes then produce androgen. However, the "target organs" of this hormone throughout the body fail to respond appropriately. Accordingly, the external genitals develop as those of a female. At puberty the small amount of estrogens produced by the testes cause these patients to appear physically female. Lacking a uterus, they do not menstruate, and their vagina tends to be smaller than that of a normal female. The coexistence of testes in the groin is embarrassing and uncomfortable so that these are usually removed surgically.

Because these individuals look like girls at birth, they are invariably raised as girls. Remarkably, among the many recorded cases of testicular feminization there are few if any instances of gender identity disturbances. Subjects all regard themselves as females, tend to marry and have families by adoption, and to make good mothers. In this case, early rearing influences appear to override completely the effects of both chromosomes and fetal androgen secretion.

The andrenogenital syndrome: female pseudohermaphroditism

Hermaphrodites are organisms with both male and female gonads, that is, testes and ovaries. True human hermaphrodites occur very rarely. Biological females with adrenogenital syndrome have the external genital appearance of a male, but since their gonads are completely female they are only pseudohermaphrodites. Their adrenal cortex lacks the enzymatic mechanisms to complete the synthesis of its normal hormone, hydrocortisone. Instead, the gland releases a precursor of hydrocortisone which happens to possess androgenlike activity. The androgenic secretions do not build up to high levels until the ovaries and other internal reproductive organs have been formed. They do appear in time to cause the external genitals to develop along male patterns. In some individuals a completely normal penis and scrotum (lacking testes) develop. More commonly, the penis does not develop completely so that the urinary opening is approximately in the female position.

A somewhat analogous problem occurs in genetic females whose mothers are treated with synthetic progesterone hormones during pregnancy, usually to prevent early miscarriage (Ehrhardt and Money, 1967). Though progesterone is a normal ovarian secretion, in large doses the synthetic progesterones used have a masculinizing effect on the genitals of the fetus. In most of these cases, the internal organs are not affected, but the external genitals develop like those of a male.

Both the adrenogenital syndrome and progesterone-induced pseudoher-maphroditism teach important lessons about the comparative influences of hormones and early rearing practices on subsequent gender identity. Children with either condition who have been raised as females differ very little in their behavior patterns from age-matched normal controls. These girls seem to behave somewhat more as tomboys than average girls, displaying considerable interest in athletics and less in doll play. However, they unequivocally regard themselves as females. Children with the adrenogenital syndrome raised as boys regard themselves as males exclusively. Behaviorally these boys differ little if at all from ordinary boys.

These conditions indicate the overriding role of social learning and psychological factors in determining a child's ultimate sexual identity. The subtle but definite signs of "boyishness" in girls exposed to androgens in fetal life suggest that hormonal effects on the brain before birth can play an important role in subsequent personality development, and perhaps in some cases they are the major determinants of adult sexual behavior.

Transvestism

Most people think of *transvestism* as simply "cross-dressing." Virtually all transvestites are male, perhaps because there is little if any social stigma attached to a female dressing in masculine clothing. Cross-dressing is not an adequate definition of this disorder. Many male homosexuals dress as females, "in drag", especially if they are relatively effeminate. Male transsexuals also dress in female clothing. By contrast, transvestites are virtually never homosexual. They are usually pleased to be males and have no intention of changing their sexual identity. For a diagnosis of transvestism, most sex researchers require that the male obtain sexual arousal by wearing female clothing. The DSM-III does not require that cross-dressing produce sexual excitation because some individuals dress in female clothing less for sexual excitement than to relieve anxiety. According to DSM-III, when "sexual arousal by clothing [is present] the additional diagnosis of 'fetishism' should be made." The great majority of transvestites undergo intense sexual arousal when cross-dressed. From their attitude toward the female clothing they wear, it is quite clear that for them cross-dressing is a fetish.

As already mentioned, transvestites are overtly heterosexual. Most of them are married (Prince and Bentler, 1972; Stoller, 1971). Virtually all aspects of their behavior are masculine. They indulge in cross-dressing only intermittently and usually secretively. Sometimes their wives join in their fetishistic fantasies; they attain sexual arousal which is consummated in intercourse with their wives. Wearing women's dresses, shoes, or underwear elicits in transvestites strong erections, unlike transsexuals, who detest their penises. Transsexuals rarely show penile erections when they cross-dress.

Though the causes of transvestism are by no means clear, interviews tend to reveal typical family backgrounds (Stoller, 1970). Most transvestites report that the first instance of cross-dressing occurred while they were preadolescents. Usually another girl dressed them in girls' clothes, often simply to humiliate them. At that time there was no sexual excitation associated with the cross-dressing. The fetish of erotic cross-dressing appears later during adolescence.

Transsexualism

Transsexualism is defined by DSM-III as "a heterogeneous group of chronic disorders in which there is a persistent sense of discomfort and inappropriateness in one's anatomic self and a persistent wish to be rid of one's own genitalia and to live as a member of the other sex. The diagnosis is only made if the disturbance has been continuous for at least two years and is not symptomatic of another mental disorder such as schizophrenia and is not associated with physical intersex or genetic abnormality." Some psychiatrists label all transsexuals as schizophrenics on the grounds that such an intense desire to change one's gender identity is, by definition, a psychotic delusion.

However, careful psychological evaluation of transsexuals has failed to show major deviations from the general population, except for the presence of depressive symptoms which are clearly related to the individual's usually untenable life situation.

Much research in the past decade has focused on psychological profiles of these individuals. Numerous transsexuals have been described who, according to their own reports as well as those of their parents, felt they belonged to the opposite sex when they were two or three years old (Pauly, 1965; Walinder, 1967). Depressive feelings after many frustrated attempts to change their life situation may explain the suicide attempts noted in about 20 percent of patients (Pauly, 1965, 1969; Walinder, 1967). In one study of 34 transsexuals, no evidence of psychotic ideation was found. Moreover, there was not even a marked degree of neuroticism. Strikingly, more than half the transsexuals had IQ scores in the bright-normal range, and there were six times as many as expected in the superior group. On Thematic Apperception Tests (TAT) transsexuals were lucid, highly productive, and tended to emphasize love and sex relationships. When asked to "draw a person," these individuals invariably drew a female first (Doorbar, 1969). Two-thirds of a series of forty-three transsexuals "played [before puberty] exclusively with children of the other sex, acted like and played games of the other sex, were embarrassed in front of the same sex" (Walinder, 1967). At this early age essentially all the subjects felt that they belonged to the other sex. At puberty they all "became increasingly disgusted with their developing male anatomy, became increasingly convinced that they belonged to the female sex, wanted to be accepted by society as female, and desperately desired a change of sex operation." Indeed, 18 of 100 transsexuals in another series mutilated their own genitals when frustrated by doctors hesitant to perform sex change surgery (Pauly, 1965).

Transsexuals differ from homosexuals and most individuals with sexual paraphilias in the degree of sexual urge or libido. Homosexuals might appear to have stronger libidos than most heterosexual individuals, since their frequency of sexual activity to the point of orgasm is considerably greater than that of the normal population. A high frequency of sexual activity to orgasm is also manifested by most individuals with sexual paraphilias. However, about 20 percent of male transsexuals report only very weak sexual desires and about 60 percent describe moderate sexual interests (Walinder, 1967). Libidinal drives are rarely a prominent part of the transsexual perception of being an "other sexed" person. For them gender reversal has much more to do with overall life style, while narrowly sexual aspects are less important than with most sexual deviations.

Is the fundamental psychological functioning of a male transsexual more "male" or "female"? In one investigation, fourteen male transsexuals were evaluated by detailed interview and psychometric tests of masculinity-femininity (Money and Primrose, 1969). Male transsexuals scored lower on masculinity measures than 90 percent of the normal male population. Strikingly, seven out of eleven scored more feminine than 60 percent of normal females. This finding suggests that the male transsexuals are working very hard to mimic the stereotype of female behavioral norms. In detailed interviews, these individuals described their imagery during sexual experience either when having intercourse with their wives or when being the insertee in anal intercourse with other men. The transsexuals tended to visualize themselves with complete female characteristics: breasts, long hair, vagina, and a female body shape. These fantasies made for certain paradoxes. In one case a man could not attain an erection with his wife unless he had such a fantasy: "He reported that successful achievement was dependent upon his ability to disregard his penis.

He was aroused only when in his imagination his wife had the penis and he had the vagina'' (Money and Primrose, 1969). This pattern of behavior is suggestive of the dissociation which occurs in conversion hysteria.

Transsexualism appears to be much more common among men than women. In most series, 80 percent of applicants for sex change operations are male (Hoopes et al., 1968; Pauly, 1965). Nonetheless, there are a substantial number of female transsexuals, and operations have been developed to transform their external genitals with procedures which include construction of a penis that can be employed in sexual intercourse.

In general, female transsexuals report childhoods similar to those of male transsexuals. In one series of fifty-seven patients, 64 percent thought of themselves as boys "as long as I can remember," often from the age of 2. The mean age at which the girls were convinced they were born into the wrong bodies was 7.25 (Pauly, 1974). Before the age of puberty almost all of them crossdressed frequently. At the onset of puberty 81 percent tightly bound their breasts to minimize their female appearance. Interestingly, about half of them described a late onset of menarche with scant and irregular periods. They had explicit sexual relationships with other females, sometimes during adolescence, beginning at a mean age of 18.2 years. About 50 percent did have intercourse with men but usually only once or twice and then with little pleasure. In this sense, their behavior patterns are very much like those of female homosexuals. However, transsexuals feel quite different from lesbians and after some experimentation tend to avoid lesbian groups.

Major differences between female and male transsexuals are found in their social adjustment. Female transsexuals seem better adjusted in a male role than do male transsexuals in a female role. The females tend to have less psychopathology, with a lower incidence of depression and only infrequent suicidal attempts. Requests for sex change operations are less pressured and frantic than those of male transsexuals. Presumably these differences relate to the attitude of society toward masculine women, who are regarded with less derogation than effeminate men.

The cause of transsexualism is unknown. The fact that self-perception in the opposite gender often stems from earliest childhood suggests that transsexualism depends on some biological substratum, much like the development of genital abnormalities. To assess possible psychogenic influences, researchers have interviewed patients and their families in detail. Stoller (1970) was struck by certain consistent patterns in the relationship of the patients' mothers to future male transsexuals. The mothers tended to be domineering and extremely close to their sons. The sons described many instances of "physical contact, which may have been seductive." Unlike similar seductive relationships between mothers and future homosexual boys, Stoller noted that the mothers of transsexuals tended to be competitive and to have been tomboys themselves as young girls. In a series of nine transsexual families, Stoller believed that the mother was bisexual in eight instances. Such a consistent pattern of family interactions suggests but does not establish a psychogenic etiology of the disorder. If transsexualism were associated with a specific genetic vulnerability, one might expect the mother to be partially afflicted and so to differ behaviorally from the general population norm.

Therapy

The first well-known case of surgical treatment for transsexualism was that of Christine Jorgenson, an American ex-soldier (Hamburger et al., 1953). Very little systematic evaluation, surgery, and follow-up were conducted until the mid-1960s, when the Johns Hopkins University initiated a major research and treatment program. Only recently has it been possible to evaluate critically the effect of treatment on the life patterns of transsexuals. One controlled study has been conducted at Johns Hopkins by Dr. J. K. Meyer and Dr. D. J. Reiter (1979). A total of 100 individuals were selected for follow-up, of whom 34 were operated and 66 (the control group) were unoperated. The rationale for not operating varied considerably. In some patients, the evaluating physicians felt that surgery might not be useful, while in other cases there were financial or professional considerations. At follow-up social and professional adjustment had improved for both the operated and the unoperated groups. Both groups showed a 70 percent decrease in the incidence of psychiatric contacts over a six-year period. Thus, though none of the operated patients voiced any regrets at reassignment, operation provided no greater enhancement of overall adjustment than the simple passage of time coupled with limited emotional support from the clinic. Failure to detect any unique enhancement of adjustment following operation is reminiscent of the difficulty in demonstrating the efficacy of psychotherapy in controlled studies. Thus nonspecific placebo effects in both unoperated and operated groups may have obscured genuine improvement in operated transsexuals. Perhaps whatever factors precluded operation in the unoperated group also favored their improvement without surgery. Clearly, studies of the therapeutic effect of surgery for sexual dysfunction are difficult to evaluate.

References

Doorbar, R. R. Psychological testing of male transsexualism: A brief report of results from the Wechsler adult intelligence scale, the thematic apperception test and the house-tree-person test. In *Transsexualism and sex reassignment,* eds. R. Green and J. Money. Johns Hopkins University Press, 1969, pp. 189–200.

Ehrhardt, A. A., and Money, J. Progestin-induced hermaphroditism: IQ and psychosexual identity in a study of 10 girls. *J. Sex. Res., 3:*83–100, 1967.

Gorski, R. A. Localization and sexual differentiation of the nervous structures which regulate ovulation. *J. Repro. and Fertil., 1:*67–88, 1066.

Hamburg, D., and Lunde, D. Sex hormones in the development of sex differences. In *The development of sex differences,* ed. E. Maccoby. Stanford University Press, Palo Alto, 1966.

Hamburger, C., Sturup, G. K., and Dahl-Iversen, E. Transvestism: Hormonal, psychiatric and surgical treatment. *J. Am. Med. Assoc., 152:*391–396, 1953.

Hoopes, J. E., Knorr, N. J., and Wolf, S. R. Transsexualism: Considerations regarding sexual reassignment. *J. Nerv. and Ment. Disorders, 147:*510–516, 1968.

Jost, A. A new look at the mechanisms controlling sex differentiation in mammals. *Johns Hopkins Med. J., 130:*38, 1972.

Meyer, J. K., and Reiter, D. J. Sex reassignment: Follow-up. *Arch. Gen. Psychiat.* 36:1010–1015, 1979.

Money, J. Cytogenetics and psychosexual incongruities with a note on space-form blindness. *Am. J. Psychiat., 119:*820–826, 1963.

Money, J., and Ehrhardt, A. A. *Man and woman/boy and girl.* Johns Hopkins University Press, Baltimore, 1972.

Money, J., and Pollitt, E. Cytogenetics and psychosexual ambiguity: Klinefelter's syndrome and transvestitism compared. *Arch. J. Psych., 11:*589–595, 1964.

Money, J., and Primrose, C. Sexual dimorphism and dissociation in the psychology of male transsexuals. In *Transsexualism and sex reassignment,* eds. R. Green and J. Money. Johns Hopkins University Press, Baltimore, 1969, pp. 115–136.

Money, J., and Wang, C. Human figure drawings: Sex of first choice in gender identity anomalies, Klinefelter's syndrome and precocious puberty. *J. Nerv. and Ment. Diseases, 143:*157–162, 1966.

Pauly, I. B. Male psychosexual inversion: Transsexual. *Arch. Gen. Psychiat., 13:*172–181, 1965.

Pauly, I. B. Adult manifestations of male transsexualism. In *Transsexualism and sex reassignment,* eds. R. Green and J. Money. Johns Hopkins University Press, Baltimore, 1969, pp. 37–58.

Pauly, I. B. Female transsexuals. *Arch. Sex. Behav., 3:*487–507, 1974.

Phoenix, C., Goir, A., and Young, W. Sexual behavior: General aspects. In *Neuroendocrinology,* eds. L. Martini and W. Ganong. New York Academic Press, 1967.

Prince, V., and Bentler, P. M. Survey of 504 cases of transvestism. *Psychol. Rep., 31:*903, 1972.

Stoller, R. J. Psychotherapy of extremely feminine boys. *Int. J. Psychiat., 9:*278, 1970.

Stoller, R. J. The term "transvestism." Arch. Gen. Psychiat., 24:230, 1971.

Walinder, J. *Transsexualism.* Akademiförlaget, Göteborg, Sweden, 1967.

22. Homosexuality

Homosexuality is most simply defined as a preference for sexual activity with members of the same sex. Frequently homosexuality is confused with transvestism and transsexualism. Transvestites are usually heterosexual men who achieve sexual arousal from dressing as women, often while masturbating. Some homosexuals like to dress as the opposite sex, but this is not a source of sexual arousal for them, nor is it a common pattern. For many years, transsexuals were grouped together with homosexuals. However, it is now widely accepted that their behavior pattern can be readily differentiated from homosexuality. Transsexuals actually want to *be* members of the opposite sex (Cauldwell, 1949). They have a sense of belonging to the sex opposite their anatomical one and often feel that they were born into the wrong sex. By contrast, homosexuals generally have a strong sense of identity as members of their biological gender; they simply prefer to have sexual relations with other members of that gender.

Many people assume that the word "homosexuality" refers primarily to male-male sexual relationships on the basis that "homo" derives from a word relating to "man." In fact, the word's root is the Greek *hom* or Latin *homo,* which means "the same." Thus, homosexuality refers to same-sexed relationships, whether male or female.

Female homosexuality is sometimes referred to as *lesbianism* or *sapphism.* These terms derive from the poet Sappho, born about 612 B.C., who lived on Lesbos, a Greek island in the Aegean. Sappho formed a female literary society, one of the first historical instances of women's liberation. The Greek playwright Aristophanes appears to have introduced the term *lesbian* in the sexual sense into popular culture through his play *The Frogs,* written about 405 B.C.

Much controversy has surrounded the question of whether homosexuality represents an emotional disturbance. For many years, official psychiatric diagnostic manuals placed homosexuality in the group of "psychopathic personalities" as an instance of "pathological sexuality." DSM-II, issued in 1952, still labeled homosexuality as a "sociopathic personality disturbance." As such, it was grouped with other sexual deviations, including transvestism, pedophilia, fetishism, and sexual sadism. After heated debate, in May 1974 a majority of the voting members of the American Psychiatric Association voted to change the classification of homosexuality. Homosexuality was no longer to be regarded as a mental disorder. Instead, a diagnosis of "sexual orientation disturbance (homosexuality)" was to be restricted to "individuals whose sexual interests are directed primarily toward people of the same sex and who are *either disturbed by, in conflict with or wish to change their sexual orientation.* This diagnostic category is distinguished from homosexuality which by itself does not constitute a psychiatric disorder" (DSM-II, 1974). The most recent stage in the evolution of the official position of the American psychiatric establishment toward homosexuality is marked by DSM-III (1980), which omits all reference to homosexuality in its classification of psychiatric disturbances.

Attitudes toward homosexuality have varied markedly in different historical periods and different cultures. There seems to have been a high incidence of homosexuality in most societies that condoned the practice. In ancient Greece homosexual relationships among men were regarded as desirable human relationships. Plato apparently expressed the contemporary attitude when he wrote, "He who grants sexual favors to his male lover in the hope that he will be improved through the friendship shows himself to be virtuous . . . it is honorable for a man to grant sexual favors to the good among men" (Plato as quoted in Tripp, 1976). In certain Peruvian Indian tribes, homosexuality is sufficiently dominant that heterosexual contacts occur only a few times a year (Schneebaum, cited in Tripp, 1976). In the Kiwi tribe of New Guinea homosexual rites are a standard part of puberty initiation.

Evidence that homosexuality has existed in various cultures throughout history, statistical studies of its incidence in the United States, and psychological studies of homosexuals all help in answering the question of whether homosexuality is a form of psychopathology. The conclusion from these varied sources of evidence is that the American Psychiatric Association voted correctly in 1974: Although homosexuality represents a difference in sexual preference from the norm in our society and nearly all others, there is nothing intrinsically psychopathological about it.

Incidence

In the first half of the twentieth century, several studies evaluated the frequency of homosexual activity. In the United States interviews with young men of about college age indicated that 17 to 30 percent had had some homosexual experience.

The most definitive studies were conducted by Alfred Kinsey and his associates, and in their investigation of male sexual behavior 5,300 men were interviewed. Kinsey had expected to find a 1 or 2 percent incidence of homosexuality. He was surprised to find that it was much higher. Deciding that people cannot be separated into exclusively homosexual or heterosexual groups, Kinsey rated individuals on a seven-point scale ranging from 0 for an individual who had no homosexual experience through 6 for someone who was exclusively homosexual in thought and behavior. He was struck by the occurrence of considerable homosexual behavior in men who were predominately heterosexual. Specifically, 37 percent of the total male population had engaged in some overt homosexual activity to the point of orgasm between adolescence and old age. Another 13 percent had reacted erotically to other males without having overt homosexual contacts after adolescence. Thus, half the entire male population that was interviewed had had some homosexual experience at one time or another. Clearly, homosexual experience itself could not be an aberration.

Among individuals who had only a few homosexual contacts, the experiences often represented adolescent experimentation. Yet 25 percent of the male population had "more than incidental homosexual experience for at least 3 years between the ages of 16 and 55." Moreover, 18 percent reported as many homosexual as heterosexual episodes, while 13 percent had more homosexual than heterosexual involvement. Finally, about one out of ten of those interviewed were more or less exclusively homosexual (Kinsey et al., 1948).

At the time of Kinsey's studies, homosexuality was classified as a manifestation of a "psychopathic personality," a derogatory term usually reserved for incorrigible criminals. Kinsey felt strongly that homosexuality was in no way fundamentally psychopathological:

. . . the opinion that homosexual activity in itself provides evidence of a psychopathic personality is materially challenged by these incidence and frequency data. Of the 40–50% of the male population which has homosexual experience, certainly a high proportion would not be considered psychopathic personalities on the basis of anything else in their histories. . . . Males do not represent two discrete populations, heterosexual and homosexual. . . . The living world is a continuum in each and every one of its aspects. The sooner we learn this concerning human sexual behavior the sooner we shall reach a sound understanding of the realities of sex. . . . (Kinsey et al., 1948).

In the Kinsey study of female sexuality, a substantially lower incidence of homosexual behavior was found. Only about 28 percent of the women interviewed had ever had homosexual contacts. The percentage of women who were primarily or exclusively homosexual was a half to a third of the percentage of men. Women appeared to be less promiscuous in their contacts; 71 percent of them had one or two partners, while only half of men with homosexual experience had fewer than three partners.

A lower incidence of homosexuality among women has also been observed in preliterate societies. Of seventy-six preliterate societies evaluated in one study, some form of homosexuality was considered to be quite normal for men in more than sixty, while homosexuality among women was observed in only seventeen (Ford and Beach, 1951).

Though our society seems to have condemned homosexuality in men more than in women, there are several possible reasons for its lower frequency in women. For a man, one motivation toward homosexual activity is his fear of performance in heterosexual activity. In the sexual act itself, a woman can more easily feign competence than can a man, so that fear of performance would not force many women to retreat from heterosexual relationships. Indeed, the relative ease with which women can perform heterosexually may account for the fact that the degree of exclusive homosexuality in women is quite low. It may also be easier for a woman to achieve a feminine identity in our society than it is for a man to attain a masculine identity, so that there is less of a social motivation for a woman to change her sexual role.

If women retreat from heterosexual behavior, abstinence from sexual activity seems less difficult for them to accept than is the case for men (Marmor, 1976). Thus, women have an alternative to homosexuality that few men are willing to consider.

Though most researchers agree with Kinsey's conclusions, some now believe that he overestimated the frequency of homosexual behavior in males. Much of his information on homosexuality came from interviews that were probably not representative (Karlin, 1971). Also, the impression conveyed to the public by the statement that 37 percent of males have had homosexual experience to orgasm fails to convey the fact that most of these experiences occurred in adolescence and that the great majority of the individuals involved lived completely heterosexual lives thereafter. Pomeroy, one of Kinsey's main collaborators, concluded that the group erred in the "gathering of homosexual histories so that the sample was not representative of the whole spectrum of homosexuality" (Pomeroy, 1972).

Patterns of homosexual life

There is no uniform pattern for male and female homosexuality. The stereotype of effeminate, "swishy" young men, "fairies," is unwarranted, since only a small proportion of male homosexuals display such exhibitionist behavior. Most are covert, attempting to pass for heterosexuals in their professional and social activities. Many are married and have children, leading double lives. Among overt homosexuals, relatively few display their chosen life style blatantly. Most overt as well as covert homosexuals are not easily differentiated on superficial observation from the general population.

One striking feature of male homosexuals is their promiscuity. Kinsey interviewed some homosexuals who by the age of fifty had had more than 1,000 sexual partners (Kinsey et al., 1948). The consequence of promiscuity among male homosexuals is a lack of long-term emotional commitment. Many writers have suggested that the aging male homosexual is therefore an exceedingly lonely, pathetic figure. However, surveys suggest that as male homosexuals become older, their declining sexual relationships may be replaced by more meaningful friendships (Weinberg and Williams, 1974).

This promiscuous behavior pattern involves constant screening for new sexual contacts, which is often referred to as "cruising." Most large cities have a number of locations where male homosexuals conventionally congregate, such as certain parks, gay bars, and public toilets or "tea rooms." Because of the threat of arrest, contact in these locations is often hazardous. And homosexual prostitutes often blackmail covert homosexuals.

Male homosexuals are more promiscuous than females. Fully 94 percent of male homosexuals have had more than fifteen partners, and most have had so many that they can't recall the number. By contrast, only 15 percent of women have had more than fifteen partners (Saghir and Robins, 1969; Saghir et al. 1969). Women are much more steadfast in their relationships. Almost all homosexual women report relationships of longer than a year, and during these the women tend to be faithful. By contrast, among men only about 20 percent have faithful relationships of this duration.

One possible explanation for the greater promiscuity of male homosexuals has to do with basic psychological differences in sexual responses of all men and women. Men tend to be more responsive to visual stimuli than women and so become aroused before they make physical contact, whereas women tend to become aroused after making contact. Another explanation for promiscuity among male homosexuals is the greater social stigma attached to male than to female homosexuality. Homosexual men tend to share society's low opinion of their self-worth and similarly to devalue their partners. Lacking self-respect, male homosexual partners thus have difficulty maintaining mutual respect, which is the basis for long-lasting intimate relationships.

Deprivation homosexuality refers to homosexual behavior when men are deprived of female companionship, usually in jail or the armed forces. In prison, homosexuality may become a means through which a social hierarchy is established. More powerful inmates will take submissive prisoners as their "mistresses." Homosexual attacks often represent a release of pent-up rage. Many prison murders derive from such relationships.

In their sexual relationships, male homosexuals follow a variety of patterns. Some always prefer the dominant and others the passive role, but most alternate (Hooker, 1965). The active-passive distinction is relevant only in the case of anal intercourse. Many homosexual activities, such as mutual masturbation and oral-genital contacts, do involve dominance of one or the other partner. The American legal term for anal intercourse is *sodomy;* in England it is called *buggery*. A social revulsion against sodomy has persisted since the days of the Old Testament. The destruction of Sodom in Genesis was ordered when Sodomites came to the house of Lot and demanded that he release two male house guests to them as partners in anal intercourse. The house guests turned out to be angels of God who then devastated the city. In England the death penalty was prescribed for anal intercourse until the latter part of the nineteenth century. Femoral intercourse, in which the penis is inserted between the thighs, is also a common practice.

Symbolic gestures may be as important for homosexual as for heterosexual partners. A stroke, a simple touch, or a kiss on the shoulder may be as exciting as direct sexual stimulation. Lesbians lay greater emphasis on subtle, gentle, and peripheral stimulation than do male homosexuals. As in heterosexual relationships, women tend to desire more protracted, subtle tactile stimulation. Intimacy seems to play a large role in sexual experience for women than for men. Whereas men often initiate sexual activity within hours of a first meeting, two women usually require a long period of social interaction before they become involved in erotic behavior. Often women who have lived together for years will still confine their activity to kissing and such body contact as occurs in heterosexual petting without any direct genital stimulation.

When they do engage in direct genital activity, lesbians may be very adept at eliciting intense sexual arousal and orgasm in each other. Because they know their own bodies, they can stimulate each other more effectively than most men can stimulate a woman. For instance, thumb pressure applied in the lower side of the vaginal portion of the vestibule simultaneously with mouth-clitoral contact can produce more intense sexual stimulation than any form of intercourse with a man (Tripp, 1976). In tribadism, women stimulate each other's genitals simultaneously while one lies atop the other. The greater efficiency of female-female sexual stimulation than of heterosexual activity is attested to by the finding of the Kinsey group that lesbians experience orgasm more frequently than do married women.

Female homosexuals tend to have had more heterosexual experience than males. In one series of homosexuals, 80 percent of the women had experienced sexual intercourse, in contrast to only 48 percent of the males. One reason for this difference may be that a woman need not perform in order to experience intercourse, but instead may assume a passive role and function acceptably even in the absence of sexual arousal. The male, on the other hand, must be sexually excited in order to perform. Fully 33 percent of interviewed male homosexuals who had experienced intercourse with women cited a fear of impotence as a major reason for avoiding it.

One must be cautious in generalizing from interview studies of homosexuality. Individuals who volunteer for these interviews have generally "come out" and openly acknowledge their homosexual behavior. Covert homosexuals who do not want to be interviewed may have quite different sexual feelings and activities.

Biological correlates

Whether or not homosexuality is classified as a disease, it is reasonable to ask if it has any biological determinants. Genetic studies do provide some evidence that biological factors may determine a predisposition toward homosexuality. Among his many studies of the incidence of various disorders in twins, Kallman also examined homosexuality. In a study of eighty-five twin pairs of which forty were monozygotic and forty-five dizygotic, Kallman found striking differences between the groups in their concordance rates for homosexuality. At least one member of each pair was homosexual. All the twin partners of the single-egg pairs he could locate were homosexually inclined, twenty-eight of them exclusively so. Of twenty-six nonidentical co-twins only three had homosexual tendencies, a percentage which does not differ from the rate in the general population (Kallman, 1952). A concordance rate of 100 percent in monozygotic twins, coupled with a much lower concordance rate in dizygotic twins, is usually regarded as proof of a major genetic component.

There have been some objections to the Kallman study. Criminals and sociopathic personalities were overrepresented, and there were many schizoid and alcholic subjects in the study. Though others have also found a greater concordance rate for homosexuality in monozygotic twins than in dizygotic twins (Heston and Shields, 1968), there have been reports of monozygotic twins discordant for homosexuality (Kolb, 1963; Parker, 1964; Ranier et all., 1960). Also, because self-image is so relevant to homosexuality, perhaps identical twins experience "identity diffusion" with regard to their homosexuality. This might be less likely to occur in dizygotic twins, who cannot pass for each other. If identity diffusion were relevant to the higher concordance rate for homosexuality in monozygotic twins, one would expect the overall incidence of homosexuality in all monozygotic twins to be greater than the incidence in the general population. Studies addressing this question have not yet been reported.

Several researchers have compared chromosomal patterns of homosexuals and heterosexuals, but they have failed to find any consistent difference. Homosexuals tend to be the younger ones in groups of siblings. This "shift to the right" in the birth order of homosexuals compared to heterosexuals could conceivably reflect some chromosomal abnormality. On the other hand, it might simply indicate that younger children are exposed to psychological influences that are more conducive to developing homosexuality than those experienced by their older brothers or sisters.

In one study of 100 male and female homosexuals, about 80 percent of both sexes reported emotional attachments to individuals of the same sex before they were fourteen years old, while only 15 to 20 percent had any emotional attachments to or fantasies about members of the opposite sex by that age. Yearnings for homosexual relationships invariably preceded any overt homosexual activity. These findings suggest a very early derivation of same-sexed desires and argue against theories that homosexuality is a behavioral accident which results from the "priming" effect of one or two adolescent seductions (Saghir and Robins, 1969; Saghir et al., 1969).

Some sex researchers have hypothesized that homosexuality, at least in the male, results from an excess of libido. According to this model, young males who are oversexed lack heterosexual outlets at such a young age and so satisfy themselves by homosexual activities and then retain these behavioral patterns throughout adult life. Interviews show a surprisingly high incidence of sexual activity in male homosexuals. In one study, 70 percent of male homosexuals between the ages of twenty and twenty-nine had homosexual relationships four times or more a week. In addition, 97 percent of the population also engaged in masturbation an avarage of four to five times a week (Saghir et al., 1969). This greatly exceeds the frequency of sexual activity in married men of the same age, who presumably have ready access to sexual activity and yet average only about three times a week for both intercourse and masturbation (Kinsey et al., 1948).

In fetal and newborn animals, gonadal hormones acting upon the brain deter-

mine adult patterns of sexual behavior (Geral, 1973). This suggests that variations in hypothalamic pituitary or gonadal hormone secretion in early life might
determine the presence or absence of later homosexual behavior. No prospective studies addressing this question have yet been performed. However, several investigators have measured urinary and plasma levels of gonadal hormones in homosexuals and heterosexuals. Loraine et al. (1970) reported
abnormally low twenty-four-hour urinary testosterone levels in homosexual
males. Kolodny et al. (1971) observed low plasma testosterone levels in homosexuals compared to a matched group of heterosexual males. Subsequent investigations have muddied these waters. Some failed to replicate the initial observations (Birke et al., 1973; Pillard et al., 1974; Tourney and Hatfield, 1973).
One group even found elevated levels of testerone in homosexual men (Brodie
et al., 1974). Detailed evaluations of a large number of hormones later confirmed that homosexuals have high levels of certain testosterone-related compounds and showed that these can be attributed to greater secretion of luteinizing hormone by the pituitary (Doerr et al., 1976). Another study, however,
indicates that luteinizing hormone levels are normal in the blood of homosexuals (Friedman et al., 1977).

Clearly one cannot draw any firm conclusions as to the role of sex hormones
in determining homosexual behavior. The variability in findings suggests that
even if hormonal secretions differ between heterosexual and homosexual men,
the differences might not reflect determinants of homosexuality. Instead, they
may reflect responses to emotional stress that vary among subjects in the different studies. Hormonal secretion could also differ in heterosexuals and homosexuals in response to the frequency and type of sexual outlet.

Psychological theories of homosexuality

In the nineteenth century, physicians and psychiatrists felt that homosexuals
suffered from degeneration of the brain. Presumably this view was an intellec-
tualization of prevailing moral attitudes. "Homosexuality is found in people
who exhibit no other serious deviations from the normal . . . whose efficiency
is unimpaired and who are indeed distinguished by especially high intellectual
development and ethical culture" (Freud, 1953). In one of his essays Freud
stated that, but elsewhere he took the position that it is a deviation from normal
sexual impulses. His views on the causes of homosexuality were influenced by
new discoveries in embryology showing that male and female embryos have
analogues of both female and male sex organs. He inferred that all people are
inherently bisexual and that the "proper" choice of object is worked out as one

passes through the various psychosexual stages. According to this view, homosexuality derives from conflict and arrest at some stage of psychosexual development, with the Oedipal conflict playing a major role.

The classic psychoanalytic view of homosexuality, based on the work of Freud and other early analysts, was well summarized by Fenichel (1945). Since "homosexual men make good friends with women and respect them highly, but any idea of genital contact is repulsive or frightening," they reject sexual relationships with women. This repulsion represents "castration anxiety," and its rationale is twofold:

1. The recognition of the fact that there are actually human beings without a penis leads to the conclusion that one might also become such a being; such an observation lends effectiveness to old threats of castration.
2. The female genitals, through the connection of castration anxiety with old oral anxieties, may be perceived as a castrating instrument capable of biting or tearing off the penis (Fenichel, 1945).

The way this revulsion to female genitals becomes translated into homosexual yearnings is that "most homosexuals, however, cannot so easily free themselves of their normal biological longing for women. They continue to be attracted by women but, not being able to endure the idea of being without a penis, they long for phallic women, for hermaphrodites, so to speak. This acute longing for objects with a penis compels them to choose boys, but the boys must have a maximum of girlish and feminine features" (Fenichel, 1945). Thus, male homosexuals should seek out effeminate partners. This theory is contradicted by the well-established fact that male homosexuals usually prefer "masculine" partners (Hoffman, 1968; 1977).

The difficulty with evaluating such psychoanalytic formulations is that they deal primarily with a highly abstracted psychosexual stage of development. There is virtually no way in which such theories can be subjected to experimental tests.

In psychoanalytic theory, female homosexuality is also explained by Oedipal conflicts. "The sight of a penis may create the fear of an impending violation; more frequently it mobilizes thoughts and emotions about the difference in physical appearance . . . which disturb the capacity for sexual enjoyment to such a degree that sexual pleasure is possible only if there is no confrontation with a penis." The homosexual resolution of the problem is more straightforward in the woman than in the man because "the first love object of every human being is the mother; all women, in contra-distinction to men, have had a primary homosexual attachment, which may later be revived if normal heterosexuality is blocked" (Fenichel, 1945).

A more modern psychoanalytic approach to homosexuality is evident in a study by Bieber (1965). Comparing their experiences of treating 106 male homosexuals, 10 psychoanalysts found remarkable similarities in the family relationships of their patients as children:

The large majority of homosexual mothers had a close binding intimate relationship with the homosexual son. In most cases this son had been his mother's favorite. . . . Most homosexual mothers were explicitly seductive. . . . In about two-thirds of the cases the mother openly preferred her homosexual son to her husband and allied with the son against the husband. . . . The combination of sexual overstimulation and intense guilt and anxiety about heterosexual behavior promoted precocious and compulsive sexual activity. . . . In support of these assumptions we found that homosexuals as a group began their sexual activity earlier than did the heterosexuals and were more active sexually in preadolescence'' (Bieber, 1965).

While mothers were closely attached to sons, fathers were usually distant and/or hostile. Bieber thought that the father turned against his son when he perceived that his wife preferred her son to her husband.

A major criticism of studies like Bieber's is that they are based on individuals who present themselves as patients and thus may not be representative of the whole population of homosexuals. Some studies of nonpatients have found similar family patterns (Evans, 1969; Snortum et al., 1969; Terman and Miles, 1936), but others report quite different family backgrounds. Greenstein (1966) noted that the frequency of overt homosexual experience was greater in males who as boys were close to their fathers than in those whose fathers were distant. Bene (1965) failed to find any difference between mothers of homosexuals and of heterosexuals in the degree to which they were loving, intense, attached to their sons, or protective of them (Bene, 1965).

What might account for the variations in parental backgrounds of homosexuals found in different studies? Since some of the investigators studied psychiatric patients while others interviewed individuals showing no overt emotional disturbance, the differences in family background might conceivably relate to the psychopathology of the subjects and not to their sexual orientations. Evidence supporting this possibility came from a questionnaire assessment of the parental background of 300 male homosexuals and 138 male heterosexuals (Siegelman, 1974). Both fathers and mothers of homosexuals appeared more rejecting and less loving than parents of heterosexuals. Though none of the subjects in this study had specific psychiatric disturbances, it was possible to separate them into groups with higher and lower "neurotocism" scores on the questionnaires. Subsamples of homosexuals and heterosexuals scoring low on neuroticism showed no significant difference in family relations. This would indicate that the pattern of distant mothers and fathers is related to the presence of neurotic behavior and not to homosexuality per se.

The question of whether homosexuals suffer from a neurotic disturbance has been examined directly through psychological testing. In a well-known study Hooker (1957, 1968) compared 30 homosexual and heterosexual men matched for age, education, and IQ. All were given a battery of psychological tests, including the Rorschach, the Thematic Apperception Test (TAT), and the Make-a-Picture-Story (MAPS), and they also provided detailed life histories. When the data were evaluated in a double-blind fashion by independent clinicians, it was impossible to distinguish between the two groups. Using the Minnesota Multiphasic Personality Inventory (MMPI), Dean and Richardson (1964) found no difference between homosexuals and heterosexuals except in the M-F score, which relates to male-female orientation.

References

Bene, E. On the genesis of male homosexuality: An attempt at clarifying the role of the parents. *Br. J. Psychiat., 111:*803–813, 1965.

Bieber, I. *Homosexuality: A psychoanalytic study of male homosexuals.* Vintage Books, New York, 1965.

Birke, L., Williams, G. H., M., et al. Serum testosterone levels in homosexual men. *N. Eng. J. Med., 289:*1236–1238, 1973.

Brodie, H. J. H., Gartrell, N., Doering, C., et al. Plasma testosterone levels in heterosexual and homosexual men. *Am. J. Psychiat., 131:*82–83, 1974.

Cauldwell, D. O. Psychopathia Transsexualis. *Sexology, 16:*279, 1949.

Dean R. B., and Richardson, H. Analysis of MMPI profiles of 40 college-educated overt male homosexuals. *J. Consult. Psychol., 28:*483, 1964.

Diagnostic and Statistical Manual of Mental Disorders, 2nd ed., American Psychiatric Association, Washington, D.C., 1952, p. 38.

Diagnostic and Statistical Manual of Mental Disorders, 2nd ed., 7th printing. American Psychiatric Association, Washington, D.C., 1974, p. 44.

Doerr, P., Pirke, K. M., Kockott, G., and Dittmar, F. Further studies on sex hormones in male homosexuals. *Arch. Gen. Psychiat., 33:*611–614, 1976.

Evans, R. B. Childhood parental relationships of homosexual men. *J. Consult. and Clin. Psychol., 33:*129–135, 1969.

Fenichel, O. *The psychoanalytic theory of neurosis.* Norton, New York, 1945, pp. 328–341.

Ford, C. S., and Beach, F. A. *Patterns of sexual behavior.* Harper & Row, New York, 1951, p. 171.

Freud, S. Letter to an American mother. *Am. J. Psychiat., 102:*786, 1951.

Freud, S. Three essays on the theory of sexuality. In *Standard edition of the complete psychoanalytic works of Sigmund Freud,* vol. 7, ed. J. Strachey. Hogarth Press, London, 1953, pp. 135–243.

Friedman, R. C., Dyrenfurth, I., Linkie, D., Tendler, R., and Fleiss, J. L. Hormones and sexual orientation in men. *Am. J. Psychiat., 134:*571–572, 1977.

Geral, A. A. Influence of perinatal androgen on reproductive capacity. In *Contemporary sexual behavior,* ed. J. Zubin and J. Money. Johns Hopkins University Press, Baltimore, 1973, pp. 1–16.

Greenstein, J. M. Father characteristics and sex typing. *J. Personality and Soc. Psychol., 3:*271–277, 1966.

Heston, L. L., and Shields, J. Homosexuality in twins: A family study and a registry study. *Arch. Gen. Psychiat., 18:*149–160, 1968.

Hoffman M. *The gay world: Male homosexuality and the social creation of evil.* Basic Books, New York, 1968.

Hoffman, M., Homosexuality in four perspectives. In *Human sexuality: Four perspectives,* ed. F. A. Beach. Johns Hopkins University Press, Baltimore, 1977, pp. 164–189.

Hooker, E. The adjustment of the male overt homosexual. *J. Projective Tech., 21:*18, 1957.

Hooker, E. An empirical study of some relations between sexual patterns and gender identity in male homosexuals. In *Sex research–new developments,* ed. J. Money. Holt, Rinehart and Winston, New York, 1965, p. 24.

Hooker, E. Homosexuality. In *International Encyclopedia of the Social Sciences,* vol. 14, ed. David L. Sills. Macmillan and the Free Press, New York, 1968, pp. 222.

Kallman, F. J. A comparative twin study on the genetic aspects of male homosexuality. *J. Nerv. and Ment. Diseases, 115:*283–298, 1952.

Karlin, A. *Sexuality and homosexuality.* Norton, New York, 1971.

Kinsey, A. C., Pomeroy, W. B., and Martin, C. E. *Sexual behavior in the human male.* W. B. Saunders, Philadelphia, 1948, pp. 630–661.

Kinsey, A. C., Pomeroy, W. B., Martin, C. E., and Gebhardt, P. H. *Sexual behavior in the human female.* W. B. Saunders, Philadelphia, 1953.

Kolb, L. S. Therapy of homosexuality. In *Current psychiatric therapy,* vol. 3, ed. J. Masserman. Grune and Stratton, New York, 1963, p. 131.

Kolodny, R. C., et al., Plasma testosterone and semen analysis in male homosexuals. *N. Eng. J. Med., 285:*1170, 1971.

Loraine, J. A., Ismael, A. A., Adamopoulis, P. A., and Dove, G. A. Endocrine function in male and female homosexuals. *Br. Med. J., 4:*406, 1970.

Marmor, J. Homosexuality and sexual orientation disturbances. In *The sexual experience,* ed. B. J. Saddock, H. I. Kaplan, and A. M. Freedman. Williams and Wilkins, Baltimore, 1976, p. 374.

Parker, N. Homosexuality in twins: A report on three discordant pairs. *Br. J. Psychiat., 110:*489, 1964.

Pillard, R. C., Rose, R. M., and Sherwood, M. Plasma testosterone levels in homosexual men. *Arch. Sex. Behav., 3:*453–458, 1974.

Pomeroy, W. B. *Dr. Kinsey and the Institute for Sex Research.* Harper & Row, New York, 1972, p. 464.

Ranier, J. D., Mesnikoff, A., Kolb, L. C. and Carr, A. Homosexuality and heterosexuality in identical twins. *Psychosom. Med., 22:*251, 1960.

Saghir, M. T., and Robins, E. Homosexuality, I:Sexual behavior of the female homosexual. *Arch. Gen. Psychiat., 20:*192–291, 1969.

Saghir, M. T., Robins, E., and Walbran, B. Homosexuality, II: Sexual behavior of the male homosexual. *Arch. Gen. Psychiat., 21:*219–229, 1969.

Siegelman, M. Parental background of male homosexuals and heterosexuals. *Arch. Sex. Behav.*, *3:*3–18, 1974.

Snortum, J. R., Marshall, J. E., Gillespie, J. F., and McLaughlin, J. P. Family dynamics and homosexuality. *Psychol. Rep.*, *24:*763–770, 1969.

Terman, L. M., and Miles, C. C. *Sex and personality: Studies masculinity and feminity.* McGraw-Hill, New York, 1936.

Tourney, G., and Hatfield, L. M. Androgen metabolism in schizophrenics, homosexuals and normal controls. *Bio.Psych.*, *6:*23, 1973.

Tripp, C. A. *The homosexual matrix.* McGraw-Hill, New York, 1976, pp. 108, 231.

Weinberg, M. S., and Williams, C. J., *Male homosexuals: Their problems and adaptations.* Oxford University Press, New York, 1974.

23. Paraphilias

Paraphilias are usually referred to as sexual deviations, sexual variants, or perversions. The "para" part of the word denotes the deviation from conventional behavior. "Philia" indicates that the deviation relates to that which attracts the individual.

In older texts on psychopathology the major sexual deviation dealt with was homosexuality, but as we have seen, homosexuality is no longer regarded as a mental disorder. DSM-III does include among the paraphilias *dishomophilia,* a label that is applied to a homosexual only if his or her "homosexual arousal is incompatible with the individual's conscience and leads to significant distress."

Besides homosexuality, numerous other patterns of sexual behavior that are often treated as deviations probably do not represent genuine mental disorders. Rapists may have perfectly normal heterosexual inclinations and may be aroused by appropriate stimuli from adult females. Many, if not most, convicted rapists manifest no nonsexual emotional disorder. Theirs is simply criminal behavior motivated by a gross disregard for the humanity of their victims. Pornography is often placed under the rubric of sexual deviation. It is likely, however, that most normal men and women at times enjoy pornographic literature or movies. Individuals who for one reason or another lack adequate opportunities for sexual interaction with other adults may resort to pornography more frequently, still without manifesting a mental disorder.

DSM-III restricts the use of the term *paraphilia* by emphasizing that "in this group of conditions, persistent and repetitive sexually arousing stimuli are of an unusual nature and are associated with either (1) preferential or exclusive sexual activity with non-human objects or with humans involving real or simulated suffering or humiliation, (2) sexual activity with nonconsenting partners, or (3) subjective distress regarding the stimulus that leads to sexual arousal.''

This way of viewing paraphilia differs from earlier definitions (DSM-II) of sexual deviation, which classified as abnormal any sexual behavior that ''deviated from a defined norm of heterosexual coitus between adults under nonbizarre circumstances.'' According to such definitions, homosexuality was a deviation. The present classification (DSM-III) ''only includes as disorders those deviations from standard sexual behavior which either represent gross impairments in the capacity for affectionate sexual arousal between adult human partners or where there is an acknowledged subjective distress regarding the source of sexual arousal.''

An alternative way of viewing sexual variations is to include all kinds but use the term *sexual deviation* in a way that ''implies neither health nor illness, goodness nor badness, usefulness nor uselessness''—hence, to describe but not to evaluate (Stoller, 1977).

Because of social and legal strictures, reliable data on the incidence and detailed patterns of paraphilic behavior are difficult to obtain. It is well accepted that paraphilias are substantially more frequent in males than females. Sexual deviations often coexist with other emotional disorders. People who confine their sexual outlets to bizarrely deviant fantasies often do not relate to other adults meaningfully.

One other generality that applies to most or all paraphilias is that they are resistant to psychotherapeutic intervention. The prognosis for eliminating sexual deviations by counseling and conventional psychotherapy is quite low, as it is with drug addiction and alcoholism. The reasons for resistance to treatment are unclear. Some researchers have speculated that the deviant behavior is crucial for the mental stability of the individual (Stoller, 1977). According to this view, without the deviation the patient would undergo a much more drastic emotional disintegration. Another notion is that the specific deviations are linked with forceful positive rewards. For instance, paraphilics whose activities make them liable to arrest, such as exhibitionists, voyeurs, or pedophilics, may have a strong need to run such risks and may be ''turned on'' by the constant danger of arrest as much as by the sexual activity itself.

Fetishism

Fetish, as anthropologists use the term, refers to an object perceived with awe as the embodiment of habitation of a potent spirit. As a sexual deviation, fetishism involves behavior patterns in which ''non-living objects are utilized as a preferred or exclusive method of stimulating erotic arousal'' (DSM-III). Fetishism is thought to occur almost exclusively in males. Common sexual fetishes are female panties and women's leather boots. Most normal men are aroused by such objects to some degree. Fetishism is diagnosed only when sexual arousal depends almost exclusively on the fetish.

Fetishes usually serve to generate fantasies during masturbation. Sometimes they are employed to secure arousal during heterosexual intercourse. Often fetishism is combined with other deviations. For instance, a masochist may prefer to be whipped by women dressed all in leather.

Male fetishists often commit burglary to secure their desired fetish and thus enhance sexual arousal by combining the danger of burglary with the excitement of the fetish itself (Karpman, 1954).

Transvestism is a type of fetishism, but it is usually treated as a discrete disorder. Almost invariably transvestites secure sexual arousal to the point of orgasm by dressing in women's clothing.

Some researchers regard kleptomania as a fetish. Kleptomaniacs steal goods they do not need for any particular purpose. The theft is often associated with sexual excitement to the point of orgasm. If labeled as fetishism, kleptomania is the only type that is more prevalent in women than in men.

The causes of fetishism are by no means clear. In some cases it seems to develop from simple behavioral conditioning. For instance, if a man felt his first sexual interest as a young boy when he saw a lovely woman removing pink, lacey panties, he might later come to prefer such panties as a means of arousal. Learning theorists have studied such ''imprinting'' in many kinds of behavior. Psychoanalytic theories of fetishism also make use of the imprinting concept. For instance, Fenichel (1945) expressed the Freudian view that most typical fetishes such as shoes, long hair, or earrings are penis symbols, while fur may serve as a symbolic substitute for pubic hair. A typical psychoanalytic case study describes a foot fetishist who became fixated after seeing his governess expose her foot when he was a young boy (Fenichel, 1945). According to the psychoanalytic view, the boy immediately equated the foot with the penis, so that in his eyes the governess had a penis. This allayed the boy's castration anxiety and permitted sexual feelings to arise. The psychodynamic process operates as follows: "The thought that there are human beings without a penis and that I might myself be one of them makes it impossible for me to grant myself sexual excitement. But now I see here a symbol of a penis in a woman; that helps me to shut out my fear, and thus I can permit myself to be sexually excited'' (Fenichel, 1945).

Some analysts of behavior also regard pyromania, or compulsive fire setting, as a form of fetishism. Witnessing the fire is sexually exciting for pyromaniacs, who are almost invariably young men and usually masturbate to orgasm while watching the fire. As soon as orgasm occurs, the individual often "comes to his senses" and will join in efforts to extinguish the fire. Pyromaniacs are often more disturbed mentally than most fetishists. Many pyromaniacs are grossly schizophrenic (Robins et al., 1969).

Zoophilia

Zoophilia, often referred to as *bestiality,* is a rare condition in which animals are the preferred or exclusive source of erotic stimuli. Sexual contact with animals, on the other hand, is not rare. Though in the total population of males Kinsey found that only about 8 percent had any sexual experience with animals, the rate among boys raised on farms was considerably higher. About 17 percent of farm boys had reached orgasm through animal contacts (Kinsey et al., 1948). An approximately equal number of boys had animal contacts that did not result in orgasm, while others had sexual contacts with animals before adolescence. The great majority of animal contacts reported by Kinsey occurred during adolescence, before much sexual activity with girls or women had developed. By the time they were adults, most of Kinsey's subjects had abandoned animals.

The criteria in DSM-III for a diagnosis of zoophilia require that "the animal is preferred no matter what other forms of sexual outlet are available. Moreover, the fantasy of sexual activity with animals produces erotic arousal." Thus, the frequent animal contacts cited by Kinsey would not conform to a diagnosis of zoophilia.

Among those interviewed by Kinsey, vaginal coitus with animals such as calves or sheep was the most frequent technique employed by adolescent males. Another common pattern, especially prevalent in urban individuals who reported animal contact, was for household pets such as dogs, and sometimes even cats, to fellate the individual.

Pedophilia

Pedophilics prefer prepubertal children as sexual stimuli and engage in sexual activity with them. Pedophilic activities are against the law in all states, and child molesters are more abhorred than rapists. Adult pedophiles are oriented toward opposite-sexed children about twice as frequently as toward the same sex. The popular conception of the child molester is of a "dirty old man" who kidnaps a little girl he does not know, takes her to a dark alley or woods, and rapes and kills her. But a study of sex offenders by the Kinsey group shows that pedophiles are far less dangerous than is popularly assumed (Gebhardt et al., 1965). Pedophiles generally are not violent, and physical injury to the child occurs in only about 2 percent of instances. The typical pedophile does not "attack" strangers. In about 85 percent of cases the pedophile is a family friend, neighbor, or often a relative of the victim. Advances usually take place in the child's own home, where the pedophile is an invited guest, or in the pedophile's home. The most typical pattern is for the man to hold a young girl on his lap, to caress her, and then to fondle her genitals. A high proportion of pedophiles are impotent, which probably explains in part why intercourse is attempted in only about 6 percent of cases and successful penetration occurs in only 2 percent. Students of pedophilia tend to concur that more psychological damage is done to the children by the frantic overreactions of their parents than by the sexual episode itself (McCary, 1973; McGaghy, 1971).

Pedophilia is probably more common than most people think. In their survey Kinsey and his colleagues found that about 23 percent of middle-class females had been sexually approached between the ages of four and thirteen by adult males. The incidence appeared to be even higher in lower-class females (Kinsey et al., 1953). In a study of college students, about a third of all men and women interviewed reported some sexual encounters with adults when they were children. For about half the women these episodes involved exhibitionism on the part of an adult male. In contrast, 85 percent of the encounters for males were homosexual approaches (McGaghy, 1971).

Pedophiles form a substantial proportion of all sex offenders, averaging between 30 and 35 percent in most studies (Ellis and Brancale, 1956). The vast majority of pedophiles are men. They tend to be older than other sex offenders, with the possible exception of those who commit incest. The average age at conviction is thirty-five, and about a quarter of convicted pedophiles are over forty-five (Gebhardt et al., 1965; McGaghy, 1971; Revitch and Weiss, 1962). About 15 to 20 percent of child molesters are mentally retarded and another 5 percent are senile men. However, the majority appear to have normal mental capacity, with no clear psychiatric disturbance apart from their sexual deviation. Surprisingly, child molesters tend to be conservative, moralistic, and frequently quite religious. When interviewed in prison, they often display stern attitudes about the sexual propriety of female behavior, classifying women as "good" or "bad" and demanding that the ones they marry be virgins (Gebhardt et al., 1965). Their sexual adjustment is generally poor, with a high incidence of impotence. While definite psychiatric disturbance is not often apparent, most of these individuals display marked emotional immaturity. Though they frequently exhibit themselves to their victims, the pattern of pedophilic sexual activities usually differs strikingly from that of exhibitionists. Exhibitionists deal almost exclusively with strangers, while pedophilics much prefer small children who are well known to them and for whom they feel genuine affection. By definition, exhibitionism is confined to exposure involving adult victims.

A substantial number of convicted child molesters probably should not be regarded as pedophiles, for men can be deceived by the mature dress and appearance of eleven- or twelve-year-old girls. The girls may be socially adept and sexually experienced. Hence, the man thinks he is about to have relations with a sexually mature individual and is greatly surprised when he is arrested.

Exhibitionism

Exhibitionism is a condition in which the act of exposing the genitals to an unsuspecting stranger produces sexual arousal. Since there is very little social stigma attached to female seductiveness through partial exposure, what would border on exhibitionism in a man may be conventional behavior in a woman. Exhibitionism is the most common of sex offenses, accounting for 35 percent of all arrests (Allen, 1967). As with pedophilia, the outrage of the community and the severity of the punishment are usually well out of proportion to the social danger of the exhibitionist's act. Exhibitionists almost never do anything more violent than exhibiting their genitals, nor do they approach their victims closely. The act is usually performed at a distance of ten to seventy feet from the victim.

When exposed, the exhibitionist's penis is usually erect. However, he does not usually ejaculate when exposing himself. Instead, the overall episode serves as a stimulus to vivid fantasies during subsequent masturbation. For the exhibitionist much of the sexual excitement is generated by viewing the response of the woman. He is most aroused if she shrieks in horror. Should the woman pay no attention to him or soberly tell the man that he is foolish or disturbed, his erection usually subsides and he gains no pleasure from the episode. In most cases when the woman has approached rather than retreated from the exhibitionist, he has fled. Probably linked to the desire of the exhibitionist to startle his victim is the requirement that she be a stranger. Instances of exhibitionism involving someone well known to the offender are quite rare.

Another prominent element of the exhibitionist act is the thrill associated with the danger of being apprehended. For obvious reasons, the exhibitionist is more likely to be arrested than any other type of sex offender. His latent or not so latent need to be caught is evident in data demonstrating that exhibitionists often display themselves again and again in the same place and at the same time of day.

In contrast to the seemingly aggressive nature of their act, exhibitionists tend to be introverted and shy individuals. They are typically timid and submissive, described by others as "nice" though immature individuals. They tend to have been raised by dominating mothers and often marry similarly dominating women. Approximately 60 percent are married or have been married at some time. The heterosexual adjustment of exhibitionists is usually grossly inadequate. Even among those who are married, coital activity is relatively infrequent and the exhibitionist is often impotent.

Because of the shy and timid personality of most exhibitionists, it is reasonable to speculate that their preferred sexual behavior is a way of compensating and making themselves feel like powerful men. The likelihood of being apprehended and prosecuted as criminals adds to this sensation of *machismo*. Despite the fact that conviction as a sex offender usually results in social and professional ruin, exhibitionists have a high rate of recidivism. In a study by the Kinsey group, one-third of convicted offenders had four to six previous convictions and another 10 percent had been convicted seven or more times (Gebhardt, 1965). Thus, the secondary reinforcement of a sense of manliness must be extraordinarily powerful. The psychoanalytic view of exhibitionism fits with this general picture. It is posited that by displaying his penis the exhibitionist "proves" to the world, and most importantly to an adult woman, that he has not been castrated.

Voyeurism

Although it might seem logical for voyeurism and exhibitionism to be linked and for the same individuals to indulge in both activities, in fact this is a rare correlation. According to DSM-III, *voyeurism* is "a condition in which the patient repetitively seeks out situations in which he engages in looking at unsuspecting women who are either naked, in the act of disrobing, or engaging in sexual activity. The act of looking is accompanied by sexual excitement, frequently with orgasm. The condition has only been described in males." As defined in DSM-III, voyeurism encompasses *scoptophilia,* which refers to pleasure obtained from observing sexual acts and genitals. Elsewhere scoptophilia is distinguished from voyeurism, which involves only the viewing of nudes (Karpman, 1954). Sometimes the voyeur masturbates while he is gazing upon his "victims," while on other occasions he masturbates later at home.

As one might suspect from the proliferation of pornographic literature and the popularity of X-rated movies, both men and woman enjoy and obtain sexual arousal from viewing others involved in dressing, undressing, and sexual activity. Voyeurism is regarded as a criminal offense only when the voyeur is watching people who are unaware that they are being observed. The other proviso is that the person being observed would be offended if she became aware of it. Like exhibitionists, voyeurs prefer to observe strangers. The offender derives sexual arousal from the notion that he is somehow "violating" his victims. Like other criminal deviants, the peeping tom is stimulated by the thrill of risked apprehension.

Voyeurs differ in their demographic characteristics from most other sex offenders. On the average, they are substantially younger. The mean age at first conviction for voyeurs is about twenty-four years, whereas exhibitionists and pediophiles are first arrested in their thirties. Voyeurs do resemble other sex offenders in displaying markedly deficient heterosexual relationships.

One form of sexual activity which encompasses elements of both voyeurism and exhibitionism is *troilism*. This refers to sharing a sexual partner with another person while a third individual looks on. Often two couples may have sexual relations simultaneously in the presence of each other. Assuming that all partners are consenting, troilism differs from exhibitionism and voyeurism in that it is not a sex offense. Since the popularization of group sex activities such as mate swapping and other forms of "swinging," most authorities hesitate to regard troilism as a sexual perversion.

As with the other deviations, any conceptualization of the "cause" of voyeurism is largely speculative. Psychoanalysts attempt to trace the disorder back to childhood episodes in which the individual witnessed his parents having intercourse. Alternatively, one may consider voyeurism to be merely a passive, vicarious way of deriving sexual gratification for an individual who lacks the self-confidence to enter into adult heterosexual relationships. The risk of being caught may bolster the voyeur's usually deficient sense of manliness.

References

Allen, C. Sexual perversion. In *The Encyclopedia of Sexual Behavior,* eds. A. Ellis and A. Abarbanel. Hawthorne Press, New York, 1967, pp. 802–811.

Ellis, A., and Brancale, R. *The psychology of sex offenders.* C. C. Thomas, Springfield, Ill., 1956.

Fenichel, O. *The psychoanalytic theory of neurosis.* Norton, New York, 1945, pp. 341–342.

Gebhardt, P. H., Gagnon, J. H., Pomeroy, W. B., and Christenson, C. V. *Sex offenders.* Harper & Row, New York, 1965, pp. 356–359.

Karpman, B. *The sexual offender and his offences.* Julian Press, New York, 1954.

Kinsey, A. C., Pomeroy, W. B., and Martin, C. E. *Sexual behavior in the human male.* W. B. Saunders, Philadelphia, 1948, p. 671.

Kinsey, A. C., Pomeroy, W. B., Martin, C. E., and Gebhardt P. H. *Sexual behavior in the human female.* W. B. Saunders, Philadelphia, 1953, pp. 116–122.

McCary, J. L. *Human sexuality*. D. Van Nostrand, New York, 1973, pp. 376–379.

McGaghy, C. H. Child molesting. *Sexual Behavior,* August 1971, pp. 16–24.

Revitch, E., and Weiss, R. G. The pedophilic offender. *Diseases Nerv. System, 23:*73–78, 1962.

Robins, E. S., Herman, M., and Robins, L. Sex and arson: Is there a relationship? *Med. Aspects Human Sex.* October 1969, pp. 57–64.

Stoller, R. J. Sexual deviations. In *Human sexuality in four perspectives,* ed. F. A. Beach. Johns Hopkins University Press, Baltimore, Md., 1977, pp. 190–214.

Index